JB JOSSEY-BASS™

ARTS MARKETING INSIGHTS

The DYNAMICS *of* BUILDING *and* RETAINING PERFORMING ARTS AUDIENCES

Joanne Scheff Bernstein

Foreword by
Philip Kotler

BICENTENNIAL

1807

WILEY

2007

BICENTENNIAL

John Wiley & Sons, Inc.

Published by Jossey-Bass
A Wiley Imprint
989 Market Street, San Francisco, CA 94103-1741   www.josseybass.com

Readers should be aware that Internet Web sites offered as citations and/or sources for further information may have changed or disappeared between the time this was written and when it is read.

Jossey-Bass books and products are available through most bookstores. To contact Jossey-Bass directly call our Customer Care Department within the U.S. at 800-956-7739, outside the U.S. at 317-572-3986, or fax 317-572-4002.

Jossey-Bass also publishes its books in a variety of electronic formats. Some content that appears in print may not be available in electronic books.

Library of Congress Cataloging-in-Publication Data

Bernstein, Joanne Scheff, date.
    Arts marketing insights : the dynamics of building and retaining performing arts audiences/Joanne Scheff Bernstein ; foreword by Philip Kotler.
        p. cm.
    Includes bibliographical references and index.
    ISBN-13: 978-0-7879-7844-0
    ISBN-10: 0-7879-7844-2
    1. Performing arts—Marketing.   I. Title.
PN1590.M227B47   2007
791.069'8—dc22   2006029093

Printed in the United States of America
FIRST EDITION
HB Printing   10 9 8 7 6 5 4

Contents

Foreword

The arts are essential to the health of a nation. Just as food, clothing, and housing are essential to physical well-being, art is essential to the social and spiritual nourishing of our lives. Life would be dreary in a society without music, song, dance, film, books, and the visual arts.

Joanne and I published our book *Standing Room Only* in 1997, more than nine years ago. In these times of accelerating change, nine years is like twenty years in terms of sound prescriptions for success. Today discretionary money is scarcer, time budgets are strained, and competitive activities have proliferated, with the result that filling the seats for performances is getting increasingly difficult. Furthermore, in the past several years there have been significant changes in people's lifestyles, increased spontaneity in choosing leisure time pursuits, and new expectations in terms of excellent and responsive customer service.

Contrary to many people's belief that interest in the arts is waning, there is and, I imagine, always will be a significant proportion of the population that truly enjoys attending arts events. But many of the audience development strategies that worked in the past are no longer as viable as they once were. Furthermore, marketers' insensitivity to the ways customers prefer to do business and the types of messages that will serve to attract audience members is actually creating barriers to attendance. At best many marketers are perpetually working harder to retain their audiences and attract new ones. At the worst many symphonies, theaters, opera companies, and dance companies are facing extreme financial difficulties.

Marketing is not the art of finding clever ways to fill your seats. Marketing is the art of creating genuine customer value. It is the art of helping your *customers* become better off. The marketer's watchwords are quality, service, and value.

A mark of sound management in any organization is to review the new market conditions, the competition (both inside and outside the arts world), and the mind-set of consumers, and then revise old assumptions and launch new marketing initiatives for breathing new life into the performing arts business.

To assist your thinking, Joanne Scheff Bernstein, one of the most effective consultants and educators on the performing arts, offers you a guide to the new market factors and the new strategies, based on sound marketing principles, that will improve your audience development results now and into the future. She offers not only a review of long-standing best practices but also a multitude of viable alternatives to those practices that no longer attract and retain audiences as they formerly did. She helps you to understand the customer mind-set and to leverage the many new opportunities created by the digital revolution and its manifestations, especially Web-marketing and e-mail.

I view this new book, *Arts Marketing Insights,* as the performing arts bible for the times. I encourage every arts manager and marketer, student and teacher of arts management, and board member of an arts organization to read this book and discuss every chapter with their peers. The dialogue alone will spark new ideas in your arts organization for substantially increasing attendance and funding and for creating better satisfied customers.

Philip Kotler
Kellogg School of Management
Northwestern University

This book is dedicated with boundless love
to my wonderful husband, Bob, who shares my love of the arts,
and to my darling grandchildren, Cecilia, Daniel, Ryan, and Harper,
who have just begun to experience the delights and inspiration
the arts will offer them throughout their lives.

Introduction

The behavior of arts audiences is changing dramatically. Although some performing arts organizations have successfully retained and even grown their subscriber base in recent years, since the mid-nineties many organizations have been losing ground in their efforts to both attract and retain subscribers. Competition for leisure time activities is on the rise and arts education in the schools has been sparse for decades, with the result that many arts managers fear the younger generations are unlikely to fill the gap that will be left as loyal older audiences diminish.

People have also changed in the ways they prefer to do business. Many performing arts attenders want to choose specific programs to attend, not purchase a package of performances preselected by the organization. This trend is not limited to the younger generations who are especially unwilling to plan far in advance, but long-standing arts attenders are also becoming far more spontaneous in their ticket purchasing behavior. Thanks to the advances in communications technology, especially the Internet and e-mail, people have come to expect comprehensive information and the ultimate in convenience, literally at their fingertips. Due to the strong emphasis on customer relationship management in many other sectors of society, people expect arts organizations to listen to them and respond to their needs and preferences.

All these factors, plus ever-increasing costs and fluctuating contributed income, have placed a great deal of stress on arts managers. Furthermore, the antiquated mind-sets and approaches of many managers and marketers are putting many arts organizations at risk of failure. Some have been at the forefront of designing and implementing marketing programs that respond to evolving customer needs and preferences. But too many marketers are reluctant to vary from tried-and-true marketing methods, even in the face of declining audiences and revenue. Other marketers are eager to change but do not know where to turn for direction on viable approaches.

This book's title may suggest to some readers that on these pages they will discover "quick fix" solutions. Many of the ideas suggested in this book can be and have been implemented with rewarding short-term results. However, there really is no quick fix. Specific tactics must be developed in the context of strategic marketing principles. This means that better planning is needed as well as better, more thorough, and continuous implementation, evaluation, and modification of the plans. As a result, this book consists of both new approaches to audience development and many of the commonly accepted best practices in marketing theory and plan execution that support these approaches.

Arts Marketing Insights will provide performing arts organizations significant help in focusing on the strategies and techniques that can improve their impact and practices while also ensuring that they remain true to their artistic and public missions. This book combines theory, strategy, tactics, and innovative examples, all with the objective of improving the ability of arts organizations to better meet the needs of audience segments and thereby increase audience size. It explains not only the *what* but the *why*—why some approaches that have been ingrained in the performing arts industry for decades no longer resonate with many current and potential audience members; why new ways of thinking and new strategies are essential for success.

From cultivating an organization-wide marketing mind-set, developing a strategic marketing plan, building a brand identity, doing market research, understanding your target market to delivering an effective message, designing attractive offerings for various market segments, leveraging the Internet and e-mail marketing, and delivering great customer service, this book covers everything you need to know to put a strategic marketing program in place, manage it, and adapt it for the future. *Arts Marketing Insights* offers dozens of examples of innovative and effective marketing strategies from performing arts organizations all over the world—strategies that will ensure that the performing arts will prosper in today's rapidly changing social, economic, and demographic climate.

WHO SHOULD READ THIS BOOK

Arts Marketing Insights is an indispensable tool for arts managers, marketers, fundraisers, and board members, and for arts management educators and students. It is also valuable for others who work closely with arts organizations and desire a deeper understanding of issues in arts marketing—individuals such as foundation directors, corporate executives, consultants, managers of arts service organizations, and the artists themselves.

Marketing is a mind-set for the entire organization, not simply a function of the marketing department. Therefore it is critical for upper-level management and board members to read this book and understand the principles of customer-centered marketing. This book can serve as a comprehensive text for those relatively new to the subject—students and those in the first years of their career in the arts management field—and can be an inspiration and a challenge to those more experienced in the sector to make their marketing offers and communications more relevant to current and potential audiences.

This book will be useful to people in organizations large and small. Large institutions often continue to employ the strategies that made them so successful in the past. These organizations should consider that during the 1980s, 230 companies—46 percent—disappeared from the Fortune 500 list, demonstrating that neither size nor good reputation guarantees success. At the other end of the spectrum, the smallest companies, with negligible marketing budgets, should consider that even if their primary communication with their publics is a simple e-mail message, their offer must be strategically priced, packaged, and described to best appeal to target audiences, and the message must be carefully worded, timed, and formatted. All these efforts require up-to-date, strategic marketing practices.

The Organization of This Book

Chapter One sets the stage. It presents an overview of the current state of the performing arts industry, especially in terms of audience development, and suggests the trends that affect people's arts attendance and ticket purchasing behavior. It also describes modern marketing theories and practices that have permeated society as a whole in recent years and the ways customer attitudes toward marketing messages are changing.

Many factors that determine whether or not individuals will attend arts performances vary by customer group. It is crucial for the marketer to segment the current and potential audience and develop varied programs and messages that appeal to the different targeted segments.

What are the factors that motivate people to attend the arts? What are some of the barriers that inadvertently keep people away? Some factors are based in readily identifiable demographic characteristics. Chapter Two suggests some key audience segments for now and for the future and describes demographic characteristics that are useful for marketers in reaching out to them.

Some factors are human issues—common to people across various audience segments. Chapter Three presents approaches for thinking about the consumer mind-set, such as understanding how risk and uncertainty affect behavior, how people approach decision making, and what benefits people seek from attending the performing arts.

The foundation for developing the organization's mission, objectives, goals, and plans is the strategic marketing process, the subject of Chapter Four. In addition to describing the steps in this process, this chapter offers an extended example of strategic planning from a major dance company in a large metropolitan area.

Chapters Five and Six discuss the key elements in marketing planning: defining and designing the offer, choosing performance venues and ticket outlet options, communicating the organization's messages, and developing pricing strategies—otherwise known as the four Ps of marketing: product, place, promotion, and price. These elements are discussed in light of the focus that marketers should place on customer value, rather than on factors internal to the organization.

If the strategic marketing process is the foundation of marketing planning, then market research can be considered its structural support. Research plays a critical role in understanding customer attitudes and behavior and in planning marketing strategy. Chapter Seven offers an overview of some common research approaches and an example of an extensive audience research project for four arts organizations in San Francisco.

The Internet and e-mail give marketers new power and new responsibilities: the power of instantaneous, comprehensive, and low-cost marketing tools and the responsibility to learn how best to leverage high-tech marketing potential. Chapter Eight goes into detail on the theory and practice of Internet and e-mail marketing and gives several examples of organizations that are capitalizing on these methods in creative and productive ways.

Branding has become a marketing buzz word in recent years, but what is a brand? Why is it important to have a strong brand identity? How can an organization build a brand image that resonates with its publics? Chapter Nine offers answers to these questions and shows in detail how branding strategy was developed at a midsize opera company facing significant changes.

Chapter Ten confronts a major issue facing arts marketers in the twenty-first century: declining subscriptions. From the perspective of many organizations the subscriber is the ideal audience member, and for decades, arts marketers seeking to increase their audience size have worked most diligently on their subscription campaigns. Until recent years this approach was extraordinarily effective. But since the mid-1990s, more and more audience segments are finding subscribing unattractive. Not only are arts marketers less successful at attracting new subscribers, but each year fewer current subscribers are likely to renew. This chapter presents the pros and cons of subscriptions from both the organization's and the customer's perspectives, suggests a new mind-set for the arts marketer on the definition of a valuable customer, and recommends ways to build the subscriber base and alternatives to subscriptions for audience development.

Many people *like* being single-ticket buyers. This growing preference is not short term; rather it is part of a larger societal trend that will affect arts organizations into the foreseeable future. Those arts marketers who continue the decades-old tradition of considering single-ticket buyers a necessary "evil" to fill seats not purchased by "good" subscribers are likely to watch their audience size decline over time. Chapter Eleven therefore suggests a new mind-set and approaches that marketers can adopt to help them reach new and infrequent buyers more effectively and at lower cost than ever before.

Another major societal trend is people's changing expectations, resulting from the experience of heightened customer service in other sectors. It is crucial that arts marketers listen to their customers and provide excellent customer service that meets people's needs and preferences. This is the topic of Chapter Twelve.

The purpose of this book is not only to offer insights on new theories and processes that improve the effectiveness and efficiency of the marketing function but also to help arts managers and marketers develop their own insights in the face of a changing environment and changing customer values so that arts organizations will survive and prosper, for now and into the future.

The chapters in this book need not be read in consecutive order. You can select chapters by the subject matter of interest to you and gain meaningful value. However, the material in each chapter builds on and sometimes refer to concepts and examples in earlier chapters, and the subjects are treated in a logical sequence. It is my hope that each chapter will provide value for every reader, whether a novice or experienced arts marketer.

I expect that readers of this book will have valuable insights and best practices of their own that relate to the theories presented. To broaden the nature and quantity of examples offered here and to ascertain that the concepts have an ongoing relationship to practices in the field, I invite readers to dialogue with me personally. Please share your insights, your ideas, and the results of your efforts by e-mailing me at joanne@artsmarketinginsights.com. Selected contributions will be made available on my Web site (www.artsmarketinginsights.com) and attributed to their submitters.

ACKNOWLEDGMENTS

I would like to thank the arts professionals whose insights and experiences have significantly enriched the material content and focus of this book, especially Julie Aldridge, Alan Brown, Eugene Carr, Brian Dickie, Alan Heatherington, Gayle Heatherington, Glenn McCoy, Robert Orchard, Jim Royce, Greg Sandow, and Roger Tomlinson.

Dorothy Hearst, formerly of Jossey-Bass, encouraged me in the creation of this book, and Jossey-Bass editor Allison Brunner has graciously offered extremely helpful suggestions and support throughout the process. Finally, I cannot imagine writing a marketing book without being guided by the wisdom of Philip Kotler.

Northfield, Illinois   Joanne Scheff Bernstein
September 2006

The Author

Joanne Scheff Bernstein is an educator, consultant, speaker, and author in the field of arts and culture management and marketing. She is adjunct associate professor of Business Institutions at Northwestern University and taught Arts Management at the Kellogg Graduate School of Management for eight years.

Bernstein has extensive experience as a speaker, seminar leader, and workshop facilitator for organizations and associations across the United States, such as the National Alliance of Musical Theater, Dance/USA, the Association of Performing Arts Presenters, and many other national, regional, and local arts service organizations. Internationally, she has lectured in Moscow, Valencia, Cardiff, Helsinki, Caracas, Buenos Aires, Sydney, Melbourne, Brisbane, Adelaide, Milan, and many other cities. She has consulted to theaters, dance companies, opera companies, symphonies, chamber music groups, presenting organizations, museums, and arts service organizations. Her clients include Chicago Opera Theater, San Francisco Symphony, San Francisco Opera, San Francisco Ballet, American Conservatory Theater, Ballet Memphis, Dayton Contemporary Dance Company, Lake Forest Symphony, and Arts Partners of Central Illinois.

She is the coauthor of *Standing Room Only: Strategies for Marketing the Performing Arts* with Philip Kotler (Harvard Business School Press, 1997), which has also been published in Chinese, Russian, Spanish, and other languages. She has had articles published in

Harvard Business Review, California Management Review, International Journal of Arts Management, and other arts publications. She is a member of the scientific committee of the International Association for the Management of Arts and Culture (AIMAC) and serves on the editorial board of the *International Journal of Arts Management.*

She graduated with distinction from the Kellogg Graduate School of Management at Northwestern University and is a member of the Beta Gamma Sigma honor society in business.

ARTS MARKETING INSIGHTS

I write the script, the directors and actors and designers write the production, and the audience writes the play. If there are 200 audience members, there are 200 plays.

—Paula Vogel, Pulitzer prize–winning playwright, 2005

Prologue

Candide, Voltaire's great story, which Leonard Bernstein transformed into a brilliant operetta, tells of exile, of poverty, of war and famine, of rape and murder, of torture, of longing for love, of individual misfortunes, and of earthquakes that shake an entire civilization's very foundation. Does this scenario sound all too familiar to you performing arts managers and board members who are constantly struggling with funding cuts, spiraling expenses, increased competition, and declining subscriptions? At worst you are struggling with your organization's very survival; at best you are seeking ways to sustain its vigor and mission and purpose.

In the midst of torment and chaos, Pangloss, Candide's philosophy teacher, keeps repeating that "this is the best of all possible worlds." Does Voltaire intend us to think of Pangloss as merely a demented buffoon? I think not. Voltaire is clearly advocating our responsibility to change what is in our control, regardless of the circumstances we cannot control. In effect Pangloss is saying that all is not well but all things can be bettered. Voltaire emphasizes this message with the final words in his tale: "we must cultivate our garden."

Clearly, the factors that created stability and sustenance for arts organizations in the past can no longer be depended upon, and arts organizations must take a fresh look at how they can survive and prosper. As Candide learns through his journeys, we cannot eradicate the effects of the world around us, but by limiting and focusing our activity, we can make a difference with the tasks that are within our power.

One company in the business sector, after experiencing sluggish sales of some of its products for many years, discovered that it was not the core product that was unattractive to its publics but the ways in which that product was packaged, promoted, and presented. For twenty-five years, milk, the old standby, was left behind as Americans quenched their thirst with increasingly slick, cool, consumer-oriented beverages. But today, suddenly, milk is flying off store shelves around the country—in some cases with sales increases of up to 500 percent.

It is not the taste of milk that has changed, or consumers' taste for milk. Instead people are responding to a product developed by Dean Foods Company, the largest producer of fluid milk in the United States, that changes the way consumers think about and drink milk. Milk *chugs,* small, plastic milk bottles, are consumer-oriented, on-the-go packages for milk that fit the way people live today—a standard to which traditional milk packaging has fallen short. I cannot resist describing what happens when one puts old milk in new bottles.

Old Milk in New Bottles

Milk, a $23 billion a year industry in the United States, penetrates 98 percent of households in standard half-gallon and gallon containers. But before milk chugs, today's on-the-go consumers, who consume 50 percent of their meals outside the home, had a hard time fitting milk into their daily diets. The design of the old single-serving, nonresealable, square-bottom, gable-top container, available in eight-ounce servings only, was driven by its low cost of production but provided virtually no consumer benefits. Milk chugs, in contrast, are resealable and sized for easy portability and convenience for families and individuals, fitting in car cup holders and in bags, coolers, and lunch sacks. The entire line of Dean Foods milk products is available in the new bottles—including whole and low-fat chocolate milk and fat-free, 2 percent, and whole white milk—and these products are sold in quarts, in pints, and in eight-ounce multipacks.

White milk sales in quart, pint, and half-pint chugs are up 25 to 30 percent compared to sales in the old gable-top containers. Chocolate milk sales have doubled in every market. Seventy percent of the sales are in supermarkets; the other 30 percent are in convenience stores.

Milk has always been considered a child's drink. However, the primary targets for the new chugs are young men aged eighteen to twenty-four, teenagers twelve to seventeen, and moms twenty-five to fifty-four; the latter are avidly buying eight-ounce multi-packs—chocolate or whole white for their kids, fat-free for themselves. The quart-sized containers are being bought for one- and two-person households and by blue-collar workers fueling up for a strenuous day.

The chug is not just a packaging change; according to former Dean Foods marketing director Dave Rotunno, it is a product innovation. The branding strategy began with the name itself. *Chug* elicits meanings such as "on the go" and "don't save." The product's positioning statement is "a cool refreshing body fuel for on-the-go people." *Cool* suggests not just the temperature but the desired image. *Body fuel* reinforces milk's healthy image in contemporary verbiage, without hitting people over the head with the health concept. The positioning statement also implies that milk is a good beverage, not just a good food complement. The "Got Milk" and milk moustache campaigns, designed to build primary demand for milk, emphasized milk as a good food complement but only to a limited number of primarily sweet foods. Those campaigns built top-of-mind awareness, but fell far short of the milk industry's modest goal of increasing sales 1 percent a year for four years.

The chug's award-winning advertising campaign tags the product simply: "Milk Where You Want It." This is a fairly straightforward message that says much about what traditional milk packaging has not been. Dean Foods is looking ahead to putting new flavors of milk in the new bottles.

Just as Deans Foods has discovered that it can considerably increase milk sales with packaging and messages that are relevant to its target markets, creative arts marketers are successfully and even dramatically building audiences without compromising their product by offering their art in "packaging" that fits the ways their consumers live today. All those who say the market for the fine arts of classical music, dance, theater, and opera will continue to erode as competition for the public's leisure time perpetually increases and arts education becomes even more scarce among younger generations should consider that it is up to arts marketers to discover new market segments and new ways to make their organizations' products more exciting, compelling, and accessible.

Those of us who work in arts management often find ourselves making a strong case for the value and importance of the arts. But when we attend a performance, we do so primarily because we are passionate about the arts, not because it is something we "should" do, like eating vegetables or drinking milk. Just as the positioning of milk as a *cool* drink has attracted important new market segments, describing and promoting the performing arts product as *good* (fun, exciting, entertaining, relaxing), not just *good for you* (and not something one needs to "understand" in order to enjoy or appreciate), is an approach from which arts marketers and their organizations can clearly benefit. This approach will also help to reduce the perception held by many individuals that the fine arts are "not for me." Just as the milk chug offers convenience never before available to consumers, arts organizations must package and promote their artistic offerings in ways that are relevant to people's lifestyles.

Arts marketing has come a long way in recent decades. However, many arts managers continue to rely on methods that worked well in the past, and in doing so they are missing opportunities to keep up with the changing lifestyles, needs, interests, and preferences of both current and potential patrons. Throughout this book I will offer new strategies and tactics for effectively attracting and retaining audiences, for building customer satisfaction and loyalty, and for continually analyzing the internal and external environment, so that arts managers can ride the wave of opportunities rather than be pulled down by the undertow.

Now, let us cultivate our garden.

The State of Performing Arts Attendance and the State of Marketing

If we do not change our direction, we are likely to end up where we are headed.

—Old Chinese proverb

In business, as in art, what distinguishes leaders from laggards, and greatness from mediocrity, is the ability to uniquely imagine what could be.

—Gary Hamel and C. K. Prahalad

UNLIKE THE CLASSICS, WHICH REMAIN FRESH FOR each generation, many aspects of the performing arts world are in constant flux. Especially since the turn of the twenty-first century, audience needs and preferences have changed significantly. There is much debate as to whether the art presented on our stages is the source of changing ticket purchasing behavior or whether people are responding differently to how the art is packaged and communicated to its publics. In this chapter I present the perspectives of various experts on this topic, discuss the results of significant survey research on audience behavior, and offer marketing trends and concepts that have a strong effect on consumers in this new age.

The State of Performing Arts Attendance

Among experienced practitioners and researchers in the performing arts industry there is no clear consensus as to the state of performing arts attendance. The following discussions consider the perspectives of various experts in the field and the results of several extensive surveys, all designed to help identify current attendance patterns and important audience trends.

Extinction, Survival, or Vitality?

For decades some knowledgeable observers have been predicting the morbid decline of the performing arts, especially of classical music. Says *New Criterion* music critic Samuel Lipman, "Classical music now stands, for the first time in the modern world, on the periphery of culture . . . classical music today is in deep trouble. It is not clear whether we can do more than bear witness."[1] Norman LeBrecht, music critic for the *London Daily Telegraph* and author of *Who Killed Classical Music?* has written, "Ticket sales have tumbled, record revenue has shriveled, state and business funds have dried up . . . orchestras [are] threatened with extinction. . . . The future of musical performance hangs in the balance at the close of the twentieth century."[2] Pulitzer prize–winning composer William Bolcom warns that "we are, it seems, currently witnessing a crumbling of the façade of the serious music scene in the United States."[3] Robert Schwartz, writing in the *New York Times,* summarized the reasons for orchestras' despair: "There is much unease today among those who head America's orchestras. Statistics show that audiences are aging, and the collapse of arts education in the public schools makes it difficult to find new listeners among a younger, more ethnically diverse urban population. The repertory has grown stuffy and predictable, and daring ventures tend to alienate old, reliable subscribers. Finances are shaky in all the arts, but orchestras . . . are particularly vulnerable."[4]

These concerns are not exclusive to the United States. Heloisa Fischer, founder and director of Viva Música in Rio de Janeiro, says,

"In Brazil, classical music plays only a small part in the life of most people." Asks Fischer, "Is someone working in this segment rowing against the tide? Is classical music an art form which is able to be consumed in contemporary societies?"[5]

Yet, other observers view the state of performing arts attendance with a great deal of optimism. "We live in something of a classical music golden age," insists music expert Douglas Dempster. "Classical music is more widely heard and available, performed at a higher level of preparation and artistry, both in the U.S. and, I would wager, around the world, than it has ever been before. . . . If classical music is in some kind of trouble, it is trouble that is simply not evident in tangible measures of its popularity and availability."[6] In addition, the availability of digital classical music, although in its early stages of adoption, is already having dramatic effects. Even though sales of classical CDs in the United States decreased by 15 percent in 2005, digital downloads of classical albums grew by 94 percent. More significant, several labels are finding that the classical share of the downloaded music business is about 7 percent, more than twice the share in traditional retail outlets. BBC Radio offered free downloads of Beethoven symphonies in June 2005, and the 1.4 million people who downloaded in response prove that audiences for classical music might be larger than anyone thought. And these audiences are likely to be young—Forrester Research reports that most people who listen to downloaded music are between the ages of fifteen and the mid-forties.[7]

Furthermore, reports the *Wall Street Journal*, "the American cultural barometer is rising." In the 1990s, Americans attained a historically high level of wealth, education, and cultural exposure, and as a result the lowest common denominator of American culture is rising rapidly (notwithstanding the popularity of MTV and reality TV). As proof that America is becoming a nation of culture, consider that 41 percent of Americans listened to classical music in the late 1990s compared to 19 percent in the early 1980s; 35 percent of Americans visited art museums in the late 1990s compared to 22 percent in the early 1980s.[8]

A Harris Poll has found that more Americans travel for cultural enlightenment than for sports, shopping, and theme parks combined, and a survey by the Travel Industry Association of America indicates that 46 percent of the almost two hundred million total U.S. travelers in 1998 included a cultural, arts, heritage, or historical activity while on their trip.

There is further evidence that performing arts attendance is strong. Extensive research conducted in 2003 in ten communities across the United States by the Performing Arts Research Coalition (PARC) indicates that attendance at live, professional performing arts events is an activity enjoyed on at least an occasional basis by a significant majority of adults—ranging from 61 to 78 percent of respondents in the various communities surveyed. In fact more people attended a live performing arts event at least once in 2003 than attended a professional sporting event. Frequent attenders, defined as those who attended at least twelve performances over the past year, ranged from 11 to 18 percent of respondents.[9] Moreover, the National Endowment for the Arts (NEA) has reported that a 2002 survey it conducted found that nearly 23 percent of the national audience for classical music was under age thirty-four and a whopping 43 percent were under age forty-four. Opera audiences tracked even younger: 25 percent were under age thirty-four and 44 percent were under age forty-four. Opera attendance, spurred by the use of computerized supertitles that translate lyrics, has been rising steadily and dramatically since 1982. According to the NEA survey, 6.6 million adults (3.2 percent of the adult population) attended at least one opera performance in 2002, reflecting a growth of 43 percent over a twenty-year period.[10] In the United States there are now 110 opera companies, 34 of which were founded after 1980. More than 110 symphony orchestras have been founded since 1980, and the number of nonprofit, professional theater companies has grown to more than 800, compared with fewer than 60 in 1965.

In the U.S. theater industry, some managing directors express concern that they were lulled into a false sense of security during the boom years of the 1990s, when the economy seemed to rise with no end in sight and attendance grew annually. In the five-year period from 2000 through 2004, according to a survey conducted by the Theatre Communications Group (TCG), attendance at 92 *trend theatres* declined 4 percent, and these theaters' ticket sales covered a decreasing proportion of expenses, 5.1 percent less in 2004 than in 2000. Yet during the 2003–2004 season, the 198 *profiled theatres* in the TCG survey attracted a cumulative 12.8 million patrons to more than 39,000 main series performances, numbers that hardly ring a death knell for the field. Among the 258 *universe theatres* that responded to TCG's 2005 survey of non-profit, professional theaters, a majority ended the 2004 season in the black, reversing the trend of the previous few years.[11] This rebound was the result of belt tightening and a vigorous commitment to contributed income generation, meaning that these theaters are managing more intelligently and effectively, as all businesses should do, whether in growing or lean times.

Those who claim that the primary factors inhibiting the growth of performing arts attendance are less expensive and more convenient forms of entertainment should compare the state of the performing arts with the state of the movie industry, which has experienced truly precipitous audience declines. In 1948, ninety million Americans— 65 percent of the population—went to a movie house in an average week; in 2004, thirty million Americans—roughly 10 percent of the population—went to see a movie in an average week.[12] Performing arts advocates should be encouraged that home entertainment options such as DVD players, VCRs, TVs, TiVo, and iPods do not closely replace live arts events as they do the in-theater movie experience.

Following the tragedy of September 11, 2001, fears that audiences would evaporate as people stayed closer to home proved unfounded. On the contrary theaters reaffirmed their relevance as gathering places for people in troubled times. "It was amazing how many people walked by our theatre who just wanted to come in and be a part of something that made them feel good," says Kate Lipuma, managing director of the Signature Theatre Company in New York City.[13] This is an example of the reasons why, despite the uncertainty of the times, many theater leaders are fundamentally optimistic. "The best thing we have on our side is the goodwill of our audience," says Kate Warner, managing director of the Theatrical Outfit in Atlanta. "Of course, the quality of the work on stage and the creativity of artists and administrators are crucial intangibles." By making the most of such assets, while focusing on their mission, arts organizations are positioning themselves to build toward future growth.[14]

It is my contention that the arts themselves are not less desirable than they were in past decades or to past generations. Stagnating or declining attendance can be largely attributed to the fact that the ways the arts are described, packaged, priced, and offered to the public have not kept up with changes in people's lifestyles and preferences. Some declines are and always have been, of course, a function of programming choices. Even during the years when arts organizations enjoyed overall enormous growth in attendance, ticket sales were weak when too much work that was new, unfamiliar, or otherwise undesirable to the organizations' audiences was put on the stage. Other aspects of programming and style of presentation have had an effect on audiences—especially those for symphonic and chamber music concerts—and the nature of arts criticism in the media at times has a negative effect on ticket sales as well.

But in recent years it is changing lifestyles and values that have had the strongest impact on ticket sales. Because of these changes, long-standing arts marketing practices no longer work as they once did. For example, people today are more spontaneous in choosing leisure time activities, are more eager to select exactly which productions they will attend, and in this high-technology age, expect better, faster, and more customized service. Because these trends bode well for new strategies that appeal to single ticket buyers, why do many arts marketers still produce and distribute costly *subscription* brochures, which restrict people to the packages a marketing director offers them, rather than *season* brochures, which people can use to order exactly what *they* want?

People know what they like and often do not want to take risks on what they do not know. Many arts organizations fail miserably in their marketing communications at answering the questions prospective patrons have in their minds: Will I like this show? Will I understand it? Do I need to understand it to enjoy it? Will I feel comfortable there, and will I fit in? What relevance does this performance have to my life? Arts marketers must make a sincere effort to get inside the heads and hearts of their publics. Managers who blame external forces for a decline in audience size, believing the problems are out of their control, are likely to fail. Managers who implement marketing strategies relevant to their target audiences are realizing significant success.

Trends in Arts Participation

Some strategies that were once commonly accepted *best practices* in the performing arts industry are rapidly losing effectiveness because of behavioral and attitudinal changes in the broader environment.

These trends affect not only the ways arts organizations reach out successfully to new audiences but the satisfaction and retention levels of current audiences as well. The trends, insights, and marketing principles presented in the following sections of this chapter are the foundation for the concepts and recommendations presented throughout this book.

SUBSCRIPTIONS VERSUS SINGLE TICKET SALES Subscriptions fueled the dramatic growth of performing arts audiences and the number of new organizations from the mid-1960s through the mid-1990s. But since the late 1990s, with changing lifestyles and more competition for leisure time activities, subscriptions have decreased for the industry as a whole. People have become more spontaneous in choosing their entertainment options, and younger audiences in particular are less likely to commit months in advance to specific dates or to an entire series of performances. From 2001 through 2005, subscriptions at 100 *trend theatres* surveyed by the Theatre Communications Group (TCG) in its 2005 study declined 5 percent, and the average subscription renewal rate dropped from 73 percent to 63 percent. The total number of seats occupied by subscribers declined by 10 percent. But single ticket sales at these same 100 theaters increased 13 percent during that five-year period. Average single ticket income was greater than average subscription income in each of those five years for the first time in decades.[15]

This change in ticket purchasing behavior has dramatic implications for arts marketers. Subscribers guarantee an audience for virtually all of a season's productions and allow artistic directors to produce some works that are less well known or more adventuresome and that might not attract sizable audiences on a single ticket basis. Organizations with a strong subscriber base are far less dependent on good critical reviews for each production than are organizations that rely on rave reviews and word of mouth to attract ticket buyers. Subscribers produce enormous lifetime value to arts organizations. Once a person has subscribed, renewals are far less expensive for the organization to sell than repeated single ticket sales are. Furthermore, subscribers constitute not only the most loyal audience but also the largest group of contributors. On average, the 1,490 *universe theatres* surveyed by the TCG in the U.S. not-for-profit professional theater field are estimated to have received 51 percent of their income from earned sources and 49 percent from contributions in 2005. Theaters with budgets of less than $250,000 averaged 34 percent earned and 66 percent contributed in that year.[16] Individuals are by far the largest source of contributed income for performing arts organizations. The reliance on contributions from loyal attenders means that with a continuing decrease in the subscriber base, new strategies must be developed to attract contributions from single ticket buyers as well as to sustain and grow a loyal audience.

This need has put significant strain on performing arts marketers who must work much harder and more creatively to maintain ticket sales at their former levels.

ATTITUDES TOWARD ARTS ATTENDANCE Some people want to fully engage and learn something every time they go out, whereas others prefer a more passive, disconnected experience. A small segment of the arts-going public seeks to be challenged by unfamiliar art, but many more arts attenders prefer the comfort of revisiting familiar works. Of course there are always people experiencing *Swan Lake* or Beethoven's Fifth Symphony for the first time. As the range of sophistication levels in the audience widens over time, so do expectations for fulfillment. As a result, it gets increasingly difficult for an arts organization to satisfy its various patron segments.

A number of nonattenders claim to feel uncomfortable or out of place at performing arts events. Joli Jensen, in her book *Is Art Good for Us?* says that this perspective derives at least in part from the attitude disseminated, consciously or not, by arts organizations that say, in effect: "The arts are good medicine, especially in today's 'sick' society. The mass media, in contrast, are bad medicine, poisoning a healthy society." Jensen continues, "For many social and cultural critics, the passive, unproven effects of Muzak (the music heard in fast food joints and shopping malls) are a form of social control, while the passive, unproven effects of a single Mozart sonata are examples of social benefit." The problem, says Jensen, is the elitist notion that high culture *does* something (it is good for us), rather than that it *is* something (good in and of itself). Arts supporters cannot persuade people to attend the arts by defining them as "cultural spinach."[17]

People tend to make a sharp distinction between art and entertainment and have a strong, even exclusive preference for one or the other. Composer Charles Wuorinen says, "I think there's a very simple distinction, and it doesn't diminish entertainment in any way, because we all want it and we all enjoy it. Entertainment is that which you receive without effort. Art is something where you must make some kind of effort, and you get more than you had before."[18] This effort is partly a matter of repeated exposure and partly a function of arts education, something arts organizations offer in ever more creative ways to largely receptive audiences.

ARTS EDUCATION The U.S. population is becoming more highly educated. In 1976, 15 percent of adults aged eighteen and over had a college education. In 1997, that number rose to 24 percent, and projections for 2010 indicate the number will rise to 30 percent. This fact is highly significant to arts marketers in that a high level of educational attainment—a bachelor's degree or more—is the single most important socioeconomic factor influencing cultural participation.

In the PARC study conducted in ten communities the idea that the performing arts do not appeal was identified as a big barrier by between 6 and 14 percent of respondents.[19] This barrier was closely tied to educational level and, as might be expected, clearly differentiated attenders from nonattenders.

Yet, the lack of arts education in the schools in recent decades has created at least one generation of young adults who feel that the arts are not for them, that the arts are elitist and something not easily accessed or appreciated. It is anticipated that future generations will reach adulthood with similar attitudes. Results of a study conducted by Arts Council England in 2002 suggest that the arts face a "personal relevance gap." Among the respondents to the survey, 73 percent said the arts play a valuable role in the life of the country, but only half as many (37 percent) said the arts play a role in their own lives.[20]

A Harris Poll conducted in May 2005 of American attitudes toward arts education offered a more promising response. Survey results revealed that 93 percent of Americans agree that the arts are vital to providing a well-rounded education for children. Additionally, 54 percent rated the importance of arts education a "ten" on a scale of one to ten. The survey reveals additional strong support among Americans for arts education:

- 86 percent of Americans agree that arts education encourages and assists in the improvement of a child's attitudes toward school;

- 83 percent of Americans believe that arts education helps teach children to communicate effectively with adults and peers;

- 79 percent of Americans agree that incorporating arts into education is the first step in adding back what's missing in public education today.[21]

TICKET PRICE ISSUES Although ticket price is commonly assumed by arts managers to be a primary barrier to attendance, research repeatedly shows that this factor ranks relatively low among both attenders and nonattenders. Most people who do not attend would not do so even if the tickets were half price. Deep discounts do serve to motivate more frequent ticket purchases and to sell more subscriptions, but small variations in ticket price have little effect on sales. Research demonstrates that people want to choose exactly which performances to attend and are typically willing to pay to have the best possible experience. In fact many arts marketers report that their highest-priced seats tend to garner the most sales. This is part of a larger trend toward *trading up* to premium products and experiences. But as the price of admission goes up, the willingness to risk an unsatisfactory experience goes down. (I will cover pricing in depth in Chapter Six.)

THE HIGH-TECHNOLOGY AGE As more and more businesses leverage the power of high technology to personalize their product offerings, consumers have grown to expect more customized experiences. TiVo users choose exactly which television shows to watch and when to watch them. Netflix patrons order DVDs online, receive them in their mailboxes, return them when they please without any late fees, and receive the next film in their queue two or three days after the previous one is returned. Netflix also builds a recommendation list for each patron, based on that customer's reviews and on what other people with similar taste have liked. When people listen to music in their daily lives, they choose one kind of music while dining and another kind while exercising and upload just what they want to hear to their iPods. Contrast these examples with arts organizations that offer preset programs at a fixed time in a single location and ask patrons to purchase a series of these programs many months in advance. Furthermore, high technology has made it not only possible but common for people to place orders twenty-four hours a day, seven days a week, and find virtually any information they seek. Many arts organizations offering real-time, online ticket sales are experiencing dramatic sales growth, especially among new and younger audiences. This is what people expect today. In the not-so-distant future people may expect that tickets will be sent to their mobile phones, they may expect podcasts of performances, and they may expect that preperformance lectures be made available to them so they can listen in their cars when driving to the venue.

"'Time is becoming the currency of the new millennium,' said Shellie Williams, former senior consultant with LORD Cultural Resources Planning & Management Inc. 'In 1973, the average American had 26 hours of leisure time per week; in 1997, leisure time shrank to 17 hours. A recent study found that half of busy executives would rather take less pay for more time off. With the rise of home offices and electronic accessibility—e-mail, cell phones—people's work follows them everywhere—to the little league field, the dinner table, and the arts venue. With less leisure time available, people are getting very choosy.'"[22] Arts organizations that have not as yet capitalized on the power of Internet and e-mail marketing to simplify and speed up information searches and ticket purchases are missing huge opportunities for growth and for satisfying current audiences.

AUDIENCE TREND EFFECTS "The sum of all these trends," says arts consultant Alan Brown, "is higher demand for more intense and more pleasurable leisure and learning experiences." As people visit interactive museums, play video and computer games, and attend multisensory, highly stimulating events, they are moving further and further away from enjoying fixed, static experiences. There have been false predictions about the demise of the fine arts for decades, primarily triggered by the introduction of such alternatives as television, home videos, and the cocooning trend. Despite these changes the arts have not only survived but have thrived and grown. However, says

Brown, arts managers who think that their organizations are "immune to the shifting sands of demand are sadly mistaken. . . . We cannot invent a more viable future for our institutions and agencies without a deep understanding of how consumers fit art into their lives."[23]

THE STATE OF MARKETING

Presenting quality art is and always will be the primary objective for all arts organizations in realizing their mission. Yet the ultimate artistic experience is the *communication* that happens between the performers and the audience. Without an audience our arts organizations would have no reason to exist. *Marketing* is what facilitates this communication. Effective marketing is an absolute prerequisite for success, and to be consistently successful, marketing managers must continually monitor their environment and keep in touch with changing preferences of their current and potential markets.

Marketing is customer centered. This does not mean that the artistic director of a symphony, opera company, dance company, or theater must compromise his or her artistic integrity. It does not mean presenting more Broadway shows and less Shakespeare. Nor does it mean that an organization must cater to every consumer whim and fancy, as many managers fear. It does mean creating a *total* experience that makes the production more accessible, enjoyable, and convenient and a better fit with more people's lifestyles.

The Marketing Mind-Set

Marketing is a sound, effective technique for *creating exchanges* and *influencing behavior.* When properly applied it is necessarily beneficial to both parties involved in the exchange. The highest volume of exchange will always be generated if the way the organization's offering is described, priced, packaged, enhanced, and delivered is fully responsive to "where the audience is coming from." Marketing directors often ask for ideas on *attracting more people* to their organizations' performances. In addition to determining how best to attract patrons, marketers must also learn how to *break down barriers* that prevent people from attending. These barriers are a function of the customer's needs, interests, attitudes, and preferences, some of which can be influenced by the marketer and some cannot. Attitudes are very difficult to change; many needs can be met easily by flexible and open-minded thinking. This means, however, that it is necessary to truly understand the customer.

A marketing mind-set requires that the organization systematically study customers' needs and wants, perceptions and attitudes, preferences and satisfactions. What gives the marketing manager power is knowledge of the customer. Marketing involves answering questions such as, Who is the customer? What does the customer value? How can we create more value for the customer? Then the organization must act on this information by improving its offerings to better meet its customers' needs.

The traditional marketing mind-set is a *command-and-control* approach that relies on selling to passive customers whose demands and perceptions can be influenced and manipulated. Marketing directors need to evolve to a *connect-and-collaborate* mind-set that ascertains the organization collaborates with customers to create, deliver, and share value.

Marketing is a way of thinking for the entire organization, whether it is in the nonprofit or the business sector. Says Steve McMillan, CEO of the Sara Lee Corporation, "Business success is a function of how well the marketing mind-set is integrated in the entire company. Furthermore," says McMillan, "the perfect offering or cost remains perfect for a fleeting instant. The only advantage that remains *sustainable* in the long term is innovation."[24] A key responsibility of the performing arts organization then is to focus on unmet demand, on opportunities with long-standing, loyal patrons; with infrequent ticket buyers; and with potential audiences. Because audience interests, preferences, and needs keep changing along with changes in individuals' lifestyles and in the broader environment, flexibility and responsiveness are chief objectives of all those in the organization attempting to build and retain audiences.

The Experience Economy

The curtain has risen on "a new economic era in which every business is a stage and companies must design memorable events" that engage customers in an inherently personal way, say Pine and Gilmore in their book *The Experience Economy.*[25] Trendy cafes offer the ambience of cushy sofas, roaring fires, soft jazz, and wireless Internet so that their patrons are happy to pay a premium price for a cup of coffee; sports stores feature rock-climbing walls to keep parents browsing and returning to the store, but cultural institutions have the great advantage that by their very nature they offer authentic, unique, quality experiences with their core offering—what is being performed on stage. We must ascertain that every encounter the public has with our organizations— from our marketing materials to the ticket purchasing transaction and the experience in the lobby—anticipates and enhances the experience of viewing the performance.

A visitor-centered philosophy affects every part of an institution, from the amenities it offers to its programs and even its architecture and institutional site plan. Suggestions for enhancing the visitor's experience will appear throughout this book.

The New Economy

The Internet, other advances in technology, and globalization have combined to create a new economy. The old economy was built on managing industries; the new economy is built on managing information. Previously, say Kotler, Jain, and Maesincee in their book *Marketing Moves,* "the company had been the hunter searching for customers; now the consumer has become the hunter." Instead of acting as hunters, smart managers perform as gardeners, nurturing their customers.[26] Marketers can put this *reverse* marketing into action by paying attention to the customer's four C's: "enhanced customer value, lower costs" (tangible and intangible, perceived and real), "improved convenience, and better communication."[27] Businesses need to shift from focusing on products to focusing on the customers. This requires shifting the marketing mind-set from make-and-sell to sense-and-respond, from mass markets to markets of one, and from seasonal marketing to real-time marketing. Using the Internet the customer can readily tell the organization what he or she wants, and the organization delivers. "Thus," say Kotler, Jain, and Maesincee, "the customer changes roles from 'consumer' to 'prosumer.'"[28]

The emergence of the new economy does not mean the extinction of the old, but it does require a new focus overlying existing approaches.

Attitudes Toward Marketing

Recent research by Yankelovich Partners indicates that people feel they are under siege by marketers. It is estimated that in the 1970s the average person was targeted by 500 to 2,000 ads each day. Thirty years later ad exposure has grown to 3,000 to 5,000 ads per day. This figure is not hard to believe once one considers all the places where brand logos, promotions, and ads show up these days. As a result of overwhelming marketing saturation, marketing resistance is widespread and growing and is a defining characteristic of today's marketplace.[29]

Yet people do not want an end to marketing, say J. Walker Smith, Ann Clurman, and Craig Wood in their book *Coming to Concurrence.* "People just want marketing that is less annoying, less intrusive, less dominating, less saturating, more respectful and more informative."[30] As it has become technologically feasible for people to get just what they want, that is what they are demanding from marketers. What people want these days is more meaning and fulfillment, so the emotions and aesthetics inherent in the arts-going experience are a natural draw for modern-day consumers. But people do not want only a more meaningful experience with a product or experience, they want a better experience with the product's marketing.

ARTS MARKETING INSIGHTS

As we have already seen, we live in a dynamic environment with changing attitudes, preferences, values, lifestyles, and demographics among our current and potential audiences. So in order to *be* current and *remain* current as marketers, we must go beyond learning and adopting trendy marketing strategies and tactics. We must be fluent in marketing principles and approaches to understanding consumer behavior, and we must employ this knowledge as the foundation for the *insights* that will continually keep our organizations and our offerings relevant and appealing.

Gaining Customer Insights

Insight is defined by Microsoft's *Encarta* as "the ability to see clearly and intuitively into the nature of a complex person, situation, or subject." A *customer insight* can be further described by the following characteristics.[31]

IT IS A NOT-AS-YET OBVIOUS DISCOVERY *Wisdom* is sometimes defined as a "penetrating view of the obvious." Insights seem eminently logical in hindsight, but they are not obvious before they are discovered. The incredibly successful launch and implementation of subscription campaigns derived from the insight that many people who attend performing arts events would eagerly buy a series, thereby guaranteeing that they would see an entire season of performances in preferred seating locations and often receive other benefits as well. Although subscription sales have declined since the turn of the twenty-first century, it is just now becoming obvious to many arts marketers that many people now value flexibility, spontaneity, and the ability to choose which programs to attend more highly than they value "their" seats or a subscriber discount.

Marketers are also learning that many people have drawn the unfortunate conclusion that the performing arts are stuffy, elitist, and boring—an assumed "knowledge" in the absence of real exposure. In response the Pittsburgh Symphony Orchestra, which had been losing subscribers for years, invested in several *season preview* concerts in surrounding communities for the 2004–2005 season. The concerts included repertoire from the coming season, meaningful commentary from the stage, insights about the organization, discussions about famous myths surrounding the industry, and a chance for the audience to get to know the musicians. As a result of these events and follow-up phone sales, new subscriptions for that season increased by 60 percent.[32]

IT IS A UNIQUE AND FRESH PERSPECTIVE Insights often emerge from looking at a problem differently. Rather than continuing their ineffective efforts to encourage businesspeople to spend a weekday evening attending a two-hour concert beginning at eight o'clock in the evening, some orchestras in major cities have adopted the *rush hour concert,* typically a one-hour concert offered at 6:30 P.M., so people can attend a concert, avoid heavy traffic, and still spend a good part of the evening at home. This program has been very effective in that many orchestra marketers report that their seats are filled for these concerts and the aisles are lined with briefcases.

IT IS OFTEN ROOTED IN AN OBSERVED ANOMALY In the effort to uncover insights it is important always to ask *why.* This question leads to opportunities for those who find the status quo ineffective and at odds with what should or could be. Dayton Contemporary Dance Company (DCDC), a company with which I consulted in the mid-1990s, could not understand why its well-priced family ticket offer (a discounted price for two adult tickets plus $5 for each child) for its Saturday matinee was selling so poorly. After considering that many child-centered activities are taken on by one parent, due to either divorce or busy schedules, I suggested that DCDC initiate an offer for one adult with one or more children. Also, many parents do not consult the Friday arts section of their local newspaper, where the dance company had historically advertised, for ideas on how to spend an afternoon with their children. So DCDC placed two smaller ads that its target customers would come across in their daily lives—one in the Monday sports section (a young boy looks up at his father and says, "Hey Dad, Let's do DCDC!") and another in the Wednesday women's section (a young girl looks up at her mom and says, "Hey Mom, Let's do DCDC!"). Family tickets for that Saturday's performance sold out.

Developing Customer Understanding

Arts marketers should use two very different approaches for developing customer understanding. Deductive reasoning is the basis of quantitative research, such as the audience surveys organizations often insert in program booklets. Through this approach you try to get specific answers to well-defined questions. In contrast, inductive reasoning relies on observation to formulate an idea or hypothesis and is the basis of qualitative research. Qualitative research generates insights, whereas quantitative research validates insights. You need both in order to devise strategies that are both insightful and viable.

For example, when I was doing market research for several arts organizations in San Francisco, I traveled frequently between that city and my hometown of Chicago. At airports and on planes I chatted informally with frequent business travelers, flight attendants, parents with young children, and others about their interests and habits in attending performing arts events. Surprisingly often, people told me there were many performances they would like to attend, but given their uncertain schedules, they could not buy tickets well in advance, and they assumed there would be no seats remaining—certainly no good seats—if they tried to buy tickets within a few days of the show. I asked these people if they would purchase tickets in advance if they had the option of exchanging their tickets for another performance for a small handling fee. Most responded enthusiastically. Arts organizations are typically highly reluctant to offer ticket exchange privileges to single ticket buyers because this is a benefit for subscribers and creates extra work for box office personnel. However, if the organizations charge single ticket buyers a fee for this privilege, it would not diminish the free subscriber benefit and would cover the costs of the extra effort. The San Francisco arts organizations with whom I was working were then in the process of designing a survey about ticket pricing and related issues and were able to add questions to test out these insights I had gained qualitatively in my conversations. (The encouraging results of this survey can be found in Chapter Eleven.)

Looking Ahead

When tickets can be exchanged, the benefits to both the organization and the customer go far beyond those each gains from attendance at the performance itself. People who come once are much more likely to come again. Customer satisfaction is greatly increased; imagine how much better people feel when they hear, "These tickets can be exchanged for another performance, for a small fee, according to availability. We hope you like the show!" rather than, "All sales are final; there are no refunds or exchanges."

During the first decades of the twenty-first century, we can look forward to a population that is larger, more ethnically diverse, and more highly educated and that also has an increasing number of mature adults with more discretionary time, income, and interest in the arts.

Rather than bemoaning the environmental changes of recent years that are decreasing the effectiveness of the traditional tried-and-true strategies, arts marketers should embrace the opportunity to become relevant and meaningful to new lifestyle segments and new demographic segments and to be responsive to perpetually changing behaviors.

This book is replete with examples of customer insights that have led to new and effective strategies. Some strategies will be generalizable to other arts organizations, but each manager must evaluate the specific needs and opportunities within his or her organization and among its publics. I hope that these insights, along with the principles, trends, and approaches to understanding consumers and developing viable strategies presented throughout this book, will inspire you to realize insights of your own.

Finally, we would all do well to remember Michael Hammer's insight about organizations: "One thing that tells me a company is in trouble is when they tell me how good they were in the past. . . . When memories exceed dreams, the end is near. The hallmark of a truly successful organization is the willingness to abandon what made it successful and start fresh."[33]

Exploring Characteristics of Current and Potential Performing Arts Audiences

You really don't have a play until the audience comes along.

—Robert Brustein

Look at the past . . . and from that extrapolate the future.

—Marcus Aurelius, *Meditations*

EFFECTIVE MARKETING COMMUNICATIONS APPEAL TO a target customer's core values, lifestyles, and interests. However, marketing managers typically replay those strategies that worked in the past and do not take into account changing attitudes and expectations among their customers. Furthermore, a primary focus on current customers will serve only to deplete audiences of the future, because it fails to reach potential new audiences adequately. Arts marketers must develop and implement strategies that develop new audiences while continuing to build loyalty and frequency among current audiences.

In this chapter I will address age and life cycle status, gender, and ethnicity and the ways these characteristics affect various audience segments' attitudes, behaviors, expectations, and preferences. As we will see in Chapter Five, there are numerous segmentation variables that marketers can and should employ when analyzing and developing strategies to reach viable audience groups. The demographic analysis that follows is just the beginning.

SEGMENTING BY AGE AND LIFE CYCLE

Arts organizations face the challenge of appealing to four very different age and life cycle groups: mature adults; baby boomers; thirty- and forty-somethings, who often have children at home; and the younger set, the members of Generation X and Generation Y. Each of these generations is characterized by a different level of exposure to and interest in the arts, by different life cycle factors that affect their propensity to attend arts events, and by differences in lifestyle that strongly affect which marketing messages and media are most effective in attracting them.

The Aging Population

In the year 2000, 34.4 million people in the United States, or 12 percent of the population, were aged sixty-five or more. It is predicted that our older population is going to grow steadily through the early part of the twenty-first century and that by 2010 53.2 million people, or 16.4 percent of the population, will be sixty-five or older. One study, for example, shows that although Chicago's metropolitan region will grow by 16 percent over the next twenty years, the retirement population—those fifty and older—will grow by 40 percent.[1] In Great Britain, it is estimated that over the next twenty-five years the number of people between sixteen and fifty years of age will decrease by 1.5 million and the number of people over fifty will increase by 6 million.

In the United States, Great Britain, and other countries, the generation born during the *baby boom* that took place between 1946 and 1964 is now going through middle age. Baby boomers have the greatest wealth of any generation, and their financial resources will grow as they age and as they inherit from their parents. The one in four Americans aged fifty and older control half of the nation's buying power and three-fourths of its assets. This mature market represents $150 billion in annual discretionary income. Current estimates suggest that in Britain people over forty-five control 80 percent of the national wealth.

American Demographics magazine calls today's fifty and older population "the youngest, the wealthiest, the healthiest, best educated and most ambitious group of retirees ever." Their wealth will be much less important than the values they bring to the idea of growing older and the ways those values influence their spending. The *Future of Retirement* survey, sponsored by HSBC Bank, which interviewed nearly 11,500 adults in ten countries across four continents, has provided valuable insights about how people view the period stereotypically called their *golden years*. Not only do people reject retirement, they also do not want to continue their current lifestyles. Instead, says Ken Dychtwald, CEO of Age Wave, "a totally new model of maturity is emerging—a vibrant landscape filled with new beginnings and personal reinvention, where people remain involved, productive, and connected. People don't like the idea of becoming out of touch, distant, or unnecessary—which are all too often descriptors for many of today's seniors. I don't think it's aging that frightens people. It's the fear of becoming uninspired and unwilling to try new things. In essence, opening yourself up to new experiences and making new friends is the ideal antiaging medicine."[2] This is good news for arts and cultural organizations.

We know that individuals' participation in cultural experiences climbs through middle age and peaks between the ages of forty-five and sixty-four. Arts managers and marketers who bemoan the graying of their audiences should reconsider not only the enormous importance of mature adults as a strong audience base but also these adults' ability to help develop audiences of the future.

MATURE ADULTS Mature adults are a substantial, vital, loyal, and fortunately, growing segment, offering great opportunities for arts marketers to harness. Mature adults tend to have significant discretionary time and income and prefer *being* experiences, of nonmaterialistic origin, to purchasing and possessing products. Mature adults tend to spend more tightly on goods and more loosely on lifestyle enhancement experiences. Some arts organizations offer discounts to seniors for all performances and in all sections of the hall, not considering that many people in this segment are fully able and even eager to pay full price. Arts marketers should address the needs of low-income seniors by offering discounts for one or two performances per week or for specific (nonpremium) seating areas.

Mature adults respond more favorably to marketing messages that emphasize introspective or altruistic values than to those that emphasize selfish values. Marketers should keep in mind that mature consumers tend to be motivated more by the capacity of a product or service to be a gateway to experiences than by the nature of the product itself. This means that mature adults have a propensity to seek the type of fulfillment arts performances offer.

Barriers to attendance for this group are likely to be functional factors, not the arts themselves. An example of one response to a functional barrier is that some theaters and music organizations have moved the time of their Wednesday matinee from 2 P.M. to 10 or 11 A.M. to better accommodate the lifestyles of mature adults, who tend to be early risers and like to avoid rush-hour traffic in the late afternoon.

Mature adults are excellent candidates for group sales. Senior centers and senior residences often have their own program directors and these individuals are likely to be receptive to group sales offers from performing arts organizations. Typically, senior centers and homes provide their own transportation and their program directors would eagerly arrange with an arts marketing director to provide a pre- or postshow lecture and reception with refreshments.

Depending on the city, the neighborhood, and patrons' needs, such transportation services can be door-to-door or patrons can be picked up and dropped off at local shopping centers that have bus service and ample parking.

GRANDPARENTS   About one-third of American adults are grandparents. There are currently 70 million grandparents in the United States, and with more and more baby boomers now approaching grandparent age, this number is expected to swell to over 115 million by 2010.

Today's grandparents have higher levels of education and income than their predecessors and are more likely to participate in arts and culture. They also play a larger role in their grandchildren's lives, in-

Getting There in Gateshead and Newcastle

Getting There, predominantly funded by Arts Council England, is a British program that aims to bring older audiences to the arts and to take new arts to audiences. Members of Getting There pay a flat fee (£5 for three months) and in return receive substantially subsidized taxi fares to arts and cultural events in Gateshead and Newcastle. Members also have opportunities to meet together once a month for an outing to various visual and performing arts centers. Getting There was developed in response to the fact that many older people, particularly those living in areas with little public transportation, find it difficult to get out and often venture on trips only when helped by family or out of necessity. This plan gives people their independence back and has meant that many people who would otherwise be virtually housebound are getting a new lease on life. Participants have universally responded that the ease of door-to-door service was one of the main benefits of the scheme, and 80 percent of those consulted have said that the opportunity to bring a friend was very important to them and supported either their physical or psychological needs. All of the participants consulted said that the Getting There program helped them to feel confident, comfortable, and safe.[3]

cluding their grandchildren's education and cultural enrichment, especially now that many parents work long hours.

As a group, grandparents now spend more than $30 billion a year on their grandchildren, a twofold increase over what was spent a decade ago. It is estimated that grandparents account for almost 17 percent of toy sales in the United States, yet today's grandparents are even more interested in spending money on structured activities they can do *with* their grandchildren.

Grandparents traveling with their grandchildren accounted for one in every five trips taken with children in the year 2000. Six million Americans reported vacationing with their grandchildren in a typical month. *Grandtravel,* grandparents traveling with grandchildren, is becoming so popular that tour operators, hotels, cruise lines, and even Elderhostel have developed programs and promotions tailored to this market.

Arts marketers should capitalize on these trends by offering a special grandparent or child and grandparent membership and promotions tailored to grandparents and their grandchildren.[4]

Singles

As of 2002, there were eighty-six million single people aged eighteen or over in the United States, representing more than 40 percent of the adult population. In 1970, only one in ten men remained single until age thirty-four, but in 2003, one in three remained single through that age. Percentages are similar in the United Kingdom, where, as of 2003, 37 percent of adult men and 41 percent of adult women are neither married nor cohabiting.

It is clear that many arts organizations are either unaware of the huge number of singles (and of odd-numbered groups) or simply do not take them into consideration when they offer *twofer* promotions (two tickets for the price of one). This problem can be resolved simply by offering half-price tickets instead.

Singles nights for young adults have become an effective strategy to attract this market segment. Singles subscriptions are often so popular that they sell out. One of the primary benefits of such events is that they appeal to a young crowd whose members enjoy participating when more people like them are in attendance. These events often feature special programs such as preshow casual dinners or postshow discussions about the performance, sometimes with a wine and cheese reception that encourages socializing. Somewhat ironically, singles do not usually attend these events alone, but they prefer attending when their peer group is well represented.

Too many marketers ignore the significant potential market of older singles, people who like to frequent the arts but often do not do so for lack of a companion with whom to attend or lack of access to transportation. The arts organization can increase the chance that older singles will attend and will have a more satisfying, interactive experience by creating opportunities for conversation. Arts organizations can successfully reach out to this market by, for example, reserving a bloc of *mature singles* seats for certain performances so that these patrons will have a like-minded person at hand with whom to chat before the show, during intermission, and at postshow events. People like to share their thoughts about a production and frequently do so with congenial seat neighbors.

Young Adults

Young adults, those born between 1965 and 1980, number fifty million in the United States and make up 17 percent of the population. They have vast amounts of discretionary income—$125 billion annually—to spend on cars, entertainment, travel, computers, and clothes. Furthermore, young adults will be around to spend money for a long time to come, and they will have more of it in the future.[5] It is both a major challenge and a major opportunity for arts organizations to reach out to young adults in ways that are concurrent with their lifestyles, attitudes, and experiences.

In the 1980s, the young adult segment was stereotypically characterized as the Me Generation—flashy, overambitious, and status conscious. By the 1990s, the newly dubbed Generation X was characterized by genuineness, authenticity, and simplicity. For the Me Generation, on the one hand, effective promotion focused on star performers, the attraction of the best (most expensive) seats, the importance of being there and being *seen* there. Generation Xers, on the other hand, respond best to an approach that emphasizes humanism and honesty, offers value, and is presented with a touch of irony. Generation Xers are skeptical of advertising claims and look at things critically, trying to spot a lie. Marketers must be sure to deliver what is promised. Xers are impressed by messages with a little humor, sarcasm, or irreverence. They value vibrancy and respond to quick-paced ads with lively graphics and music.[6] Because Generation X members spend a lot of time in front of the computer and are comfortable with e-commerce, high-impact Internet marketing techniques play into their propensity to purchase online.

Arts organizations everywhere are discovering it is the highly sought after, younger potential audiences who are most likely to be attracted to purchase tickets to performances through online access. At the San Francisco Opera, Internet ticket sales exploded from $1.5 million during the 1998–1999 season to about $4 million through the first half of the 2000–2001 season. The great majority of these sales were to the new, younger audiences classical organizations crave.[7] Similar results at many other organizations offer clear evidence that it is not the art itself that is at issue for many previous nonattenders, but how and when information and tickets are made available.

Casual Fridays at the Los Angeles Philharmonic

To remove hurdles between young people and orchestral music, the Los Angeles Philharmonic offers Casual Friday concerts. Conductor Esa-Pekka Salonen appears sporting jeans and a T-shirt; the orchestra wears khaki pants and various antifashion ensembles. The audience is invited to arrive in its "rumpled finest." Concerts are somewhat shorter than usual, and patrons are invited to mingle with musicians at a postconcert reception. However, the music is serious business. Recent concerts have included music by Shostakovich, Scriabin, Mahler, Dvořák, Smetana, and Ravel.[8]

Symphony with a Twist in Baltimore

The Baltimore Symphony's new effort to make its musical offerings more intriguing to a younger demographic is called Symphony with a Twist. This series of four Saturday night concerts, according to the symphony's Web site, comes complete with a "lobby full of martini bars, live jazz, tapas and more—each show brimming with unique surprises and great music."[9]

U27 in Canberra

Canberra Arts Marketing, an organization serving the arts in Canberra, Australia, offers a program called U27 (Under 27), a free membership plan that offers cheap tickets to art venues around town for eighteen- to twenty-seven-year-olds. Says the organization's Youth Zone Web site, "The Canberra Theatre Centre wants to make it easier for young people to access our shows and venues, and so do many other performing arts venues." U27 offers discounted tickets at a wide variety of arts organizations and some restaurants in the region and speaks to young people in their own language.[10]

Big Deal at the New York City Opera

The New York City Opera offers Big Deal, a membership program with deep discounts for twenty-one- to thirty-five-year-olds. After an initial enrollment fee of $47.50 ($62.50 for a *duet* membership), members can purchase one ticket to every opera for only $33 for weekday performances or $38 for weekend performances. Members receive the best seats available, and most members sit in the orchestra, which amounts to a savings of up to $67 per ticket. Members receive e-mail invitations to Big Deal parties and special events throughout the season. Members can buy tickets up to two weeks in advance, either at the box office or online for greater convenience. Claudia Keenan, marketing director at the New York City Opera, reports that as of February 2005, there were more than 1,000 Big Deal members and on average they were attending 3.5 performances per year. Approximately 30 percent renew annually, yet the opera realizes some growth each year in the program. Once members reach age thirty-five, the opera sends them a birthday card and lets them know of other ways to get discount tickets to the opera, hoping to eventually "ease them into subscription."[11]

Teenagers

Another major demographic group with important buying power is youths aged twelve to nineteen. In 2000, there were thirty-one million Americans in this age group; by 2010, the number is expected to grow to thirty-four million, or 11 percent of the population. The 1997 National Longitudinal Survey of Youth found that U.S. kids are richer and more sophisticated about money than ever before. Teenagers between the ages of twelve and sixteen are getting allowances from $30 per week in the South to $75 per week in the Northeast. In addition to these allowances, teens are working part-time jobs. In 1998, they spent $141 billion of their own and their parents' money. A teen money Web site called DoughNET records that the kids using the site say they are saving

15 percent of their money and that they are donating 2 to 5 percent to charitable organizations.

Teens are the most informed and media-aware consumers in history. They are especially tech savvy, having grown up using cell phones, faxes, CDs, the Internet, and e-mail as a way of life. Teens rapidly adopt state-of-the-art products, then adapt them to their ever-evolving lifestyles. Not only is the opportunity for arts marketers to target teenagers in their interactive environment great, but only those marketers who appeal to teens technologically and interactively are likely to succeed.[12] Each arts organization should consider designing part of its Web site to be particularly appealing to teens and should offer click-throughs to online ticket sales for older teens who have access to credit cards.

Teens are also marketing savvy, having been exposed to more than 1,200 advertising messages per day during their lifetimes. Consequently, they're more immune to traditional ad messages than any other generation before them. Teens don't want to be told by advertisers that something's cool; they would rather find it on their own or through their peer group.

Word-of-mouth and *viral marketing* are the best ways to reach this generation. Arts organizations can try enlisting other teens to distribute free tickets, specially priced group offers for teens, and other incentives. Marketers might consider efforts to excite this age group to become participants in a teen club or teen membership program.

No matter how respected and successful an arts organization may be, it must plan for the future by building audiences among today's youths. Arts marketers can follow the lead of Stéphane Lissner, artistic director of La Scala, the world-famous opera house in Milan and long the exclusive playground of the rich, who announced in summer 2005 that he will welcome the younger generation into the luxurious theater with a series of Sunday concerts that will be free for anyone under age eighteen who is accompanied by an adult.

Children

Many arts organizations have been proactive and creative in educating youngsters about the organizations' art forms by presenting in-school programs and special student performances and by offering a wide range of educational material.

High 5 Tickets to the Arts in New York City

High 5 Tickets to the Arts is an exemplary organization. It was created in New York City in 1993 to develop new audiences for dance, theater, music, film, and art by making New York City's cultural life affordable and accessible to teenagers. The High 5 calendar presents incredible variety and selection, offering thousands of tickets each season to events at more than 500 of the most prestigious concert halls, off-Broadway theaters, avant-garde performance venues, and world-class museums in New York and New Jersey. These arts organizations donate tickets to their performances and exhibits, and High 5 markets, promotes, and sells these tickets to teenagers for just $5. High 5 serves teenagers from every segment of the population, but makes a special effort to reach into communities where teenagers are economically disadvantaged, culturally diverse, and at risk. By July 2005, High 5 had sold more than 93,000 tickets.

Teens can purchase High 5 tickets at Ticketmaster outlets up to one day before the event, free of service charges; at the box office at least thirty minutes prior to the start of the event; and online at www.high5tix.org. Small groups can purchase group tickets by calling the High 5 office. Group tickets are six for $25, and groups may include up to two adults. For performances Monday through Thursday, teens can buy two tickets for $5. This allows them to bring a friend or sibling or a teacher, parent, or other adult who would otherwise be ineligible.

To market its programs, High 5 has developed a catalogue that is published three times a year and has an annual circulation of 225,000 and brochures geared toward students and adults that provide brief overviews of High 5 and how the program works. High 5 receives pro bono advertising from major publications and TV stations, has enjoyed editorial coverage in a wide variety of local newspapers and magazines in English and Spanish, and has an extensive mailing list of teens, schools, and community-based organizations. The High 5 Web site, which receives 34,000 hits per month, displays an online version of the catalogue as well as daily updates and special announcements, links to nearly fifty

High 5 Tickets to the Arts in New York City, *continued*

youth- and arts-related organizations, a section devoted to student reviews, and a Spanish language section. The High 5 weekly e-mail newsletter, sent to about 10,000 customers, contains the week's featured performances and staff recommendations.

The High 5 arts ticket offer is enhanced by several special programs. Take 5 is an intensive, guided, small-group experience that allows adults to take small groups of teens to arts events at High 5 ticket prices, and this program accounts for 60 percent of High 5 ticket sales. The Freelance Program recruits students to "freelance" for High 5 by writing reviews of performances in the High 5 calendar and then uploading them onto the organization's Web site. The Teen Reviewers and Critics Program is an honors program that selects teens to participate in a workshop series with professional arts critics. Participants spend five weeks on each discipline (such as dance, music, theater, or the visual arts) and learn how to shape their reviews. *2001: An Arts Odyssey* was a collaboration between thirty-five New York City museums and arts institutions, the New York City Board of Education, and High 5 Tickets to the Arts. For one weekend, teenagers were able to purchase one $5 ticket that gave them entry into any and all of the participating museums. Participating teens made more than 5,000 museum visits during the course of the festival, and most of these teens had never been in those museums before. In order to build its outreach efforts, in 2001 High 5 launched the Community Partnership Initiative with representatives of key youth service organizations around New York City, including the Board of Education, New Yorkers for Children, United Neighborhood Houses, and New York Cares.

High 5 has three affiliate sites in Columbus, Ohio; Freeport, New York; and Montreal, Canada. Not all cities provide conditions ideal for a program such as this, but aspects of this program can be borrowed or adapted for use by arts organizations, arts service organizations, and community groups in cities and towns with various levels of cultural offerings.

Very Young People's Concerts
at the New York Philharmonic

The New York Philharmonic has launched Very Young People's Concerts, a junior version of the Young People's Concerts that it began in 1924 and that were later made famous by Leonard Bernstein. Designed for children aged three to five, the one-hour concerts introduce youngsters to classical music through games, active listening, and hands-on music making with members of the Philharmonic. Each concert has a host and a theme, such as "Fast and Slow," "Loud and Soft," or "High and Low."

Sound Learning in Atlanta

Sound Learning, a partnership between the Atlanta Symphony Orchestra (ASO) and Georgia State University, is a new educational program in which symphony musicians visit an elementary school four or five times a year. Symphony musicians tailor their presentations to various subjects, illustrating how, for example, music fits in with math, science, or social studies. Children plan a project around the musicians' visits—making instruments or studying the cultures of various composers. They also attend a symphony performance. Says ASO bass player Michael Kurth, "It was a blast. Usually in the classes I visit, it's 'This is my instrument, this is how it sounds, thank you very much, see you next year.' But with Sound Learning, I had time to discuss with students their roles as audience members and focus on the tie between music and emotions."[13]

Teddybear Concerts in Sweden

Sweden's Malmö Symphony Orchestra, like many Swedish arts organizations, has a strong commitment to children's concerts. This orchestra's version is called Nallekonsert (teddybear concert) and is aimed at children from the age of four upward. It is estimated that 25,000 children and young people attend the orchestra's school

Teddybear Concerts in Sweden, *continued*

concerts every season. The orchestra's Web site has a special section that features music quizzes and games for kids.

Keeping Score in San Francisco

The San Francisco Symphony's Keeping Score program is another effort designed to bring the arts back into the schools in a meaningful way. The Keeping Score educational program trains teachers to integrate music effectively into core subjects such as science, math, English, history, and social studies. Teachers are trained by the symphony's educational staff and musicians and by arts educators and receive professional development training and assistance throughout the school year. The program, which began in 2005 with a pilot program involving twenty area teachers, is planned for expansion in California and then nationally over a five-year period.

Typically, the goal of special children's programs is to build the audiences of tomorrow. However, Peter Brosius, Minneapolis Children's Theatre Company (CTC) artistic director, has a more immediate goal, which he described on the occasion of the CTC's winning the first Tony award for excellence in regional theater ever given to a theater aimed entirely at kids: "Central to the mission of this theater is the belief in the power of young people—not as future subscribers or donors, but as arts audience of today." Even so, CTC, which was founded in 1965, has developed several generations of adult audiences who started out by going to CTC.[14]

Family concerts are geared to children, but parents are the ones who buy the tickets. So arts organizations market to parents, aiming to convince them that their children will have an enriching, entertaining experience. Furthermore, says Pam French Blaine, vice president for education and community programs at Orange County's Pacific Symphony, "We are educating the parents at the same time as we are educating the kids. Parents will put themselves in learning situations for the sake of their children in ways that they might never do for themselves."[15]

Unfortunately, the limited revenue potential of family programs makes them a low priority in marketing budgets. Yet arts managers and marketers need to carefully consider the long-term value of acquainting children and their parents with the organization's art form and building a familiarity that will translate into regular arts attendance when these individuals have more maturity, time, and disposable income.

Families

Some arts performances by their nature offer opportunities for marketing to families. In fact certain events, such as productions of *A Christmas Carol* and *The Nutcracker,* are typically advertised as family entertainment. Because nearly half of North American dance companies' annual earned revenue comes from holiday season productions of Tchaikovsky's *Nutcracker,* dance companies typically leverage every possible marketing opportunity to attract patrons to these performances and increase revenue with specially designed amenities. The New York City Ballet offers parents the opportunity to purchase a photograph of their child with one of the ballerinas; many *Nutcracker* performances nationwide are followed, for an additional fee, by after-concert receptions replete with tea and cookies and dancers milling about. These activities are not geared conceptually around an afternoon at the ballet but rather around the idea of family holiday entertainment. For it is the occasion of the Christmas-time celebration that induces families to attend and to spend more than they would ordinarily, not the cultural event in and of itself.

Of course there can be many opportunities for marketing to families throughout an organization's entire season of performances.

SEGMENTING BY GENDER

There is substantial evidence that gender affects how people process information, respond to messages, and make decisions. It is believed that these differences emerge in part due to socialization and in part for biological reasons.

Differences Between Women and Men

Research shows that more than 80 percent of purchasing decisions in the United States today are made by women. Furthermore, since the late 1980s, women have been earning 57 percent of the college degrees awarded and about half of the professional graduate degrees. Today, women bring in at least half the income in a majority of U.S. households and control 51.3 percent of the private wealth in the United States. The largest wealth transfer in U.S. history is occurring as baby boomers inherit from their parents. Because women outlive men, family assets will be concentrated in the hands of boomer women.[16]

Undoubtedly, women are the largest and most important market segment, and marketers should seriously consider what approaches are most effective in reaching women. Women's communal focus prompts them to consider both the self and others in making a decision. The fact that females tend to be more detailed processors of disparate bits of information than men manifests itself in women's greater likelihood of processing message information that includes different types of product benefits. Women want comprehensive information, want to compare more options, and often have many questions they want answered. Women think laterally and notice things peripherally, so it is helpful to be subtle when marketing to them. In contrast, men respond better to messages that focus directly on a single benefit. Men tend to be highly goal directed and prefer messages that help them make a quick and simple decision.[17]

Women also like stories; they like to hear them and they like to tell them. Because women are predisposed to share information with their friends, especially information based in emotional contact, marketers should create messages that not only influence the reader but help the reader to transmit the message. Martha Barletta, author of *Marketing to Women,* suggests that it is much easier for women than for men to recall and recount an ad that contains sound bites, strong visuals, and stories.[18] Marketers should also capitalize on the fact that women thrive on connecting with one another, says Faith Popcorn in her book *EVEolution.* A brand must be differentiated not in the way you bring components together but in the way you bring women together. Successful brands host relationships among their consumers; brands will become the fulcrum for connecting. Women will bond over brands, form clans and clubs and communities around brands. Says Popcorn, "A customer of the moment is the one who buys your brand; a customer for life is the one who joins it."[19] What better catalyst for connecting people is there than the performing arts, which bring people together and stimulate ideas, curiosity, and conversation?

Marketing to Women

"We have to market toward women," says Jon Teeuwisen, executive director of the Joffrey Ballet. "Our audience is 60 percent female, and most of the men who come do so because women bring them." The Joffrey's ads were changed to show less athleticism, which appeals to men, and more grace and inspiration, which attracts female balletomanes. "We wanted to reach the inner ballerina in women who have taken classes," Mr. Teeuwisen explained. "We also started a very successful women's board, and organized affinity groups which featured professional women as keynote speakers before performances."[20]

Gays and Lesbians

It is estimated that 4.8 percent of the population in the United States, or about fourteen million people, are gay. "The average household income for gay people is $61,300 compared with $56,900 for heterosexuals. . . . Nineteen percent of both gay men and women have postgraduate degrees, compared with 14% of heterosexual men and 12% of heterosexual women."[21]

"Gays are twice as likely to have graduated from college, twice as likely to have an individual income over $60,000 and twice as likely to have a household income of $250,000 or more." Moreover, "gays comprise a $350 billion market fiercely loyal to brands that advertise directly to them."[22] In fact research shows that 94 percent of gays and lesbians "would go out of their way to purchase products and services marketed directly to them."[23]

In the early nineties it was sufficient to run mainstream advertising in a gay publication to capture the attention of the market. Today, with more marketers vying for the gay consumer dollar, the bar has been raised. Gay consumers now expect advertisers to address them for who they are, directly and openly. In focus groups nationally, gay men and lesbians express a definite preference for advertising that specifically reflects their mind-set and sensibilities.

Rarely can gay marketing efforts rely on traditional advertising alone. Extending your reach among this audience requires understanding the community infrastructure available to access them. The result is often a sophisticated mix of advertising, direct marketing, community presence and Internet promotions.[24]

SEGMENTING BY ETHNICITY

The ethnic composition of populations in the United States is changing dramatically. In 1990, one out of six U.S. workers belonged to an ethnic minority; by 2000, the proportion was one in three. It is projected that by 2020, the U.S. population of African Americans, Hispanic Americans, and Asian Americans combined will double. These three groups' combined spending power is in excess of $600 billion a year, and it will only rise as their populations grow at a faster-than-average rate. The search for new patrons for now and into the future means looking to these nontraditional markets. Arts organizations must learn how to include members of diverse minorities among their audiences, boards of directors, donors, and volunteers.

Says David Brooks in the *New York Times,* "Communications technology hasn't brought people closer together; it has led to greater cultural segmentation, across the world and even within the United States . . . as people are empowered by greater wealth and education, cultural differences become more pronounced, not less, as different groups chase different visions of the good life."[25] This places new demands on arts marketers to understand how to break down physical, psychological, and cultural barriers to participation and how to help people feel that our arts organizations and our offerings are for them.

"Cultural programming in America often has been comprised of bringing in the latest popular ethnic production, without feeling the need to make any connections with the affiliated ethnic groups in the surrounding community," says Susan Lipman, former executive director of the now-defunct presenting group Performing Arts Chicago.[26] The only way to make these connections work is to invest a great deal of staff time in locating the business, religious, social service, media, and educational leaders in target ethnic communities, setting up an advisory group composed of these people, and soliciting as much information as possible to learn cultural biases and preferences and how best to meet the needs and interests of each group to develop compelling communication strategies, special pricing offers, and so on. Grassroots community efforts require an intensive time investment, which pays off in understanding, learning, and long-term audience development.

Hispanics

According to MarketResearch.com, the U.S. Hispanic population grew more than four times as fast as the U.S. population as a whole between 1990 and 2002. With an estimated 38.8 million Hispanics in the United States in 2002, Hispanics are now the largest single minority group in the country, and this population is expected to continue to grow at a more rapid rate than other population segments, with a projected population of eighty-one million by 2050.

Hispanic household income has been increasing at a rapid rate; more than 3 million Hispanic households have an income of $50,000 or more and about 1.5 million households have an income of $75,000 or more. It is estimated that Hispanic disposable personal income will top $900 billion in 2008, representing cumulative growth of nearly 46 percent from 2003.

Because education is the demographic factor most closely linked with arts attendance, it is important to note that college enrollment among Hispanics shows a steady increase. In 2000, Hispanics earned 9.1 percent of all bachelor's degrees awarded in the United States, compared to only 4.3 percent in 1980. Analysts indicate that new Hispanic immigrants see the link between education and affluence; Hispanic parents are and will be encouraging educational opportunities for their children.[27]

Traditional ideas about family retain a strong hold on Latinos in the United States, whether they are foreign born or U.S. born. According to a Pew Hispanic Center/Kaiser Family Foundation survey, 89 percent of Latinos believe that relatives are more important than friends, compared with 67 percent of non-Hispanic whites and 68 percent of African Americans. The results of this research indicate that arts organizations could most effectively reach out to potential Hispanic audiences with family-oriented programming, pricing, and scheduling.

This niche market of today will become a mass market in its own right, segmented not only by nationality (for example, Mexican or Guatemalan) but also by spending behavior and other psychographic characteristics. Survey research confirms that Hispanic identity and a connection to Hispanic culture have remained remarkably strong across generations of Latinos now living in the United States. Marketers must learn how to create campaigns that resonate with Latino identity and culture.[28]

According to Packaged Facts, conventional wisdom holds that because Latinos receive only a fraction of the direct mail offerings sent to non-Hispanics, they pay more attention to them and consequently are highly desirable prospects for direct marketers.[29] A number of firms have found that bilingual direct-mail pieces draw better responses than English-only or Spanish-only pieces. However, direct mail from arts organizations to Hispanics must be extremely well targeted in order to garner a response rate that is worth the cost to the marketer.

African Americans

U.S. non-Hispanic blacks number an estimated thirty-two million, or 12 percent of the U.S. population. The mean income of African American households grew 25.8 percent between 1990 and 2000, resulting in 3.7 million African American households with annual incomes of $50,000 or more. Since the mid-eighties the buying power of African American households has more than doubled and has grown 50 percent faster than that of the U.S. population as a whole, totaling $656 billion in 2003. Other key social and economic indicators—such as home ownership and college enrollment—are also improving at above-average rates for African Americans. Another factor in the rising affluence of African Americans is a noticeable increase in the number of high-income, married-couple African American families. As a result of these long-term trends, more and more

African American households are achieving middle- and upper-income status.[30]

Despite economic changes in the African American community, values and attitudes remain the same. Home and family are extremely important to this segment, as are church, religion, education, and community involvement. In a study done by Yankelovich/Burrell, 39 percent of African Americans say the home provides all, or almost all, of their satisfaction, whereas only 25 percent of nonminorities found their home so satisfying.[31] Religion ranks very high among African Americans, with 73 percent citing religion as being very important, compared with 47 percent of nonminority populations.[32]

In order to effectively market to and ultimately win the African American customer, it is important that organizations demonstrate an understanding of and respect for African American culture in their communications, marketing programs, and sponsorships. Most African Americans are discerning shoppers and can easily perceive whether or not a business or organization is welcoming. African American consumers want to see themselves in advertisements; they want to know they are being invited to select a product or service. Organizations should place ads in media that this community trusts and, when possible, feature members of the community, whether they be artists or audience members, in the advertisements. Building relationships within the African American community through channels such as events and community-based programs is important, not only to generate business but to maintain loyalty.

The significant number of African American theaters and dance companies across the United States attests to the strong interest among this market segment in the performing arts. Many predominately white organizations are working to attract African Americans to their performances by incorporating works by African Americans on their stages, by casting people of color in their productions, by diversifying their boards and staff, and by reaching out to this segment in their local churches and community centers.

Asian Americans

The United States has nine million Asian Americans, and this population is growing at an exceptionally high rate. Between 1990 and 2000, the Asian American population increased nearly four times as fast as the U.S. population as a whole. The Asian American population is the most affluent demographic segment in the United States and presents a more favorable economic profile than the country's non-Hispanic white population. This group earns more on average than any other racial group, with annual married-couple household incomes of $83,803—8 percent more than non-Hispanic white households earn. The U.S. Asian American population had buying power of $246 billion in 2001, making it an especially important consumer segment for retailers and marketers nationwide. Nearly half of Asian Americans have a bachelor's degree or a higher degree, and Asians are twice as likely as Caucasians to enroll in college.[33]

The Asian American market consists of numerous subgroups with distinct languages and cultural frames of reference. Although the great majority of Asians in the United States have English language facility, Asians respond best to messages in their native language and delivered via their ethnic media. Furthermore, advertisements need to reflect an Asian cultural context, and some of the most effective marketing campaigns have been tied in with Asian festivals and holidays. Asians are the heaviest Internet users of all U.S. groups, and strategies to reach out to Asians should include a strong online component.[34]

People link with others who are similar to them. The implications, says Emanuel Rosen in his book *The Anatomy of Buzz*, are that first, the more similar your employees are to your customers, the easier the

Chinese Audiences at the Sydney Symphony

Xing Jin, multicultural marketing manager of the Sydney Symphony in Australia, says that he owes much of his success with Chinese audience development to his Chinese background and Chinese language skills. Says Jin, "As I came from the same community, I understand the Chinese customer's interests and concerns very well. To help to bridge the language barrier, we produced a series of Chinese language promotional materials and employed a Chinese-speaking person in customer service to handle all Chinese customers' booking. The result was phenomenal."[35]

communication between them will be. Second, people who are similar to each other tend to form clusters.[36] Identifying these clusters and reaching out to them effectively is a prime challenge for marketers.

Attracting Russian Audiences

Sergei Danilian, an Armenian promoter who has brought a steady stream of Russian performers to the United States, relies on a bevy of methods to get the word out to the estimated one million Russian speakers living in the New York–New Jersey–Connecticut area. In addition to direct mail and television and radio advertising on the Russian stations, he connects with the local communities, placing signs with Cyrillic lettering in store windows and selling tickets in the traditional fashion—in small kiosks found in bookstores, mobile phone shops, and at the box office of a large theater which features Russian performers and Russian food in its restaurant.[37]

Because of generational differences and the diversity of ethnic subgroups, locating the media outlets and messages that will target these various markets is quite difficult. As a general rule, marketers can best reach diverse groups where and how they live. "A lot of it really is guerilla marketing," said Erica D. Zielinski, general manager of the Lincoln Center Festival. "For example, for the United States premiere of *I La Galigo*, avant-garde director Robert Wilson's adaptation of an Indonesian epic, Lincoln Center marketing interns approached Indonesian mosques in Long Island City and Indonesian restaurants in Park Slope. They dropped flyers at an Indonesian-owned bank on Wall Street, a South Asian martial arts studio in the Flower District, and even a couple of yoga studios in SoHo." This sort of effort requires a knowledge of ethnic enclaves and depends on the help of specialists.[38]

The type of information offered in this chapter should be just a starting point for arts marketers in their efforts to know current and potential customers. Another important, informative element in the process is understanding the consumer mind-set, which we will explore in the next chapter.

Understanding the Consumer Mind-Set

Our mission is the orchestration of social interaction, in which the performance is a piece, but only a piece, of what we're called to do.

—Ben Cameron

If you're trying to persuade people to do something, or buy something, it seems to me you should use their language, the language they use every day, the language in which they think.

—David Ogilvy

IN HIS WELL-KNOWN BOOK *THE TIPPING POINT*, MALCOLM GLADWELL relates the story of the so-called fear experiments conducted by social psychologist Howard Leventhal in the 1960s. "Leventhal wanted to see if he could persuade a group of college seniors at Yale University to get a tetanus shot." He gave all the students "a seven-page booklet explaining the dangers of tetanus, the importance of inoculation, and the fact that the university was offering free tetanus shots at the campus health center to all interested students." The booklet was distributed in several versions so Leventhal could track the impact that his various approaches had on students' likelihood of getting a shot. "Some of the students were given a 'high fear' version, which described tetanus in dramatic terms" and included vivid photos of people suffering with tetanus. "In the 'low fear' version, the language describing the risks of tetanus was toned down and the photographs were omitted."

Results of a questionnaire administered at a later date showed that all the students appeared to be well educated about the dangers of tetanus, and that, predictably, "those who were given the high-fear booklet were more convinced of the dangers of tetanus, more convinced of the importance of shots, and were more likely to say that they intended to get inoculated." Yet one month after the experiments, only 3 percent of the students, no matter which booklet they received, had gone to the health center to be inoculated.

Leventhal redid the experiment with new subjects, keeping the messages the same, but this time he included a "map of the campus with the university health building circled and the times that shots were available clearly listed." *With this one small change,* the vaccination rate rose to 28 percent. Says Gladwell, "The addition of the map and the times when the shots were available shifted the booklet from an abstract lesson in medical risk . . . to a practical and personal piece of medical advice. And once the advice became practical and personal, it became memorable."[1]

Those who complain that people do not like the performing arts and that nothing marketers say or do attracts people to come must look more carefully at how they are packaging and promoting their offers to the public. Often functional details prevent people from attending, not the artistic offerings.

Says marketing professor Mohanbir Sawhney, "While companies have to focus on creating great products, customers think in terms of the activities they perform and the benefits they seek. For companies, products are ends, but for customers, products are means. . . . The disjunction between how customers think and how companies organize themselves is what leads to inefficiencies and missed opportunities."[2]

Music critic Alex Ross believes the name *classical music* is a "masterpiece of negative publicity, a tour de force of anti-hype. It cancels out the possibility that music in the spirit of Beethoven could still be created today. . . . When people hear 'classical,' they think 'dead.' The music is described in terms of its distance from the present, its resistance to the mass—what it is not. You see magazines with listings for

Creative Scheduling

The Cherry Lane Theater in the West Village of New York City dropped its 2 P.M. matinee after realizing great success with its 11 A.M. Wednesday show. This early matinee was initiated to lure busy mothers to attend performances of *EVEolution,* a two-woman play chronicling motherhood's bumps and triumphs. The early start allowed mothers to be out in plenty of time for the three o'clock school pickup. These performances attracted not only carloads and busloads of moms but also older adults who enjoyed beating the late afternoon rush hour.[3]

Increasing Accessibility at the City of Birmingham Symphony Orchestra

In 2001, the City of Birmingham Symphony Orchestra (CBSO) implemented a new communications strategy to get rid of anything stuffy, snobby, and dull and to be seen as friendly, approachable, and passionate about music while still adhering to its international reputation for high-quality performances and pushing the boundaries of music making.

As part of this new identity the CBSO created several programming strands aimed at nontraditional concert-goers, including Sunday afternoon family concerts—fun events that dispense with the usual traditions. For these concerts CBSO employs presenters, either from TV or radio or from the orchestra, to introduce each piece, describe some instruments, make the experience fun, and create a relaxed atmosphere. These concerts have offered such features as children conducting the orchestra, special lighting effects, magicians, and players dressed up as wizards. In the beginning most attenders were subscribers bringing their grandchildren, but now about 60 percent of attenders are new to the CBSO. Although this program targets families, other adults come without kids because they like the informality and low-key, educational presentation style. These concerts have been the CBSO's most successful venture and are almost always sold out.[4]

Popular Music in one section and for Classical Music in another, so that the latter becomes, by implication, Unpopular Music. No wonder that stories of its imminent demise are so commonplace."[5]

As these examples and comments suggest, the key to sustaining and developing cultural consumption at arts organizations is to adopt a customer-centered approach to marketing. Successful arts organizations systematically study customers' needs and wants, perceptions and attitudes, preferences and satisfactions, and then act on this information. This does not mean that artistic directors must compromise their artistic integrity or cater to every consumer whim and fancy. At its best the organization glorifies the talents and creativity of its artists and retains the primacy of its artistic vision. But it also understands that audience size and satisfaction will be maximized when the ways the organization's offerings are described, priced, packaged, and promoted are fully responsive to the customer's needs, preferences, and interests.

The success of an organization is a function of the thoughts and emotions target markets attach to the organization itself, to its offerings, and to its people. By putting themselves inside a current or potential patron's head and heart, by understanding how a person's behaviors and lifestyle affect his or her leisure time decisions in general and arts attendance decisions in particular, arts marketers can effectively generate new audiences for the arts, increase the attendance frequency of current patrons, and provide customer satisfaction in ways that enhance the quality of the audience members' experience with the art itself.

RISK AND UNCERTAINTY

Arts marketers often ask how they can *attract* more people to attend their organizations' performances. An important consideration is not just identifying the factors that will *entice* people to attend but also identifying and breaking down the barriers that *prevent* people from attending.

Nobel Prize–winning behavioral economist Daniel Kahneman, whose insights concern human judgment and decision making, has done extensive research about people's propensity to dislike uncertainty and to be extremely risk averse. Kahneman argues that people think in terms of both gains and losses but, in the short term especially, fear loss much more than they value gain.[6] In other words, when people ask themselves, "Will I be better off or worse off if I take this action?" the negative possibilities loom larger than the positive ones. Furthermore, intuitive decisions are shaped by the accessibility of different features of a situation. Highly accessible features influence decisions, whereas features of low accessibility will be largely ignored. Says Kahneman, "Unfortunately, there is no reason to believe that the most accessible features are also the most relevant to a good decision."[7]

Too often the most accessible features of an advertisement for an arts performances are the names of performers, composers, or choreographers, names that only die-hard fans would recognize. As Welz Kauffman, executive director of the Ravinia Festival, the summer home of the Chicago Symphony Orchestra, says, "rather than working to win over new audiences, the average newspaper advertisement for a classical event simply lists names that are probably unfamiliar to a majority of readers."[8]

Common risks that people face when considering attending a performing arts event are the fear that they will not understand the performance, that they might applaud at the wrong time, or that they will be bored or just not like the performance, incurring both the tangible and intangible costs of a bad experience. When considering a ticket purchase, infrequent or nonattenders often ask themselves: Will there be other people like me there? Will I feel like I belong there? Do I need a degree in music to appreciate the performance? Will I be able to get tickets? Tickets for good seats? Seats I can afford? Will I be able to find someone to accompany me?

Henry Fogel, president and CEO of the American Symphony Orchestra League, fixes blame firmly on the musical establishment for the fact that classical music has gradually been marginalized, especially in the last twenty years. "Complex program notes, musicians in white ties and tails, and dowagers who hiss if one claps at the wrong time all keep newcomers out of the concert hall," he has noted. After recently seeing a conductor wag his finger at concertgoers who applauded too soon, Fogel wondered "how many more times those people will actually pay money for tickets so they can be humiliated."[9]

It is not only the new or infrequent attenders who face risks in attending performances. People who frequent full-length story ballets may expect that they will not appreciate modern dance repertory. People who attend popular symphonic concerts may perceive it as risky to attend concerts featuring the works of modern composers. Researchers conducting a study of dance attenders in Scotland found it difficult to recruit participants for their focus groups because even frequent ballet and contemporary dance attenders became anxious when they realized that the topic would be dance. They felt uncomfortable talking about dance and were worried that they would seem stupid or ignorant. One respondent said, "I don't understand half of what they're trying to put over in dance but I just like freedom of movement." Many study participants said they were careful in their choice of programs to attend as they wanted to be sure they were going to enjoy an event before they committed to seeing it. The variability of the quality of the experience from one production to another, especially when one is choosing among different performing groups, adds another element of risk that creates a barrier to attendance.[10]

The 2002 American Express National Audience Research Project looked at the attitudes of current performing arts ticket buyers who have not made the leap to opera. More than half said that knowing the "story line" was critical to their decision to purchase an opera ticket. About 30 percent said that they would be unlikely to attend because they did not understand the art form and would feel "intimidated" and "uncomfortable." However, almost 40 percent said they would attend an opera if a friend or family member whose opinion about opera they trusted personally invited them.[11]

Not all concerns of potential patrons can be addressed by arts marketers, but many of them can. Rather than just brainstorming about what aspects of the product offering to promote, marketers should put themselves inside the head of the reluctant attender and think in terms of dispelling myths and fears and breaking down other barriers to attendance. Subsequent chapters are replete with strategies to accomplish these goals.

Decision Making

How people make decisions is crucial for marketers to consider when designing marketing offers and copy. Gerald Zaltman, author of *How Customers Think,* asserts that many managers still believe that consumers make decisions deliberately, logically processing information to arrive at a judgment. In the model of rational decision making, a person follows the steps of identifying a particular need, seeking a set of options that could meet that need, evaluating the pros and cons of each option, calculating the tangible and intangible costs of overall satisfaction per option, and then making a well-reasoned decision. Says Zaltman, "consumer decision making sometimes does involve this so-called rational thinking.". . . However, [it is] the exception, rather than the rule. As it turns out, the selection process is relatively automatic, stems from habits and other unconscious forces, and is greatly influenced by the consumer's social and physical context.". . . "More important still," claims Zaltman, "emotions contribute to, and are essential for, sound decision making. . . . In actuality, 95 percent of thinking takes place in our unconscious minds—that wonderful, if messy, stew of memories, emotions, thoughts, and other cognitive processes we're not aware of or that we can't articulate."[12]

Gary Klein, in his book *Sources of Power: How People Make Decisions,* lends the validity of scientific research to everyday decision-making techniques such as intuition and use of metaphor. The use of storytelling and metaphor enables decision makers to devise meaningful frameworks and compare their present situations to previous events. Intuition, says Klein, is not based on instantaneous insight but rather on the rapid (perhaps even subconscious) interpretation of perceptual cues.[13]

Experience is a central factor in how we make decisions. A person who does not have experience to draw on, someone who has never attended a dance performance, for example, will rely heavily on traditional decision-making models—gathering information and weighing options. For such people it is necessary to provide answers to their questions, information that will help them understand the nature of the experience. More experienced people can see a situation for what it is and quickly, even automatically, size it up and make a decision. Building on that experience is an excellent way to draw these people in to your offer.

A common marketing principle is that past behavior is the best predictor of future behavior. If we know what people have done in the past and why they made the choices they did, we can use this information to stimulate future purchases.

BENEFITS SOUGHT

Marketers are typically most effective when they tap into *outcome-based offerings*—the benefits realized by the customer—rather than *input-based offerings*—descriptions of the program being presented. People want healthy teeth, not toothpaste; they want their cars to run, not a trip to the gas station. Similarly, people want an experience at a performing arts event that is, depending on their preferences, aesthetic, sociable, entertaining, familiar, new, educational, or inspiring, and so on. For most people, a message that they will hear Mahler's magnificent Second Symphony or see a critically acclaimed play by a well-known playwright will not generate a promise about what is in this performance for *them*. Descriptions of the offering should include, either directly or implicitly, promises of the benefits various consumer groups value. Many benefits can be described better by organizations in pictures than in words, as when one sees a photo of a pair of dancers expressing an experience that is romantic and tender or athletic and exhilarating, for example.

Intrinsic and Extrinsic Benefits

The topic of what benefits and utilities people seek in attending a performance and what aspects of the experience they value was a focus of the ticket-buyer surveys in the 2002 John S. and James L. Knight Foundation Classical Music Consumer Segmentation Study (one of several studies arising from the Knight Foundation's Magic of Music Initiative, which involved surveys and other work with fifteen symphony orchestras and their audiences). The insights derived from the survey responses centered on the fact that classical consumers derive "layers of value" from the concert experience, and some value gained does not always relate to what is happening on stage. Benefits gained vary from the extrinsic to the intrinsic. Some people use concerts to entertain friends and family members ("occasion value"), whereas others use concerts as a means of nurturing and sustaining their personal relationships ("relationship enhancement value"). Respondents give high ratings to the "ritual/ambience" value of the concert experience. In focus groups classical music consumers discuss the concerts' increasingly intrinsic "healing and therapeutic value" and "spiritual or transformational value." Yet all these layers of benefits and values surround the actual artistic and educational experience, which is what the orchestras sell.[14]

Although promoting anything "less" than the artistic and educational value of the performance experience is distasteful to some who work in the arts, understanding and interpreting the complex values that consumers draw from the experience and highlighting these benefits in marketing material is likely to stimulate demand, especially among those individuals already predisposed to attending.

Self-Invention

To make their messages and offerings relevant to today's consumers, marketers must also respond to the concept of *self-invention* that has blossomed in the era of the Internet, where extensive information is just a click away, empowering consumers to make better choices, to pay lower prices, and to enrich their experiences. People have more confidence in their own abilities (72 percent) than they do in doctors (57 percent), police (39 percent), public schools (26 percent), the judicial system (18 percent), and advertising (7 percent), which ranks near the bottom of people's confidence level.[15] J. Walker Smith, Ann Clurman, and Craig Wood say, "Expectations of self-invention are blurring the lines between consuming and marketing. In a world of self-invention, people want more, if not all, of the power and the control that marketers traditionally presumed was theirs alone."[16] Consider that more and more people are configuring their iPods with the music they select for their own listening pleasure, yet few arts managers face the music that increasingly, people are resistant to subscription *packaging* because they want to choose which performances to attend. By offering a season brochure that allows people complete freedom of choice, organizations empower their customers, especially infrequent or new patrons, and are likely to sell far more tickets than if they offer a subscription only.

The Customer's Cognitive Space

According to Kazuaki Ushikubo, human wants can be described in terms of four basic desires: *change, participation, freedom,* and *stability.* These wants, which operate on the two major dimensions of *chaos and order* and *outer and inner direction,* can be further broken down into twelve factors that suggest different lifestyles. The importance of these elements changes as an individual enters different contexts or moves through different life cycle stages, describing what Ushikubo calls the person's *cognitive space*. People seeking stability may focus on relaxation and health, for example, and those seeking change may be interested in diversion ("I want to change my lifestyle occasionally"), knowledge ("I want to know more"), or creation ("I want to do something to enhance myself"). People who primarily desire participation may seek occasions to be with family and friends and other opportunities for a social life and a sense of belonging. Those who desire freedom may be most likely to respond to opportunities to be distinctive from others.[17]

These dimensions provide marketers with a framework for uncovering latent demand and suggest opportunities for positioning their offerings. For example, communicating the meaning and value of a play and other information that enhances the attendance experience appeals to a person's desire for knowledge and creation. Communicating the options available for social interaction, such as group sales, opportunities to celebrate occasions, singles nights, and so on, appeals to people's participatory needs. Creative marketers can tap into a variety of people's wants and lifestyles by communicating the various cognitive benefits of their organizations' experiential offerings.

SOCIAL FACTORS

Social factors involved in the experience of attending an arts event play a significant role, especially for those who are not avid cultural attenders. Alan Brown, who directed the Magic of Music Initiative for Audience Insight on behalf of the John S. and James L. Knight Foundation, says that "a mounting body of research suggests that who invites you to a concert has as much to do with your decision to attend as other factors such as the program and guest artists. Indeed," says Brown, "the vagaries of social context cast a long shadow on demand for arts programs."[18]

Craving Connections

The Knight Foundation study also found that even though people connect with classical music more than ever, the traditional concert hall experience is not the primary way they do so. Rather, they listen to classical music on the radio or play CDs in their cars or living rooms. When some people do attend concerts, they often come for social reasons: their friends are there, it is a good date or a spousal night out, they are entertaining visiting friends and family, or someone has asked them to go.

Among respondents to the 2002 American Express National Audience Research Project, one-third of those who did not buy their own ticket but were invited by a friend spoke warmly of social aspects of the opera-going experience, such as a group dinner before the performance or the enjoyable camaraderie with friends. About 25 percent of nonattenders said that they did not attend opera as they did not want to attend alone, noting that their spouses or friends did not enjoy opera.[19]

Yankelovich Monitor consumer surveys show a nearly universal craving for connections and relationships. Ninety-one percent of respondents say that they are looking to find more time for the important people in their lives. Seventy-three percent of people say they are looking to do things that make them feel closer to others.[20]

Programs long in use by arts organizations, such as postconcert social gatherings, are highly limited as effective tools for appealing to people's social needs because not much intermingling takes place at these events. Rather, says Alan Brown, "many individuals use arts programs as a means of investing in their personal relationships. While arts organizations sell artists and repertoire, consumers are buying spiritual journeys, emotional therapy and better relationships. . . . What's needed and quickly, are new models for customer-centered marketing relationships with the goal of offering consumers a menu of involvement opportunities that fit into their lifestyles and reinforce their self-perceptions."[21]

Initiators and Responders

How does a marketer define the customer? Is a customer someone who purchases a ticket or someone who attends a performance? For marketers the difference is important. If the definition of customer is expanded to include people who enjoy concerts but do not attend without an invitation, then a fundamental realignment of marketing strategy is called for, a shift toward strategies that create and facilitate attendance in small social groups.

The Knight Foundation's Magic of Music Initiative conducted a survey of U.S. adults that clearly identified two types of consumers, initiators and responders. The *initiators,* who constitute 18 percent of culturally active adults (people who attended any arts events in the past year), strongly agree with the statement, "I'm the kind of person who likes to organize outings to cultural events for my friends." *Responders,* 56 percent of culturally active adults, report that "I'm much more likely to attend cultural outings if someone else invites me." Initiators are constantly scanning the media for activities (specifically, 58 percent of initiators are "always looking for cultural activities to do," whereas only 16 percent of responders do this). They are more likely to be "extremely interested" in arts activities (24 percent versus 8 percent), and are more likely to say that arts activities play a "major role" in their lives (58 percent versus 23 percent). Initiators are more likely than responders to be single (36 percent versus 22 percent), younger (average age of 42 years compared to responders' 48 years), and female (60 percent versus 53 percent).

The 2002 Classical Music Consumer Segmentation Study made the important finding that the incidence of initiators is lower among orchestra subscribers than it is among culturally active adults. Subscribers make a major commitment far in advance to attend several programs and typically outlay significant money all at once. Getting other people to commit to the same purchase is not an easy undertaking. Says Alan Brown, "arts organizations must embrace the growing number of omnivorous and independent-minded single-ticket buyers who enjoy arts activities but won't subscribe. . . . Arts groups spend a lot of money trying to convert Responders into Initiators. The research suggests, however, that as many as eighty-five out of one hundred concert attendees do not have the psychological profile of an Initiator. . . . Would it not be more productive to find a new way to market to Responders indirectly through their Initiator friends?"[22]

The benefits of arts participation accrue not only to the responders but also to initiators. Focus group research suggests that some initiators derive meaning and satisfaction from the process of creating cultural experiences for their friends—the drama of putting it all together—says Brown.

So rather than making futile efforts to target responders directly, arts marketers should seek out the initiators and inspire and empower them to become *sales associates* for arts organizations.

Targeting Initiators and Responders

Capitalizing on the research findings that say that many potential attenders just need to be asked by friends or family, some arts organizations are offering a new Web-based application targeted to initiators. The Organization Relationship Building Invitation Tool (ORBIT) combines technology with an understanding of consumer attitudes and behavior and is an innovation that could lead to audience growth among younger, culturally active adults.

"The first point of contact with many customers is the web," says Rebecca Krause-Hardie, one of ORBIT's designers. "ORBIT provides a way for Initiators to start a relationship with the organization online, on their own, and at the moment of first contact."[23]

> As customers surf an [organization's] Web site and select a program, they are prompted with an unexpected proposition: "Would you like to invite friends?" Clicking on the prompt takes them into the ORBIT system. Once in ORBIT, they can personalize an invitation and e-mail it to any number of friends. ORBIT users can remain anonymous or register to use other features, such as automated response tracking. To complete the sale, users are directed back to the [organization's] online ticketing system. . . . [T]he ORBIT system treats the exchange of e-mail between Initiators and Responders as private and confidential, which means the [arts groups] cannot have the e-mail addresses of the Responders without permission.[24]

ORBIT was originally developed by SymphonyWorks for a partnership of six orchestras—the Philadelphia Orchestra, St. Louis Symphony Orchestra, Kansas City Symphony, Atlanta Symphony Orchestra, Detroit Symphony, and Long Beach Symphony. The ORBIT system requires only a low level of staff support to maintain it, and the program's online tactics are virtually free, once the initial investment has been made.

Targeting Initiators and Responders, *continued*

Several other arts groups have now installed ORBIT on their Web sites, including the Boston Symphony Orchestra and Artsopolis, which is Silicon Valley's comprehensive guide to arts and culture and is an ideal resource for social groups to use when planning their arts activities. In the first few months after installing the software, the Boston Symphony reported gaining several hundred new ticket buyers—and many more responders who came with them.[25]

Web-based invitation tools are only a partial solution to the issue of how to build peer-to-peer sales, as they are only relevant to consumers who are comfortable in and seek out the online ticket buying environment. Creative arts marketers should consider ways of developing a program for initiators that relies on the human interface, as the group sales model does. The first step in this process is for arts organizations to identify and collect the contact information for the initiators among their customers.

Attracting single ticket buyers has always been an expensive endeavor for arts organizations. But through the use of low-cost invitation tools, single ticket sales transform into small-group sales, multiplying the number of tickets sold. Initiators, in effect, become sales agents for the organization, while meeting their own social goals.

Peer Group Influences

In a study of Cleveland's cultural patrons undertaken in the mid-1980s to compare the relative importance of peer group influences and childhood arts education for later arts attendance, it was found that instruction or education in the arts during childhood is a powerful factor in shaping future attendance patterns. However, mere exposure of children to culture appears to have little effect on later attendance habits. It was also found that performing arts attenders are about twice as likely as nonattenders to have friends who participate in the same cultural activities. Adult reference groups are so important that where they are absent, the effects of childhood exposure and education tend to dissipate.[26]

One focus group participant in the Scottish Arts Council's study of dance attendance reported that she took a friend to see a traditional production of *Romeo and Juliet.* The friend is extremely intelligent, is a playwright, and has had her plays produced, yet she was frightened to attend the dance performance because, she said, "It is not for the likes of me; I've never been to ballet before." The focus group participant commented, "She didn't realize how accessible it was and she really loved it. Some people have a barrier."[27]

The implication for arts marketers is that attendance can be stimulated by promoting group sales among various membership groups and businesses, by offering gift tickets with subscriptions, and by encouraging the purchase of gift certificates.

Some organizations offer a complimentary guest ticket for one performance to people who purchase a minimum number of tickets for the season. This encourages patrons to introduce their friends to the organization and its offerings while gifting their friends with tickets they have received at no cost.

Play Money in Chicago

The League of Chicago Theaters offers gift certificates called *Play Money* that are redeemable at 192 member theaters, good for a full year from date of purchase, and sold in $25 denominations online and at the organization's three Hot Tix locations. The League's advertising for these certificates says, "One size fits all for friends, relatives, clients, employees . . ." Chicago area hotels are actively buying Play Money certificates to include in the weekend packages they offer.

Gift certificates or cards can be marketed as holiday gifts for family and friends, employees, colleagues, and suppliers; as special occasion gifts for birthdays, anniversaries, weddings, and graduations; or just as a way to introduce someone to an art form, an organization, or a specific show. They can be sold through each organization's box office, through the Web site of a trade organization or local arts council, and at local cooperating book and music stores. Gift cards purchased through collaborating organizations allow the card recipients to select the organization and performance they want to attend, and often a card acts as an incentive for people to attend events they would not have attended otherwise. Board members and other volunteers should be encouraged to offer gift cards for sale, and it may be advantageous to hire a part-time salesperson to market the cards to local businesses, alumni associations, and other organizations.

Gift cards can be sold for any amount the giver would like to spend, from the cost of one performance to a full season subscription.

A theme that is both explicit and implicit in this chapter is that the decision to purchase many types of products, services, and experiences is part of a social process. Marketing is not only a one-to-one interaction between the organization and the customer; it also involves many exchanges of influence and information among the customer and the people in his or her network of friends, family, and associates. In later chapters I will discuss other benefits sought by current and potential patrons, how to build word-of-mouth marketing, and other interpersonal approaches for attracting customers and breaking down barriers to attendance.

4

Planning Strategy and Applying the Strategic Marketing Process

Marketing is not an event, but a process. . . . It has a beginning, a middle, but never an end. . . . You improve it, perfect it, change it, even pause in it. But you never stop it completely.

—Jay Conrad Levinson

Whether you think that you can, or that you can't, you are usually right.

—Henry Ford

DEVELOPING NEW TACTICS THAT ARE RELEVANT TO TODAY'S consumers requires more than some good ideas; it requires thinking strategically—from both the top down and from the bottom up. In other words, it requires a broad understanding of the organization's current needs and opportunities, and it requires determining whether ideas old and new are a good fit with the organization's core strengths and resources. These exercises are part of strategic marketing planning.

Strategic planning has been an integral part of management and marketing literature for decades, so its importance and processes are not new insights. But just as every building, no matter what the architecture, must have a strong foundation, all marketing efforts must derive from comprehensive planning. Many managers and board members do devote precious time to fairly extensive planning, but too many arts managers admit that they create a mission statement and develop a strategic plan purely for use in their grant applications. A plan that is not used to guide the organization's activities is waste of time and effort.

THE COMPLEXITIES OF PLANNING

Nonprofit, mission-driven organizations seek to realize multiple objectives, many of which are driven by nonfinancial goals. As a result they must use various measures of success, which makes strategic planning in arts organizations a highly complex activity. Because the marketplace is increasingly changing, it is also difficult to predict funding levels, audience development, and even programming opportunities.

Furthermore, the diverse stakeholders have different perspectives on what is of most value to the organization. Due to the very nature of their role as "owners" of the organization, board members prioritize fiscal responsibility, whereas artistic directors, the keepers of the organization's vision, prioritize artistic excellence and exploration. Some artists, board members, and staff may prefer an emphasis on highly sophisticated programming that has limited appeal, whereas others may place a higher value on maximizing audience size or providing a broad spectrum of educational outreach programs in the schools. Goals can often clash when, for example, the artistic director would like to present more new works but the board would prefer to play it safe and present familiar works, or when the board wants to earmark fundraising efforts for growing the endowment for the organization's long-term security but the choreographer is eager to raise additional funds to provide live orchestral music at performances. Meanwhile managers often prioritize expanding their administrative budget in order to increase staff size, improve staff quality, and have additional funds for marketing and fundraising activities so they can best fulfill their objectives of maximizing both earned and contributed revenue.

These multifaceted conditions make strategic planning extremely important. Strategic planning directs the arts organization to identify long-term trends and their implications, helps define the key strategic issues facing the organization, opens better communication among the organization's key players, and improves management control by setting objectives and providing measures of performance. Strategic planning helps an organization to develop a shared vision of its policies, goals, objectives, and activities. It defines the organization's planned trajectory.

THE PLANNING MIND-SET

Both the organization itself and the environment with which it interacts are perpetually changing, and it is up to the marketing manager, top management, and the board of directors to be aware of the current pulse and be sensitive to potential opportunities and threats. The key to an effective marketing strategy is to maximize *relevance* to the consumer. Relevance is not a constant; as people become accustomed to changes in their environment, they develop new expectations. Adrian Slywotzky, who coined the expression *value migration,* says that "customers make choices based on their priorities. . . . As customers' priorities change and new designs present customers with new options, they make new choices. They reallocate value. These changing priorities, and the way in which they interact with new competitors' offerings, are what trigger, enable, or facilitate the Value Migration process."[1]

Slywotzky suggests that a business or organization's success depends on its understanding of the business designs to which its customers respond and its ability to adapt these designs and improve upon them for its particular customers. To assess how well an organization meets customers' most important priorities—both today and in the projectable future, managers should answer the following questions: "What are the customer and economic assumptions on which [our offer] is designed? Are those assumptions still valid? What might change them? What are the customers' most important priorities? How are they changing? . . . How well are they served? What priorities are not well served?" How can we "recapture value?"[2]

Therefore, given a primary allegiance to the organization's mission, the strategic plan should be as flexible, adaptable, and changeable as the environment in which it exists.

The Strategic Marketing Planning Process

Strategic planning is the process through which arts managers, marketers, and board members define their objectives (where they want the organization to go), their strategy (how the organization will get there), the necessary resources (what it will take to get the organization there), and evaluate their results (how they will know if the organization got there).

Steps in Strategic Marketing Planning

The strategic marketing planning process consists of four steps:

1. *Strategic analysis.* Assess the organization's strengths, weaknesses, opportunities, and threats (SWOT analysis), and analyze the organization-wide mission, objectives, and goals.

2. *Marketing planning.* Determine the objectives and specific goals for the relevant planning period, formulate the core marketing strategy to achieve the specified goals, and establish detailed programs and tactics to carry out the core strategy.

3. *Marketing plan implementation.* Put the plan into action.

4. *Control.* Measure performance and adjust the core strategy or tactical details, or both, as needed.

Strategic Analysis: SWOT Analysis

Integral to the analysis of the organization's mission is an analysis of its internal strengths and weaknesses and its external opportunities and threats. When recognizing weaknesses, planners must also determine if it is important for the weakness to be rectified or if it makes more sense for the organization to pursue other avenues. Opportunities can be seen as combinations of the organization's core competencies or strengths with unfilled niches in the external environment. Common threats are anticipated or real funding decreases and lowering prospects for future audience vitality due to an aging patron base.

It is extraordinarily illuminating for board members and staff to hear one another's views about the organization as they list in black and white everything that comes to their minds in each of these four categories and then discuss all these factors. Not only are important issues revealed, but in most cases the process helps participants arrive at a consensus on future directions.

Often it is helpful for an outside consultant to facilitate strategic planning sessions, as managers and board members may be unaware of some weaknesses and threats, or even some strengths and opportunities, and may not recognize the extent to which these factors do or could affect operations or may be unsure of how to correct the problems.

Strategic Analysis: The Mission

Although the question "What is our mission?" sounds simple, it is really the most challenging question an organization can ask. Different individuals are likely to have different views of what the organization is about and should be about. The mission statement should describe what the organization does, whom it serves, and what it intends to accomplish. The mission should be broad enough not to need frequent revision and yet specific enough to provide clear objectives and to guide programming. It should be understandable to the general public and should be stated as succinctly as possible, with a forward-looking approach and with the use of action verbs. Organizations may need to hold numerous meetings over several months to clarify their ideas and to develop consensus about the mission.

The mission is often driven by the organization's founder, who is usually the artistic director. People join the board of directors because they believe in the founder's vision and are eager to support it. Over time, as the organization matures, grows, and institutionalizes, the founder may become less central to the planning process although the mission remains essentially intact. Sometimes, a dramatic change forced upon the organization can require a major rethinking of aspects of the mission statement. For example, one symphony that had performed in and for its community for nearly fifty years was compelled to move to a performing hall in another community about fifteen miles away when its long-time venue was torn down. Because many of the original patrons were reluctant to travel to the new venue, the board had to redefine whom the symphony served.

Marketing Planning: Setting Objectives and Goals

The mission statement comprises an organization's purpose and broadly states the results the organization wants to achieve. Each organization must also develop specific objectives and goals for the coming period that are consistent with its mission statement. Objectives are usually intended to have a three- to five-year life span. The objectives of a midsize theater company planning to move into a new, larger venue in three years, for example, include raising $10 million in a capital campaign for the new building, increasing annual giving to accommodate the larger operating budget required in the new venue, increasing the subscriber base in anticipation of having 50 percent more seats to fill in the new space, building awareness of and interest in the theater to attract new patrons, and upgrading box office software so that customer-centered data can be easily accessed and real-time, online ticket ordering facilitated.

In order for objectives to be achieved, they need to be restated in operational and measurable terms, called *goals*. The objective of increasing the number of subscribers may be turned into a goal of a 10 percent increase the first year and a 5 percent increase each of the next two years. Goal setting leads managers to consider the necessary planning, programming, and control aspects: Is a 10 percent increase feasible? What strategies will be used? What human and financial resources will they require? What activities will have to be carried out? Who will be responsible and accountable? How will we track achievement?

Implementation and Control

A brilliant strategic marketing plan counts for little if it is not implemented properly. Many of the best-laid plans fail to see the light of day. Every plan should be a living document—a blueprint for the organization's ongoing activities. Adequate resources must be allocated, both human and financial. The organization's personnel, including management, artistic staff, board of directors, support staff, and volunteers, must be educated about the plan and motivated to implement it. A plan is a commitment to action—a commitment by people with their own ideas, attitudes, preferences, concerns, and needs. People must see the strategy's relevance, feel they are capable of implementing it, understand the required behaviors, know whether they have achieved the objective, and be rewarded for doing so. Ongoing activities of organizational personnel should be prioritized, or the organization may find that extraneous activities are draining valuable human and financial resources from the challenges at hand.

In order for a plan to be effectively implemented, several issues need to be considered. First, input should be sought from people at all levels of the organization during the formulation stage. Widespread participation helps to secure commitment to the new course of action as well as to highlight the major issues expected to arise during implementation. Second, human and financial obstacles to implementation must be carefully assessed. There may be ideological resistance from those who believe the new strategy is ill fated or violates deeply held values; there may also be resistance from those who are intolerant or afraid of change. It is important to ascertain that the organization has on its staff appropriately skilled people to implement the strategies and that a clear majority of board members are firmly supportive of new directions. If these conditions cannot be met, even the best-laid plans may be impossible to realize. Finally, the organization must commit adequate resources to allow for a strategy's success. Many strategies fail because resources are not decisively allocated to support them.

Performance is the ultimate test of any organization. The last step of the strategic marketing planning process, that of reviewing and adjusting the strategy and tactics and measuring performance, should actually be taken into consideration throughout the process. As experience and new knowledge are gained, strategies and tactics should be reevaluated in light of new information. Frequent evaluations can serve to validate a current approach, to stimulate the modification of an approach or of the goals themselves, or even to encourage the abandonment of a strategy altogether.

Long-Range Strategic Planning
at San Francisco Ballet

San Francisco Ballet (SFB) has been in existence for several decades, has an annual budget in excess of $30 million, and is known and respected around the world for its high-quality offerings. Strategic planning at the San Francisco Ballet was a comprehensive process, undertaken intensively over a period of several months. Smaller organizations often do not have the same level of human or financial resources to devote to such extensive planning, but they can learn to plan effectively by following the same steps in the process.

In July of 1996, key members of the artistic staff, management staff, and board of directors began a dialogue about the future of SFB. Said Helgi Tomasson, artistic director and choreographer:

> At this critical point in our history, our Company is renowned for the quality and vitality of its dancing, its diversity, and the choreographic scope of its repertory. The high caliber of our School and our outstanding outreach and education programs reflect our strong commitment to the future of dance and to being responsible and responsive to our community. All of this is made possible by our dedicated and supportive Board of Trustees, our loyal and generous donors, our highly professional and experienced administrative leaders, and most of all, by our talented artists.
>
> Yet, in order to ensure that our mission is realized, that our values remain intact, and that our artistry, our programs, and our sources of support are continually strengthened, our leadership must focus intensively on the years ahead. Our purpose is to lay the groundwork for a plan that will help us build upon our past successes, further our long-standing goals, and provide direction for bringing to fruition our newly inspired vision.[3]

What began as an informal brainstorming session developed into an in-depth process to develop a five-year strategic plan, undertaken with thoughtfulness and enthusiasm by the newly formed long-range planning committee, the staff, special workgroups, and the full board of trustees. I was brought in as a consultant to act as project facilitator and organizer and to write the plan documents.

Revising the Mission Statement

The first step in the process was to review SFB's mission statement to determine if it still met the organization's needs and aspirations. The existing mission stated: "San Francisco Ballet Association is dedicated to producing superior performances of classical and contemporary ballet, to providing the highest caliber of training for dancers aspiring to professional careers and to becoming America's model of excellence and innovation in ballet artistic direction and administration."

The planning committee recognized immediately that this mission statement was outdated. For several years the company had garnered worldwide recognition for the quality of its dancing and innovative programming; the dance school was considered one of the country's finest and was in high demand by fine, young dancers; the artistic and administrative functions were extremely well run by high-caliber personnel. This mission had been accomplished; a new mission that would be motivating, distinctive, and feasible needed to be crafted.

Over the course of many meetings among artistic staff, management staff, and the board, key elements for a new mission statement were determined. SFB wanted to recognize its status as a superior dance company and school yet motivate its staff, dancers, and students to continually improve. It wanted to expand the audiences it served, both locally and on tour, and expose as many people as possible—young and old, dance aficionados and newcomers alike—to the joys of dance. To express the characteristics that make San Francisco Ballet distinctive and that are central to its very essence, vitality and diversity were added to the ballet's longstanding focus on innovation, although it was crucial to state that no matter how contemporary and creative the choreography, it would be based in the tradition of classical ballet.

The unanimously agreed-upon new mission statement read: "The mission of San Francisco Ballet is to share our joy of dance with the widest possible audience in our community and around the globe and to provide the highest caliber of dance training in our school. We seek to enhance our position as one of the world's finest dance companies through our vitality, innovativeness, and diversity and through our uncompromising commitment to artistic excellence based in the classical ballet tradition."

SWOT Analysis

Each department—artistic, the school, marketing, development, and others—produced a series of documents for the planning committee that included historical information, a SWOT analysis for that department, a list of suggested opportunities for future growth and improvement, and a budget for each suggested project. The department heads and key board members met frequently to share ideas, develop an overall direction for the organization, and select the areas on which to focus. The SWOT analyses were a catalyst for identifying trends, both external and internal, and for focusing on the organization's most meaningful and viable opportunities. By working so closely together, personnel became intimately familiar with issues across the entire organization.

Identifying Objectives and Goals

Six primary objectives for the upcoming five-year period were identified and agreed upon by the planning committee. The committee called them *strategic imperatives* and divided them into two categories: *program imperatives* and *resource imperatives*. The program imperatives are central to realizing the mission. The resource imperatives focus on the resources necessary to implement these programs.

Program Imperatives:

1. New Works: "a dedication to the continual creation of new works as a central component of the Ballet's artistic goals."

2. Touring: "an emphasis on increased touring to broaden performance opportunities, Company visibility, and audience exposure."

3. Outreach and education: "an enhanced commitment to outreach and educational efforts to further the Ballet's mission

of sharing the joy of dance with the widest possible audience today and into the future."

Resource Imperatives:

1. Major gifts: "attracting major gifts from the Ballet's loyal supporters and other potential generous donors."

2. Brand identity: "developing and implementing a brand identity campaign to increase the awareness of and interest in the Ballet among its many publics," especially current nonattenders.

3. Board development: "building new Board leadership among highly qualified potential members, refining the Board's governance structure, and creating an International Advisory Council."

Specific goals and budgets were developed for each of these imperatives. Additionally, each department developed a detailed timeline and indicated who would be responsible for implementing each aspect of every goal over the five-year period. Because most of the goals required the involvement of several departments, managers worked together to create one master timeline. For example, touring involves the input of personnel from the artistic, development, marketing, and finance functions.

Highly detailed objectives, goals, and strategies were created for each of the plan's strategic imperatives. Some of the details established for outreach and education and for major gifts are presented here to demonstrate how specific an effective, actionable plan should be.

OUTREACH AND EDUCATION "The overriding objectives of San Francisco Ballet's outreach and education programs are to expand the audiences of today and to create the audiences of tomorrow. Outreach efforts are primarily designed to target the various demographic groups underrepresented in the Ballet's current audience and to assist schools in integrating dance into the instruction program. Importantly, in the process of realizing its outreach and education agenda, the Ballet will continue to be a vital contributor to its own community and to the other communities in which it performs."

Some of the goals are to build current audiences by reattracting patrons who could not be accommodated during the two seasons that the ballet's venue, the Opera House, was being renovated, by acknowledging subscribers who have maintained their support in ways that will build their loyalty, and by attracting new subscribers and single ticket buyers. The Ballet will also build audiences for the future by filling the gap left by the lack of arts education in the schools and by giving back to the community by providing programming for school children and adults, for people of various ethnic groups and cultural backgrounds, and for the physically and developmentally challenged.

Some of the strategies that will be employed to realize these goals are to expand the number of school children reached by the Dance-in-Schools (DIS) program to triple the current number; expand each school residency from ten to fifteen weeks; provide programs, materials, artists, guest instructors, and additional artist-teacher teams to deepen the DIS experience and make it more relevant for participants and to better integrate the program into the curricula; hire a curriculum planner to develop materials for DIS and the dance enrichment program; explore the development and use of new technology applications; establish a teacher "users group" to evaluate SFB's educational plans and programs; develop a dance enrichment program for students and teachers that makes their attendance at a special matinee performance more meaningful; create a new family membership program geared toward children seven to twelve years of age; offer an annual open house at the SFB Association Building where the offices and studios are housed; expose the general public to the myriad factors involved in producing dance; offer educational programs for the general public in conjunction with the presentation of new works; provide audio description for the visually impaired; and provide a special, free, annual performance for people with disabilities. To help expand the diversity of the audience, SFB will hold a series of receptions for conversations with community leaders who represent various constituencies at the SFB Association Building and ensure that SFB's performance tours include outreach activities in each location.

To ascertain the realization and effectiveness of these programs, SFB will develop and implement an aggressive media campaign to ensure that its outreach and education programs are highly visible, well known, and well respected by the Ballet's diverse communities;

increase the part-time administrative assistant and coordinator positions to full time, expand and diversify the network of volunteers who participate in outreach and education programs by targeting former DIS students, SFB dancers, SFB staff, and members of the ballet's corps of volunteers; develop a mechanism to acknowledge the contribution of dancers and staff who give of their free time to support SFB's outreach and education programs; and increase operating funds allocated for the outreach program from 1 percent of the annual budget to 2 percent.

MAJOR GIFTS "San Francisco Ballet's current stability and strength can be attributed to the generous and loyal support of its many contributors." The Ballet hopes to build upon this support and the fundraising success of its Bridge Fund during the two years the Ballet could not perform at the Opera House due to renovations.

The thrust of a new major gifts imperative will be to raise significant funds for new full-length productions ($3.8 million needed over five years); to fund the portion of the touring initiative not covered by earned revenue ($3.5 million needed over five years) and to do so well in advance of program presentation, due to the extensive preparation required for these programs; to fund enhanced outreach and education programs ($2.01 million needed); and to provide funding to meet the 3.5 to 4 percent annual increase in the operating budget and to compensate for anticipated diminishing government funding.

To raise these significant sums, SFB will "capitalize on the success of the *Preserving a San Francisco Jewel* Capital Campaign, which raised $31.3 million to help sustain the company during the recent eighteen-month hiatus from the Opera House" by encouraging donors to maintain their higher levels of giving; capitalize on the fact that the imperatives for new works, touring, and outreach and education are tangible, motivating factors in attracting generous donations; increase individual giving from 57 percent of the Ballet's support (not including gifts from trustees) to 65 percent over the plan period; and increase the size of individual major gifts to the Ballet with a special emphasis on gifts of $25,000 to $50,000. SFB will also "capitalize on an expanding corporate sponsorship environment" by identifying "corporations whose target markets and positioning strategies fit well with those of the Ballet, [by striving] to meet the interests and needs of each potential corporate partner, and [by ensuring] that the Ballet offers benefits comparable to its peer institutions;" seek grants "from foundations that have not supported the Ballet in the past, particularly local foundations and large, national foundations;" and focus on local government advocacy efforts to protect Grants for the Arts, SFB's largest and most stable source of government funding.

The Plan Documents

Many tables and financial statements were generated to help formulate the details of the plan. For example, the development director charted SFB's recent five-year history of major gifts from individuals in seven giving categories to identify the greatest likely opportunities for growth. It was through this strategy that a focus on gifts of $25,000 to $50,000 was determined. An analysis of contributed income from various sources over the five-year period 1993 to 1997 highlighted trends and helped managers set financial goals for corporate sponsorships and foundation grants.

Several financial tables were also created for inclusion in the long-range plan, including tables showing cost breakdowns for each new initiative and specific fundraising needs by year. (In order for managers to plan prudently, funds pledged for specific initiatives needed to be received from donors significantly in advance of the time when the costs would be incurred.)

We named the plan Building on Success.

When the planning was complete, two publications were created: a basic but highly detailed version for internal use and an elegant, two-color booklet for external use. The basic version was a comprehensive, no-frills, softbound volume that included all the details of each imperative, timelines showing when each aspect was to be undertaken and completed, who was responsible for what, and complete budgetary information. The other version of the plan, which was much shorter, was created to distribute to board members, current and potential funders, members of the dance community, and other interested parties. This version was designed to be modest, but it also reflected the organization's high standards for quality with its fine graphics and beautiful photos of Company dancers. It included the information that would build the organization's image and that would be useful and motivating to donors.

Five Years Later: Evaluation

San Francisco Ballet successfully realized virtually all the aspects of its 1998 to 2003 long-range plan. Fundraising was so successful that goals were exceeded; in the years 2000 to 2002, board giving alone increased 44 percent. Brand identity campaigns and outreach and education programs have long-term effects on ticket sales and donations and are difficult to measure. But management and board firmly agree that a continuing focus on realizing all the objectives in the plan is serving SFB well for the present and into future planning. Some adjustments to the plan were made along the way as necessary, and updates to the master plan were distributed internally every six months. For example, the new production of *Nutcracker,* originally planned for the 2001 season, was postponed until 2005 for artistic reasons.

According to Executive Director Glenn McCoy, SFB's outstanding success can be attributed primarily to its exceptionally high artistic quality.[4] This high quality attracted new subscribers in significant numbers, built loyalty among current subscribers, and has attracted increasingly large donations. Another meaningful success factor, says McCoy, is the fact that during the high-technology boom of the late 1990s, the Ballet's financial managers invested the endowment fund and other savings conservatively, so that while many other organizations and individuals were suffering losses, the Ballet earned modest gains. As a result, current and potential SFB funders were confident that their donations were prudently cared for and, by extension, used efficiently by the organization. Said Director of Development Tom Flynn in 2004, when seeking donations, it is most helpful to show that the Ballet has enjoyed thirteen continuous years of balanced budgets.

The Next Plan

In 2003, as the term of the 1998 to 2003 plan was coming to an end, work began on a new long-range plan for 2004 to 2008. The planning process was staff driven, as the highly professional and experienced staff is well aware of the Ballet's needs and opportunities and General Manager Lesley Koenig was highly qualified to lead the process.

The board and staff decided that the mission statement developed in 1997 continues to reflect the Ballet's vision and directions well, so not a word was changed. The format of the previous plan also functioned well for the planning committee, so it was followed closely in the new plan. One meaningful addition to the plan is that for each program initiative, a related phrase from the mission statement is quoted. For the creation of new works, the mission statement excerpt is "to enhance our position as one of the world's finest dance companies through our uncompromising commitment to artistic excellence based in the classical ballet tradition." For touring, it is "to share our joy of dance with the widest possible audience around the globe," and for the continued growth of outreach and education programs, it is "to share our joy of dance with the widest possible audience in the community." The use of these quotes emphasizes that all the organization's programs must serve to realize the mission.

The executive summary of the new plan states in part:

> Sustaining our internationally recognized level of excellence, while continuing both to honor tradition and to push the boundaries of creativity in ballet, is the primary goal of this new strategic plan that will usher the San Francisco Ballet into its seventy-fifth year in 2008. In the last plan, the Ballet looked outward, with program imperatives to tour more broadly and reach new audiences. In the current plan, the Ballet proposes to look inward at programs and practices that, sharpened by experience, will enable the Association to sustain and nurture its winning formula. The focus over the next five years will be on the balance of creativity with sustainability and of sound fiscal management with essential artistic flexibility. This plan is offered as a living instrument to be reviewed and updated on a regular basis by the artistic director, trustees, and staff.

THE STRATEGIC MARKETING PROCESS

Once the organization has defined its mission and developed its objectives and goals according to its strengths, weaknesses, opportunities, and threats, it is ready to begin the strategic marketing process.

Strategic marketing consists of three steps: segmentation, targeting, and positioning. The marketer first identifies a variety of dimensions along which to segment the market and develops profiles of the resulting market segments. Then the marketer selects segments to target, choosing those that offer the best opportunity to realize the organization's goals. Finally, the marketer designs marketing strategies and positions the organization and its offerings to have the greatest appeal to the target markets. Often, different strategies need to be designed for distinct target segments and for unique campaigns.

Segmentation

Segmenting is the crucial first step. All customers are not the same, and a single marketing strategy will do a poor job of serving many different customers. It is not unusual for arts managers to say, for example, that their typical customer is a fifty-two-year-old college-educated woman. But averages tell us very little. Even the actual ages, gender, and educational level of all current attenders tell us little or nothing about these people's interests, habits, lifestyles, personalities, preferences, and purchasing behavior—factors that are far more significant than demographic data for marketers in designing and promoting their offerings. Other important bases for segmenting the market are buyer behavioral factors: usage rates, the benefits sought from attendance, occasions for use, loyalty to the organization, and readiness stage.

Benefits sought may vary by numerous psychological, social, demographic, lifestyle, and other factors. One factor arts marketers should take into consideration is what the well-known psychologist Abraham Maslow described as the hierarchy of human needs. Maslow proposed that the more basic needs require gratification before a person is able to acquire substantial gratification of higher-level needs. Gratification at each level contributes to the person's maturation. First, people must satisfy their basic physiological and security needs. At the next level people satisfy their social needs, their need for love and a sense of belonging; then people pursue satisfaction of their need to attain a certain level of self-esteem. Once people attain comfort with these factors, they begin to self-actualize, preferring *being* experiences, such as watching a beautiful sunset or hearing a concert, to pursuing *possession* or *catered* experiences, such as purchasing discretionary materialistic goods or going to the most popular new restaurant. Performing arts organizations can meet the different levels of Maslow's hierarchy of needs in a variety of creative ways. For example, social needs are met when a theater offers group sales or a special night once a month for special target groups. Esteem needs are fulfilled when arts organizations develop offers that make a person feel special, most commonly through donor recognition events and listings. Self-actualization needs, which are most commonly felt among mature adults, are realized by the art itself. Approaches for targeting the mature adult market were discussed in Chapter Two.

Buyer readiness is a function of four factors—awareness, interest, desire, and action—known by the acronym AIDA. *Awareness,* the first factor, is a function of how much people know about your organization and its offerings; second is their level of *interest* in your organization and its programs; third is their *desire* to attend a performance or exhibit; fourth is their readiness to take *action*—by actually purchasing a ticket. If few people are familiar with your organization, it is necessary to build awareness and develop interest before expecting that people will purchase tickets. Sometimes people report remembering a clever ad but are still not adequately motivated to buy a ticket. Many organizations do a good job in their advertising of building awareness and interest, but they do not take people to the higher level of desire and of stimulating ticket purchase. One common strategy that creates a sense of urgency is to say that that there are only a limited number of performances remaining and that this is a show people won't want to miss.

Targeting

The decision about which and how many segments to reach out to is the problem of target market selection. A target market consists of a set of buyers having common needs or characteristics that the organization decides to serve. Before selecting target markets the arts organization should learn as much as possible about each segment under consideration to determine whether and how it can meet that segment's needs, interests, and desires. Marketing planning *starts* with the customer, but who this customer will be is largely up to the performing arts organizations to determine. The organization should select segments that are attractive and an excellent fit with its resources.

Positioning

After segmenting the potential audience and selecting viable target groups, the marketer is ready to develop positioning strategies to promote the aspects of the organization's offerings that appeal most strongly to these groups. Positioning is the act of designing the organization's image and offer so that it occupies a *distinct* and *valued* place in target customers' minds. Positioning involves creating a real differentiation and then making it known. Say Al Ries and Jack Trout, "Positioning starts with a product. But positioning is not what you do to a product, it is what you do to the mind of the prospect."[5]

The specific positioning the organization chooses depends largely on its analysis of its targeted market segments, its own strengths and weaknesses, and its competition. Many organizations develop a niche or specialty. A children's theater is a customer specialist, as it offers programs with a specific customer group in mind. A Shakespearean company is a product specialist. The large symphony orchestra in a major metropolitan area is a quality specialist, presenting world-class music and musicians. In a large city with a multitude of theaters, it is important for each theater to set itself apart from the others. For example, in Chicago both Steppenwolf Theatre and Writers' Theatre are well known for their extremely high quality productions. Steppenwolf focuses its positioning on its cutting-edge plays, often by well-known contemporary playwrights; Writers' Theatre focuses on the intimacy of the experience in its two venues, one with 50 seats and the other with 108 seats, and on the more classic contemporary works it produces.

Positioning may be based on myriad other organizational attributes, such as the charisma or fame of the director, the nature of the programming (Mostly Mozart, Music of the Baroque, Jazz in June), the star performers, the location or facilities (when the hall has a special appeal), the reputation and image, or the multiple attributes available when the organization has varied strengths or offerings. In the business sector it is not unusual for companies to position themselves against a major competitor (recall Avis's "we're number two, we try harder"), but this is rarely done in the arts, except for such lighthearted comments as "the home team hasn't sounded this good in years." Because arts attenders are generally more satisfied when they have a variety of events from a variety of organizations to attend, arts organizations benefit from a mentality of collaboration, not competition.

Maslow's hierarchy is one tool that can be used by marketers to help them position their offerings to target groups and attract people to their programs. For example, to create messages that resonate with audience members who are self-actualized, marketers can emphasize that the nature of the artistic experience allows for self-exploration, greater self-awareness, and greater understanding of the world. For those who are primarily concerned with socialization, the marketer can position messages on the social aspects of events designed for special interest groups. For those attempting to further their self-esteem, marketers can position an offering to emphasize the importance of "being there," showing that attendance provides recognition and status. Self-esteem seekers provide marketers with a good opportunity to sell the better, more expensive seats in the house, offering them to people who want not only to see but to be seen.

Maslow's hierarchy is of course only one of the myriad tools available to marketers when designing positioning strategies. Effective marketers understand the aesthetic factors that appeal to serious cultural attenders, are in touch with theories of psychology and sociology, and keep up with trends affecting not only their field but the marketplace as a whole.

Creating a Customer Scenario

Patricia Seybold refers to the "broad context in which a customer does business as the *customer scenario.* . . . By building a detailed understanding of common customer scenarios, [an organization] can often find creative ways to expand its reach into the lives of buyers." Seybold observes that many managers "think they are taking on the customer perspective, but they're really only focused on the point at which the customer comes into contact with their company. That touch point is certainly important, but it's rarely the center of the customer's experience."[6] To create customer scenarios, Seybold suggests the following steps:[7]

"Select a target customer set." *Be as explicit as possible.* For example: someone with little or no previous exposure to classical music who is interested in learning about the art form.

"Select a goal that the customer needs to fulfill." For example, the customer wants to develop familiarity with and enjoyment of classical music.

"Envision a particular situation for the customer." Offer a series of concerts with readily accessible music, with preconcert lectures, and with the conductor speaking from the podium about the music before each piece is performed. Enhance accessibility and knowledge with information about the concertgoing experience and sources for learning about the music, composers, and performers; offer the opportunity to purchase recordings or download music; make special offers for upcoming programs that are likely to be of interest, and so on.

"Determine a start and an end point for the scenario." The key is to focus on the total customer experience, from the time a need or interest is identified through postconcert contacts to build an ongoing relationship with the customer. Consider likely opportunities and media for reaching out to these potential customers to make the initial contact and approaches for maintaining a relationship with them.

Throughout this process, marketers should map out as many variations of each scenario as they can think of and mentally walk through each step as the customer would. To accomplish this, think of the individual activities the customer performs and the information needed at every step. What can your organization do to support those activities and supply that information? In what ways can you increase convenience to the customer by streamlining the decision-making and purchase processes? The exercise should be undertaken for a number of different target customers, customer goals, and customer situations.

Marketing expert Leonard Berry advises, "offer customers superior solutions to their needs, treat them with real respect, and connect with them on an emotional level."[8]

Lateral Marketing

In the most developed and competitive markets, strategic fundamentals of marketing (segmentation, targeting, and positioning) are becoming increasingly limited as mechanisms for generating new opportunities; over time marketers typically find increasingly smaller subgroups that may be interested in their offerings. In the long term this fragmentation effect often overwhelms expansion efforts. Philip Kotler and Fernando Trias de Bes suggest complementing this traditional marketing with lateral marketing, which provides a viable new framework for generating ideas.

Kotler and Trias de Bes describe traditional segmentation, targeting, and positioning as *vertical marketing,* which consists of creating modulations within a given market. In contrast, *lateral marketing* restructures markets by creating a new category through new uses, situations, or targets. The lateral marketing process creates, whereas the vertical marketing process selects. "Vertical marketing innovations have a high probability of success, but a low incremental volume in mature and fragmented markets. . . . Lateral marketing innovations, on the contrary, may have a much lower probability of success, but if they do succeed the obtained volume can be extremely high."[9]

Lateral marketing comes up with answers to such questions as these: "What other needs can I satisfy with my product if I change it? . . . What nonpotential consumers could I reach by changing my product? . . . What other things can I offer to my current [patrons]? In what other situations can my product be used?"[10] Once the lateral marketing process comes up with a valid new offer, then vertical marketing comes into play, developing segments, targets, and positioning.

One lateral marketing strategy may be to reverse the process by which the patron and the box office make contact. Typically, the organization distributes marketing information through a variety of media and *hopes* ticket buyers will contact the box office. With today's sophisticated databases that keep a record of what programs people have attended in the past, the organization knows what types of events individuals prefer (whether classical or avant-garde theater, chamber or symphonic music, or full-length or modern dance, for example) and also their preferred day of the week and seating location. With this information the organization can reach out directly to individual patrons with phone calls made by box office personnel during their downtime or with e-mail messages saying, in effect, "Because you came to X and Y, we thought you'd be interested in seeing our upcoming production. We have center section seats for you for the matinee performance you have preferred in the past. May I hold these tickets for you while you check your calendar?"

This book is replete with examples of effective marketing strategies developed by people thinking laterally. Taking a lateral marketing approach can help marketers think creatively to develop viable and valuable marketing innovations.

Using Strategic Marketing to Define, Deliver, and Communicate Value

People don't want to be marketed to, they want
to be communicated with.

—Flint McGlaughlin

We read advertisements . . . to discover and enlarge our desires. We are
always ready—even eager—to discover, from the announcement of a
new product, what we have all along wanted without really knowing it.

—Daniel Boorstin

TRADITIONALLY, MARKETERS HAVE RELIED ON THE FRAMEwork, the marketing mix, of the four P's—*product, price, place,* and *promotion*—to develop marketing plans. This functional approach is unidirectional, coming from the organization and being imposed on the customer and thus typically representing the seller's mind-set rather than the buyer's. Robert Lauterborn suggests that marketers think in terms of the four C's instead: *customer value* (not product), *customer costs* (not price alone), *convenience* (not place), and *communication* (not promotion).[1] In the same vein Mohanbir Sawhney suggests that marketing should be organized around processes—processes for understanding, defining, realizing, delivering, communicating, and sustaining value.[2] What both of these experts have in common is their focus on *customer value*. Philip Kotler says that once the marketer thinks through the four C's for the target customer, it becomes much easier to set the four P's.[3]

Throughout this book I focus on various aspects of customer value. In this chapter I focus specifically on the product, place, and promotion—the organization's offerings, venues, and communication approaches—from the customers' perspective. The next chapter will be devoted to pricing.

PRODUCT: THE OFFERING

In the marketing mix the most important element is the offering. The works presented on our stages are the raison d'être of performing arts organizations. Yet the product tends to be the element of the marketing mix that is most misunderstood by arts managers. The product consists not only of the performances themselves; it is the complete bundle of offerings and experiences provided by the institution to the public. All aspects of customers' experiences must be taken into account by arts managers and marketers.

The product can therefore be described as having two different levels.

Core Product

The *core product* is that which is visibly and centrally being offered to the target market for purchase or consumption—the works seen on the stages of performing arts organizations are core products. The core offering of a theater may be thought of as the performance of a single play; as the performance of a specific series, such as a Mamet Festival; or as the programs and series for an entire season. It may also be considered in terms of the performers, the directors, the playwrights, and so on.

People place different values on various aspects of the core product. For example, at the Ravinia Festival in Highland Park, Illinois, some patrons attend primarily to hear a famous soloist perform with the Chicago Symphony Orchestra; others may be most interested in the specific concerto being performed; for some people, picnicking on the lawn on a warm summer evening while listening to music is the primary draw.

According to marketing professor E. Raymond Corey, "the product is what the product does; it is the total package of benefits the customer receives when he buys."[4] People acquire products or services or seek experiences for what these products or experiences can do for them. Leo McGinneva points out that a person shopping for a drill bit is not interested in the bit itself but in what it provides: a hole in a wall.[5] Similarly, people attending arts events are seeking an aesthetic, intellectual, emotional, entertaining, or social experience, or some combination of these experiences. Of course the desired and satisfying experience varies not only from segment to segment; it can vary for each individual as well, which complicates the marketer's task. A first-time operagoer will respond far differently to a production of *La Traviata* than will someone who has seen it five times. Furthermore, each patron's experience will vary according to his or her knowledge, preferences, background, and mental state at the time of the performance.

The core product choice is typically and appropriately in the domain of the artistic director. Yet programming is only partially driven by the artists' and the artistic decision makers' vision. Selecting programming is a complex activity, requiring that the artistic director and the managing directors work together to solve a perpetual problem: how to create a series of programs that has artistic merit; is congruent with the organization's mission, competencies, and constraints; and serves the needs and interests of the community.

Ideally, an organization's programming is both highly artistic and highly satisfying to the audience. That being said, an art organization's season is best designed to balance artistic exploration with the preferences of the current and potential audience. In the United States, it is estimated that 30 percent of dance performances are of Tchaikovsky's *The Nutcracker,* and 50 percent of dance company ticket revenue derives from these productions. This revenue makes it feasible for the companies to present less popular repertory the rest of the season to much smaller audiences.

Art by definition is provocative, challenging, and often unfamiliar and disturbing. Therefore it can never be expected that large segments of the population will have or develop a taste for much of what is presented on our stages. Entertainment, which is market centered, has customer satisfaction as its core goal. The fine arts, however, are centered on artistic vision. If fine arts patrons were all satisfied, artistic directors would not be living up to their responsibility to challenge and provoke.

A performance is essentially a communication between the artist or performer and the audience. This communication cannot take place if the audience does not relate to what is happening on the stage. Therefore arts organizations should capitalize on their many opportunities to help facilitate communication with their audiences.

Modifications to the product that do not affect the artistic nature of the core product offer opportunities to attract different and larger audiences. Companies tend to think in terms of related *products.* Customers think in terms of related *activities.* The Pittsburgh Symphony initiated a program in its 2003–2004 season that keeps this customer perspective in mind. Please read about Symphony with a Splash in Pittsburgh in the box on the next page.

The concept of *edutainment* may be offensive to certain artistic directors and serious, culturally oriented attenders, but their attitude may interfere with success in attracting new and varied audiences. The separation of arts from entertainment is intimidating and causes some people to think they won't enjoy art and certainly won't understand it. The Sunday leisure section of the *Chicago Tribune* is called "Arts and Entertainment," which to my mind, furthers this dichotomy. Besides, those of us who love the arts do find them highly entertaining, and marketers who do not capitalize on this fact are doing their organization and their patrons a disservice.

Augmented Product

The augmented product consists of features and benefits created by the marketer to stimulate purchase and enhance consumption of the core product. Augmentation includes all ticket offerings such as subscription packages, ticket exchange privileges, newsletters, pre- or postperformance lectures, other educational programs, and so on. The challenge for marketers is to improve the communication between the arts organization and its current and potential audiences, reaching out to people in ways that are relevant and compelling to them. It is in the

Symphony with a Splash in Pittsburgh

Symphony with a Splash was an annual series of four concerts that combined a happy hour, starting at 5:30 P.M., with a short concert of humorous and provocative looks at serious music. These Pittsburgh Symphony Orchestra concerts were jointly planned by moderator and musicologist Greg Sandow, Vice President of Artistic Planning Bob Moir, and Conductor Daniel Meyer. Their goal was to create concerts of interest to everyone, the musicians as well as the untapped audiences the organization was trying to attract. The symphony offered an intriguing concert combined with an opportunity to socialize and introductions to the pieces during which the audience not only learned about the music they were hearing but did so in an enjoyable format. According to Greg Sandow, "the information was mainly designed to create the proper mood for enjoying the music. . . . We had a lot of fun. At our last concert, we shaved someone's head (a volunteer from the audience) while the orchestra played the Bacchanal from Samson and Delilah."[6] Said classical music critic Andrew Druckenbrod, Sandow doesn't see classical music as ivory tower-bound, and he discussed the pieces "without an air of sanctuary and all the solemn talk of masterpieces. . . . It's edutainment at its best."[7]

Unfortunately, the series was cancelled after two seasons for financial reasons. Sandow reflected his disappointment in saying he was sure that with proper marketing, the series would have grown in popularity over time.

ways that the core product is packaged, priced, and promoted to the publics and the ways that information is shared, accessibility is engendered—from well-lit parking lots to online ticket sales—and that interest is built that is in the domain of marketing.

Says Greg Sandow in his online book in progress: "People in classical music haven't learned to communicate any real interest, any excitement, any tangible artistic commitment, any reason, in short, why anyone should care about classical music. . . . Classical composers charm us, touch us, caress us, transport us, challenge us, hurt us, warm us, scare us. Yet, how much of this comes across in performance? We are all prevented from having these experiences because of the music world's failure to communicate about anything other than the structure of a piece."[8]

The Internet has provided arts marketers with a dynamic and powerful tool for sharing information, developing accessibility, and building interest. I devote all of Chapter Eight to online marketing.

Accessibility can be achieved in many other ways as well. Offering performances at times that fit people's lifestyles, in addition to expecting people to readily arrange to attend at traditional performance times, has proven to be successful at many organizations. Special events and festivals are effective tools for building interest and enthusiasm. It is important, though, that an event not be created as an end in itself; marketers should plan for the celebration to be the onset of an ongoing relationship with customers. People are hungry for knowledge, and arts marketers can capitalize on this fact when building accessibility and interest.

An Audiovisual Brochure for the Delaware Symphony

In 2004, the Delaware Symphony Orchestra produced *Guidebook,* an *audiovisual brochure* for its upcoming season of twenty-two subscription concerts. *Guidebook* is hosted by the orchestra's music director, David Amado, who talks about the various pieces to be played, with accompanying musical excerpts. J. Edward Cambron, the Philadelphia Orchestra's marketing chief, says that he has seen many orchestras, including his, accompany marketing pieces with CDs, but no other brochure disc that marries text and sound so closely. In just the first month, the brochure generated $20,000 per week in ticket sales. The orchestra sent out 23,000 copies of the *Guidebook* at a cost of $1.90 each, including postage. Audience members have been picking up six copies at a time, no doubt because, "even divorced from its role as a sales tool, the booklet explains some things about classical music that need explaining."[9]

Product Life Cycles

Over time, managers need to periodically adjust or reformulate their marketing and positioning strategy. There are ongoing changes in the environment, such as growing competition and evolving audience preferences. The organization may undergo a major internal change such as a move to a new venue or the arrival of a new artistic director. The organization is also subject to change according to its life cycle stage—from introduction to growth and maturity, and one hopes, staving off decline. The organization itself, its core products, and its augmented products are all subject to life cycle analysis.

In the *introduction* stage the primary challenge is to build awareness of the organization or the product offering or both. New organizations will rely heavily on public relations and other low-cost promotional approaches. More established organizations may offer special events and educational programming to introduce new composers or playwrights.

During the *growth* stage the organization capitalizes on the audience's strong response and seeks to develop patron loyalty. It also employs several strategies to prolong the growth stage. It may add new product features and benefits such as visible improvement in the performance hall, the quality of the productions, and customer service. It may cultivate new market segments with, for example, rush-hour concerts and special student subscriptions. It may add new products such as plays performed on a smaller, second stage or matinee concerts. It may consider new distribution channels, such as performances in neighborhood churches or on local cable channels, collaborations with area businesses, or tours.

When the growth rate slows, often to the point where managers are working harder just to maintain past years' audience level, the organization has entered the stage of *maturity.* It can try to expand its number of users by converting nonusers, by encouraging more frequent use among current users, and by increasing the amount of use per occasion—for example, by encouraging patrons to bring friends or family members. The organization can also stimulate demand by modifying the product. This can take the form of *quality* improvement, usually by investing more heavily in production values, or *feature* improvement, such as offering family programs or adding multimedia technology to a performance. Some organizations, especially orchestras, are offering modifications to their core products, and many of these modifications have been extraordinarily successful at filling the hall.

New Programs at the Chicago Symphony Orchestra

In the fall of 2003, the Chicago Symphony Orchestra (CSO) introduced a MusicPlus series that highlights the orchestra combined with other art forms, including a collaboration with Hubbard Street Dance Chicago. This program was so successful that it was repeated annually. In 2004, the CSO introduced a series titled *Friday Night at the Movies*. The three-concert series opened with the CSO providing accompaniment for a screening of Charlie Chaplin's *City Lights*, with the classic 1931 film projected on a giant screen above the orchestra. This series was such a hit that it was made a part of the CSO's annual schedule, with such offerings as a screening of the 1925 version of *Phantom of the Opera* and an evening of *Comedy Classics*.

The marketing director should also consider what modifications could be made to each nonproduct element of the marketing mix to stimulate demand. For example, could aesthetic appeal be increased with an upgrade to the hall or simply a redesign of the logo and brochures? Could emotional appeal be built with new branding and positioning strategies? Would customers be more likely to browse the organization's Web site if it were easier to navigate and more comprehensive?

At some point many products outlive their value to consumers. If a product or organization has not sustained itself or been rejuvenated through the maturity stage, its sales will eventually decline. The most striking example, pervasive in the performing arts industry as a whole, is the overall decline in recent years of the full-season subscription. Some organizations have been able to not only maintain but build their full-season subscriptions with their high-quality offerings, attractive benefits, and usually, the audience's understanding that this is the only way to guarantee tickets. But for most of the industry, alternative packages such as mini-plans, flex passes, and an emphasis on single ticket sales online have served to maintain or build audience size in the face of declining subscriptions.

Creative arts managers and marketers who think broadly enough to imagine what changes will attract new attenders and build frequency among current attenders are likely to avoid decline. Adaptation must come from within the organization.

As Steve McMillan, CEO of Sara Lee, says, "There are no mature markets; only mature marketers."[10]

PLACE: MANAGING LOCATION, CAPACITY, AND TICKET DISTRIBUTION

For the marketer, *location* has three possible meanings. First, it may refer to managing the benefits and constraints of the organization's own performance venue in efforts to realize audience-building and customer satisfaction objectives. Second, it may refer to alternative venues where the organization could consider performing or providing lectures and demonstrations. Third, it may refer to all the ticket distribution sites and methods the marketer may use to make the product offering available to the public. Decisions about facility size and features, performance location, and ticket delivery systems should be consciously related to the organization's overall marketing strategy and its specific marketing objectives.

The Performance Venue

Special venues, such as Carnegie Hall, the Royal Albert Hall, the Sydney Opera House, and Frank Gehry's Walt Disney Concert Hall for the Los Angeles Philharmonic, are a draw in and of themselves. Not only are their productions world-class in quality but the venues themselves have tremendous symbolic, social, and political significance that serves to attract audiences. At the other end of the spectrum are storefronts, churches, and school auditoriums used as performance halls. The appeal of these venues is based on convenience and, typically, lower ticket prices. Whatever the nature of the venue, it is up to the marketer to ascertain that the facilities are responsive to audience needs, with comfortable seating, adequate restroom facilities, and efficient box office lines. Audience-responsiveness also affects the design of circulation spaces, lobbies, education spaces, concession stands for refreshments and souvenirs, and spaces for special events.

Audiences identify organizations closely with their performance venues and often depend on consistency of location. The San Francisco Ballet and the American Conservatory Theatre performed in alternative yet convenient venues while their usual performance halls were undergoing extensive repairs of earthquake damage. During this transitional time they lost many audience members who returned when the venues reopened. Organizations that perform in a variety of halls, especially presenting organizations that offer a wide variety of performing groups, have difficulty building a strong brand identity and a loyal following for the organization itself.

Organizations that consider moving their venue from one part of town to another must take into account that they are likely to lose a significant portion of those audience members who live in and around the "old" neighborhood. And organizations that offer select performances in an alternative location to attract new audiences usually find that most of these new patrons are not motivated to attend performances at the regular venue, no matter how much they liked the show. When an organization loses its performing venue and is forced to make a move, it is important to promote the benefits of the new space to patrons, rather than be apologetic. For example, the new space may be further from home and work for many patrons, but it may have superior acoustics and more convenient parking.

Managing capacity is the marketer's primary challenge. Organizations that could sell more tickets than they have seats for can either offer additional performances or consider a move to a larger hall. More commonly, organizations perform in halls where the capacity exceeds their usual demand. Too many empty seats in the house can have a devastating effect not only on financial return but on the quality of the experience for both the audience members and the performers. A full house makes the experience more festive and compelling. People like to be a part of something highly sought after and tend to think there is something wrong when many seats do not fill. As Charles Dickens wrote in *Nicholas Nickleby,* it is "a remarkable fact in theatrical history, but one long since established beyond dispute, that it is a hopeless endeavour to attract people to a theatre unless they can be first brought to believe that they will never get into it."

The choice of performance venue may be a function of the availability of a space that meets the organization's production needs for such things as acoustics, sets, and lighting, rather than a function of the space's alignment with current and potential ticket sales. In one midsize city the local opera company performed for several years in a hall with 2,500 seats but sold only about 700 tickets per performance. In such situations there are several strategies marketers can employ to improve the experience. First, they can consider closing off balconies, so the main floor, boxes, and mezzanine are relatively full, and keeping the balconies dark so people are unaware of them. Alternatively, they can continue to sell tickets in the balconies, as many people prefer paying the lower prices typically charged for these seats. Then, when balcony ticket holders arrive for the performance, these customers can be moved into available main floor seats. This will no doubt delight these customers and will improve the experience for everyone in the hall as it will feel more full. Marketers should also distribute free tickets (*comps*) for a sparsely sold performance to artists, colleagues, staff, people who are likely to serve as opinion leaders and spread the word about the organization, and other special groups. They can also offer deeply discounted tickets, such as rush or standby tickets, described in the next chapter. Of course the best solution, if possible, is to perform in a venue that better matches audience size.

Performing arts organizations also commonly experience fluctuations in demand. A heavily subscribed organization is far less susceptible to fluctuating demand than one that relies primarily on single ticket sales. An organization that offers a wide variety of programming will also experience high fluctuations; an evening of contemporary chamber music will not attract the same size audience as Beethoven's best-loved symphonies do. In most other industries, supply can be adjusted to meet demand. For example, grocery stores provide more shelf space for cheddar cheese than for blue cheese. But arts organizations, driven by their artistic vision to offer works they know will draw smaller crowds, must creatively manage the fact that their costs and capacity remain virtually the same no matter what the ticket demand. This is a major dilemma that the nonprofit arts have always and will always face. Sometimes organizations are able to manage these issues by using a second stage at their own venue for certain productions, by offering performances at another location in the area, or by taking performances on tour.

Alternative Venues

Many arts organizations worldwide are responding to the idea that they should bring art to the people before they can hope to bring people to the art. The purpose is to show people in compelling ways and situations that the performing arts can make a difference in their lives. Some fine examples of bringing classical music to people in meaningful ways are the performances during memorial ceremonies for the victims of the September 11, 2001, tragedy, the performance by Yo-Yo Ma at the opening ceremonies of the 2004 Olympics, and local orchestras performing at halftime during regional sporting events. Additionally, music groups may perform at area churches (then invite church members to a concert at a significant discount), present performances and discussions in the lunchrooms of corporate offices, offer free concerts in a park during the summer, and engage in other such projects that expose people to the arts in their own world.

Touring enables the organization to share its performances with a broader audience and serves to establish a regional, national, or international reputation and raise the organization's public profile. It also provides enrichment for the performers as they are exposed to other arts professionals and new audiences. Touring is usually a very costly endeavor but is well worth the expense when the conditions are right. Orchestras and dance companies that have year-round contracts with their artists often depend on touring to provide them enough work throughout the year. Sometimes performing arts organizations can share the financial risks—and revenues—of a production on tour with the presenting organization.

Ticket Distribution

In addition to determining the location and nature of performance spaces, managers must make strategic decisions about how and where tickets to performances will be made available. For some consumers ease of access to tickets and information about availability is crucial if they are to actually make the ticket purchase. For regular at-

Bringing Music to the People in England

National Orchestra Week (NOW) is an annual event in which orchestras across Britain perform a wide range of concerts and special events in nontraditional venues. "It is an ideal opportunity for members of the general public to experience the thrill of live orchestral music for the first time," said Adam Powell, project manager for the Association of British Orchestras, which runs the event. In 2002, the City of Birmingham Symphony Orchestra entertained diners at a popular Birmingham restaurant every Monday in March.[11]

As part of the Pop-Up Project, an innovative three-year collaboration between the BBC Philharmonic and North City Arts, shoppers at a supermarket in Manchester, England, in April 2003 were treated to a surprise performance of the Supermarket Symphony. This symphony was specially composed by the BBC Philharmonic to be performed on items from the supermarket shelves as well as on traditional instruments. Orchestra members were joined in the fruit and vegetable aisle by seventy schoolchildren, supermarket workers, and local residents who played (among other things) "pan lids, food baskets, wooden spoons, packets of cereal, shopping trolleys, and tin cans fashioned into cowbells." The Pop-Up Project, conceived to help stimulate social regeneration in the region, featured a variety of cultural events "popping up" in unlikely places, including the outpatient department of a local hospital, pubs, offices, and street markets.[12]

tenders, satisfaction with the ticket purchasing process is increasingly important to their commitment and loyalty.

THE BOX OFFICE The organization's own box office can be a key link with the customer. The well-informed ticket seller should be able to provide detailed information about the productions and venue and should be prepared to respond to a variety of customer questions and special needs. Box office personnel may use the call they receive as an opportunity to suggest additional programs to the caller.

The phone works both ways. When box office personnel have downtime, they can mine their database to identify past patrons who may be interested in an upcoming production or a special offer. Patrons can be called or e-mailed with messages that show the organization understands their interests and needs, from the types of performances they like to their preferred day of the week and seating location.

CENTRALIZED TICKET AGENCIES Some arts organizations, especially those that rent a venue with its own ticketing agency contract, use intermediary ticketing services, such as Ticketmaster. These services offer ease of setup and operation but are far from ideal from the marketing perspective. They typically charge customers high fees, which has negative implications for the organization's pricing strategy and customer satisfaction levels. Also, they usually do not share their data with the arts organizations, so the marketing department cannot access all-important patron information. Furthermore, ticket agency personnel, who serve multitudes of venues, cannot be expected to provide detailed, or indeed any, information about each organization and its offerings, something the organization's own box office personnel should be trained to do.

Performing arts groups that are not required to use their venue's ticketing service but cannot afford their own systems can avoid the disadvantages of intermediary ticketing agencies by collaborating with other arts organizations in their area to form a centralized ticket agency. Hours of operation could be extended beyond those of each organization's box office if many organizations shared the costs. Specially trained and well-informed salespeople could provide valuable information to callers about each organization's offerings. Furthermore, the organizations could share patrons' names and addresses for marketing purposes and, when appropriate, develop joint offers, such as a sampler series.

ONLINE TICKET SALES In a 2004 survey of 5,500 patrons of several of its client arts organizations from around the United States, Patron Technology investigated how people prefer to transact their ticket purchase. Among arts patrons over age fifty-five, 44 percent claim that they call the box office or a ticketing agency; about 15 percent say they go to the box office in person; 11 percent mail in their orders via the U.S. Postal Service, commonly known as *snail mail;* and 28 percent order online. Among arts patrons under age thirty-five, the proverbial audience of the future, 25 percent call the box office, 14 percent visit the box office, only 1 percent use snail mail, and 55 percent order tickets online.[13] The percentage of people using the Internet to order tickets is not only considerable but continually growing among all age segments.

The Internet and e-mail have become so central a part of how we all do business that an entire chapter—Chapter Eight—is devoted to this topic.

PROMOTION: COMMUNICATING THE OFFER

An arts organization exists to enable and facilitate the communication between the artists on stage and the people in the audience. In an important sense every aspect of a performing arts organization communicates something to its publics. The programs, the facilities, the ticket price, the packages offered, and the character of the marketing messages all tell about the organization's quality and value and about the nature of the core experience the public can expect to have. Therefore the whole marketing mix must be orchestrated for maximum marketing impact.

The Communication Process

Communication is perception. This means that it is the recipient of the message, not the sender, who is central to communication. The message transmitter can only make it possible for a recipient, or *percipient,* to perceive. Perception is based on experience, not on logic, so one can perceive only what one is capable of perceiving. Therefore, in order to make communication possible, one must first know the recipient's language and experience. To further complicate matters, people respond best to communications that fit in with their aspirations, values, and motivations. If a message fits with what people believe, how they view themselves, or how they aspire to be, the message will be powerful; if the message does not correspond with these qualities, it is likely not to be received at all or, at best, likely to be resisted.

Communication and information are different yet interdependent. Whereas communication is perception, information is data. Information is impersonal rather than interpersonal. The more it can be freed of the human component—of emotions, values, expectations, and perceptions—the more valid, reliable, and informative it becomes. Yet information's effectiveness depends on the prior establishment of communication. Perception, then, has primacy over information. True communication exists when the recipient perceives what the transmitter intends.

Marketing as Influencing Behavior

Marketing is a matter of influencing behavior—either changing behavior (such as encouraging attendance at a performance of avant-garde works) or preventing it from changing (such as encouraging people to renew their subscriptions). As we have seen, in order to influence behavior it is crucial to understand where the customer is coming from. If a message is not designed to address target customer interests, needs, and mind-set, it will fall on deaf ears. Once the marketer has developed an understanding of targeted market segments, he or she will develop messages and use media that *inform, persuade,* and *educate* people in compelling ways.

INFORMING   In order to make a decision whether or not to attend, people need basic information about the event itself (what will be performed and by whom) as well as about the date, location, time, cost of tickets, and how tickets may be purchased. This may sound obvious, but some organizations do not prioritize this information properly in their advertisements and sometimes do not even include it all. For example, marketers who refrain from stating ticket price ranges in their ads may be doing themselves a disservice. Some people who are interested in the program will buy tickets no matter what the price; some already know the organization's pricing. But some people are likely to think, for example, that ticket prices at the midsize opera company are as high as prices at the city's major opera company and may choose not to attend because of this assumption alone. When an organization moves to a new venue, information about the location is probably much more important to potential ticket buyers than the names of unfamiliar performers and set designers. When creating messages, it is important for marketers to consider what is most important to consumers, not to the stakeholders within the organization.

PERSUADING All advertising, public relations efforts, personal selling, and sales promotion tactics are intended to persuade. Unfortunately, much marketing copy is filled with hype, exaggerating consumer expectations or causing people to be skeptical of the claims.

Performing arts organizations should make their purpose and positioning clear to their target audiences, and adjectives used to describe the experience should accurately reflect what the patron is likely to feel. If a play is a serious drama with a few moments of comic relief, it should not be billed as "hilarious." If music is quiet and sublime, it should not be described as "thrilling." If patrons are repeatedly unmoved by performances, then they will think either that they are missing something or that they just do not enjoy the art form. A major source of dissatisfaction is not inferior quality but exaggerated expectations. Disappointment can be avoided if the organization uses realistic methods of persuasion.

Furthermore, observes music critic and commentator Greg Sandow, "What you'll almost never read is anything that might make an intelligent person want to go to a concert—something about how the music is going to be played, what it will feel like to hear the music, or why this concert might be different from any other. Mostly we brag that we offer 'acclaimed' musicians, predictably playing—no surprise here!—'great music.' Every concert, if you believe our advertising, seems more or less the same—uniformly 'great' and uplifting. Why should anybody care?"[14]

Many focus group participants in a qualitative study of dance attenders in Scotland had a cynical attitude to marketing copy and simply did not believe what companies and venues said about events. Said one participant, "It's taken me years to learn to read through all the write-ups. All these words: 'stupefying,' 'electric,' 'dramatic,' 'never to be forgotten' and I used to believe it. All this hype."[15]

Similarly, elitist attitudes among those who produce and present the arts work against what are otherwise good efforts to attract new audiences. *New Yorker* music critic Alex Ross articulates the problem this way:

For at least a century, music has been captive to a cult of mediocre elitism that tries to manufacture self-esteem by clutching at empty formulas of intellectual superiority. . . . Music can be great and serious; but greatness and seriousness are not its defining characteristics. . . . Music is too personal a medium to support an absolute hierarchy of values. . . . Some discerning souls say, in effect, "The music you love is trash. Listen instead to our great, arty music." . . . They are making little headway with the unconverted because they have forgotten to define the music as something worth loving. If it is worth loving, it must be great; no more need be said.[16]

The marketer's goal is to persuade. The more the marketer's field of experience overlaps with that of the message recipient, the more effective the message is likely to be. Much of what is called persuasion is allowing the recipient to engage in self-persuasion. Please read about Charlotte the spider's persuasive talents on the following page.

EDUCATING   For most people an appreciation of the performing arts is learned or acquired over time. But education is a difficult task. A great deal of information has to be conveyed, a great deal of time and effort is required, and often people's long-held attitudes and beliefs must be changed. This is a primary reason why arts organizations have traditionally focused their efforts on informing and persuading current cultural patrons rather than on the much more daunting task of educating nonattenders. Yet creative arts managers can and do offer a wide variety of educational programs and resources, in person and online. The Internet has opened new vistas that make it possible for arts organizations to educate their publics, no matter what their level of sophistication, efficiently and cost effectively. Some examples of these educational approaches appear in Chapters Two and Eight.

The Communications Mix

Current marketing practice is simultaneously exemplified by the seemingly paradoxical extreme goals of mass branding and one-to-one relationship marketing. The marketing communications mix consists

Charlotte: Precursor to the Modern Spin Doctor

In *Charlotte's Web,* E. B. White's famously endearing classic tale, Wilbur the pig is about to be sold off by the Zuckerman family. Sensing the threat of Wilbur's impending death, Charlotte the spider has a plan to save him.

"Some Pig!" Charlotte weaves neatly, in block letters, in the middle of her web, to be noticed in the morning by the hired hand. "Some Pig!" The word of Charlotte's message spreads quickly.

"Edith, something has happened . . ." [farmer Zuckerman informs his wife "in a weak voice"].

> ". . . Our pig is completely out of the ordinary. . . ."
> "Well," said Mrs. Zuckerman, "it seems to me you're a little off. It seems to me we have no ordinary *spider.*"
> "Oh no," said Zuckerman. "It's the pig that's unusual. It says so, right there in the middle of the web."[17]

"Such is the power of publicity," says Marjorie Garber in her book *Symptoms of Culture.* "'Some Pig' is, of course, superbly chosen as an epithet of praise, since it could mean anything, and shortly does."[18]

> "You know [says Mr. Zuckerman, this time "in an important voice"], I've thought all along that that pig of ours was an extra good one. He's a solid pig. That pig is as solid as they come. . . ."
> Long before Sunday came, the news spread all over the county. . . . Everybody knew that the Zuckermans had a wondrous pig.[19]

of several major tools, each of which addresses one or the other of these goals.

ADVERTISING Advertising is any paid form of nonpersonal presentation and promotion of ideas, goods, or services by an identified sponsor. Advertising serves many purposes, from the long-term buildup of the organization's image and brand identity to information about a particular production or a special price offer. Paid advertising permits total control over the message content and substantial control over the scheduling of message delivery. It is a highly public and pervasive medium. Its public nature confers a kind of legitimacy on the product, and large-scale advertising by a seller says something positive about the seller's size, popularity, and success. Advertising provides opportunities for dramatizing the organization and its offerings through the artful use of print, sound, image, and color. However, paid advertising permits no control over the way the audience decodes the message, and it results in little or delayed feedback on the message. The audience does not feel obligated to pay attention or respond to advertising. Unlike personal selling, advertising is able to carry on only a monologue, not a dialogue, with the audience.

Aside from brochures and other direct-mail pieces, arts organizations have traditionally advertised most extensively in newspapers. But daily readership of newspapers dropped from 52.6 percent of adults in 1990 to 37.5 percent in 2000. The drop is much steeper in the twenty- to forty-nine-year-old cohort, a generation that is, and as it ages will remain, comfortable with electronic media in general and the Web in particular. Says Richard A. Posner, in an article in the *New York Times,* "the audience decline for newspapers is potentially fatal [to the newspapers themselves]."[20] In a survey of arts patrons, radio advertising and features received the highest ratings among people who were asked which publicity and marketing tools were most effective in influencing ticket purchases.[21] With this information and with the ever-growing pervasiveness of the Internet and resulting changes in consumer behavior, marketers must rethink how best to spend their marketing budget.

SALES PROMOTION Sales promotion offers encourage purchase of a product or service by incorporating some concession or incentive, such as coupons, premiums, or discounts that give value to the consumer. Promotions serve to gain attention and usually provide information that may lead the consumer to the product. For example, a small, young opera company uses an e-mail promotion to offer $5 off the $25 regular ticket price for one week only about a month before a weekend of performances. A theater offers two tickets for the price of one for its

Tuesday evening performances, which are not selling well. Another theater's subscription offer includes five shows for the price of four. Organizations use sales promotion tools to create a stronger and quicker response. Sometimes they help create interest in attending further offerings at the organization. However, their effects are usually short run; they are generally not effective in building long-term results.

In designing sales promotions managers must take care to not give away too much, as people value more what they pay for.

PUBLIC RELATIONS Marketing public relations is defined as "the process of planning, executing, and evaluating programs that encourage purchase and consumer satisfaction through credible communication of information and impressions that identify organizations and their products with the needs, wants, concerns, and interests of their publics."[22] Although the main function of marketing is to influence *behavior,* the primary task of public relations is to form, maintain, or change public *attitudes* toward the organization or its products.

Public relations offers high credibility. Even though the public's confidence in newspapers dropped from 49 percent in 1987 to 19 percent in 2003, news stories seem more authentic and credible to readers than do advertisements, which have consistently received only 7 to 8 percent confidence level ratings during the same time period.[23] The public relations message gets to the buyers as news rather than as sales-directed communications, so people are more likely to pay attention. Importantly, public relations is extremely low cost, requiring only a fraction of the expense of advertising. The organization does not pay for the space or time obtained in the media. It pays only for staff to develop and circulate the stories and manage certain events.

DIRECT AND DATABASE MARKETING Direct marketing encompasses several tools, including but not limited to direct mail, telemarketing, e-mail marketing, and efforts to build word-of-mouth marketing. Direct marketing allows the marketer to customize messages to appeal to select individuals and target groups. Typically, people respond better and more frequently to messages directed specifically to them. However, too extensive a reliance on direct marketing can prevent the organization from broadening its audience, so marketers must find a good balance between direct-marketing tools and other communication forms such as advertising and public relations.

A major component and advantage of direct marketing is the ability to track customer response behavior over time through a database. Leveraging the power of database marketing is an important key to direct-marketing success as a good database is a crucial tool for deriving information that will help organizations develop future marketing strategies for both current and potential audiences.

Arts marketers often exchange mailing lists with other, similar organizations. For instance, a classical theater company and a Shakespearean company might exchange lists, hoping to generate crossover attendance. Targeting within these lists is usually done by zip code. However, people enjoy attending a wide range of arts and entertainment events, and limiting crossover mailings to a specific cultural sector and geographical area misses the mark on many other opportunities.

A 1997 study commissioned by the Arts Marketing Taskforce and Arts Victoria in Melbourne, Australia, exhibited in valuable detail the strong cross-attendance patterns of Victoria's arts attenders. The study showed, for example, that 28 percent of people who had attended a chamber music concert in the previous twelve months had also been to the ballet. This datum is particularly significant when one considers that 5.9 percent of the Victoria population overall attends the ballet. Similarly, 26 percent of contemporary dance attenders had also attended performances at small or midsize theaters, compared to 7.2 percent of the general population. Operagoers had consistently high proportions of attendance across all other art events. Eighty-two percent of people who attended orchestral music concerts also visited art galleries. Although only 19 percent of the people who visited art galleries also attended classical concerts, arts marketers who have measured typical responses to direct-mail, advertising, and other promotional efforts know that a 19 percent response rate is highly desirable.[24]

Studies such as this demonstrate that arts organizations should think beyond their own boundaries and that cooperating in marketing ventures will enliven audiences rather than exhaust them. Although arts organizations are concerned about losing patrons to one another through joint subscriptions, collaborative box offices, and other cross-promotional efforts, the economies of acquiring new pa-

The Smart Database in Pittsburgh

To capitalize on the fact that past ticket purchasing behavior is a good predictor of attendance, consultant John Elliott has developed the SmArt database, data about 425,000 households in the Pittsburgh area based on fourteen years' worth of ticket sales. Elliott uses detailed computer analysis on consumers' purchasing patterns and statistical models to track down the most likely ticket buyers for six organizations participating in Pittsburgh's Cultural District. The data provide crossover information so that each household is scored on its likelihood of buying tickets for each Cultural District organization or product offering. Elliott's data inform him, for example, that of the people who saw *The Lion King* in early 2004, about 17,400 households have made $1.2 million in additional ticket purchases for Cultural District offerings. Besides being likely ticket buyers for Broadway shows such as *Cats* or *Les Miserables,* some bought subscriptions to the Civic Light Opera and Pittsburgh Ballet Theatre. Marketing directors of the six participating organizations turn to Elliott for his suggested list of people to target before they print and send direct-mail pieces. Since the SmArt database began operating in 2002, single tickets and subscriptions have risen by 13 percent among the six participating groups, amounting to a $4.2 million ticket revenue increase. Laura Willumsen, marketing director for the Pittsburgh Opera, says that with this tracking system, she can accurately predict the response rate from her internal list and from crossovers, depending on the popularity of the opera. "It's the difference between throwing darts while blindfolded and hoping you hit your target, versus having a scope with a magnifier on it."[25]

trons through these techniques are likely to more than offset the occasional loss of a patron to another organization.

BUILDING WORD-OF-MOUTH MARKETING With all the time and expense involved in creating and disseminating marketing communications—advertisements, direct-mail pieces, press releases, and so on—marketers know that word-of-mouth is the most influential factor in most people's ticket purchasing decisions, often more influential than all other marketing efforts combined. Although arts marketers are well aware of the significance of word-of-mouth marketing, it is not a common practice to implement strategies that encourage patrons to spread the word. Says Emanuel Rosen in his book *The Anatomy of Buzz: How to Create Word of Mouth Marketing,* "most of today's marketing still focuses on how to use advertising and other tools to influence *each customer individually,* ignoring the fact that purchasing many types of products is part of a *social process.* It involves not only a one-to-one interaction between the company and the customer but also many exchanges of information and influence among the people who surround that customer." Len Short, executive vice president of advertising and brand management at Charles Schwab, sums up the situation this way: "The idea that a critical part of marketing is word of mouth and validation from important personal relationships is absolutely key, and most marketers ignore it."[26]

Among the benefits of word-of-mouth marketing is that it empowers the customer; it puts the customer in the position of being the marketer. Having the customer as the marketer addresses the problems of the distracting "noise" in the mass media and the fact that customers are skeptical of advertising claims. In fact, claims Rosen, people will talk more about what they discover themselves. People enjoy their own credibility, and when they back a product, they know that they're putting their reputation on the line. Buzz capitalizes on the fact that people are connected—connected in their personal relationships, through blogs, and through e-mail. Buzz travels most smoothly through channels built on trust.

Rosen says that the products people buzz about are those that create high involvement. First and foremost in importance are the quality of the product and the emotional response the product evokes, the excitement of loving a product or experience and the delight that comes from having your expectations exceeded.

Before they attempt to stimulate buzz, Rosen suggests marketers and managers first ask themselves the following questions: "Am I offering a quality product or service? . . . Does my product enhance the lives of people who use it?" Is something about my offering "fresh and different?" Is there something I can do to make my "product or its users more noticeable in a positive way?"[27]

To create viable conditions for buzz, marketers must invest energy behind the product, in terms of both time and money. The key is to build networking by reaching people who can spread the news to many others. In his book *The Tipping Point: How Little Things Can Make a Big Difference,* Malcolm Gladwell describes the power of connectors—acquaintances who give us access to opportunities and worlds to which we don't belong. Gladwell claims that the *opinion leaders* among those acquaintances are the ones who garner the most respect and therefore have the most power to influence others.[28] Arts marketers can capitalize on the influence of opinion leaders by offering tickets for performances early in the run of a show to people who are likely to be interested and who will talk about it to others.

Seth Godin says that it is much easier to get a message in front of someone than to get that person to pass it along. Godin names powerful customer-to-customer dialogue the *ideavirus,* and he encourages marketers to create an environment where their ideas can replicate and spread.[29] As important as it is to think of your relationship with each individual customer, also think of customers as part of a network. Central to creating that environment, says Rosen, is listening to the networks. Your objective is to maximize the number of positive comments about your product that flow within this network and to other networks. And work to accelerate contagion in the network. Intense personal effort may be required to push the word and to leapfrog directly to the most productive hubs or into untapped clusters.

Regularly talk with customers on an informal basis. Subscribe to blog services. Know what people are saying about your organization and about your competitors. Identify the hubs to which customers belong—both the expert hubs and the social hubs—and try to distinguish who are the connectors, bridging the distance between clusters. Use all available techniques to find even more hubs, and as you find them, be sure to keep good records of your contacts. Develop a profile for each person including his or her name and address, what type of influence he or she has, and what types of useful connections.

Finally, regularly provide your hubs with updated information and offers, and acknowledge referrals, rewarding customer loyalty. Use a sneak preview to capture the interest of a select group of customers, and take your customers behind the scenes to share the excitement of a production coming together. People love hearing about any human drama that takes place in the creation of your show, not only the drama unfolding on stage. If you have a charismatic leader, bring him or her before your customers as often as possible. Also, make it easy for customers to talk to you, and be receptive and responsive to their feedback and input. Generating buzz about your organization's offering calls for an attitude different from the perspective marketers are used to. Rosen also encourages marketers to operate in a spirit of truth, honesty, and directness, as openness and candor are key to developing strong, long-term, grassroots support.

Viral marketing, so-named because it is intended to spread widely, is most efficiently undertaken through your Web site and e-mail messages. Make sure your Web site and e-mail messages have a simple-to-use pass-it-on mechanism that is presented in a friendly way. Although the social contacts are usually their own reward, sometimes it is helpful if the messages include special benefits that come from successfully spreading the news.

In line with the concept that the social promise might be what triggers attendance, some arts organizations are beginning to use high technology in new, creative ways.

The most important policy, says Rosen, is to keep your customers involved. "If you involve them, engage them, make it interesting for them, they will talk. Involvement translates to action, which in turn translates to buzz."[30]

Viral Marketing at the Louisiana Philharmonic

Before the devastation caused by Hurricane Katrina, the Louisiana Philharmonic designed its Find the Phil series specifically as a viral marketing event for young, Web-savvy potential audiences. The concerts, which featured small ensembles playing unusual repertoire, took place at various unannounced locations around New Orleans. The orchestra provided a series of clues on the FindThe Phil.com Web site and via e-mail. People were asked to forward the messages to friends, who in turn were invited to register on the Web site. At the concerts everyone was registered, due in no small part to a ticket discount incentive.

Integrated Marketing Management

To promote an organization, a season, or an individual production most effectively, marketing managers should plan and implement an integrated marketing approach. *Integrated* marketing means using a multiple-vehicle, multiple-stage campaign. The multiple vehicles might include a combination of paid ads in such media as newspapers, radio, billboards, TV, and the Internet; direct mail, brochures or postcards or both; telemarketing; e-mail; and public relations. Multiple stage refers to the time line developed to best leverage each of these media.

For example, a subscription campaign might start by mailing brochures to current subscribers, followed up with another mailing about one month later to people who have not renewed. About two weeks after the second mailing, begin telemarketing to reattract subscribers who have not renewed by mail. At about this time also begin the campaign to attract new subscribers. Send postcards to prospects, with a response mechanism for people who want more information. Place an ad in the local newspaper and on select radio stations to create product awareness and stimulate inquiries. Anyone who requests further information should be sent a brochure. Be sure to drive people to your Web site and clearly offer opportunities for people to request more information via e-mail or snail mail. Try to capture the e-mail addresses of anyone who comes in contact with the organization, and maintain ongoing communication, even if the person is not ready to buy.

An integrated marketing plan to attract single ticket buyers making their buying decisions within a week or two of a performance should guarantee intense visibility in multiple media all in the same key time frame. To accomplish this, use a strategy known as *roadblocking:* air a radio ad at the same time on several stations frequented by your target markets. For example, plan that consumers will hear your ad on the rush-hour commute from work and again in the early morning rush hour, when a radio personality will pitch your show and an opportunity to win free tickets. Send postcards so they are waiting in the consumer's mailbox when he or she arrives home, and send e-mail messages with links to your Web site where in-depth information can be found. Place ads in the newspaper during this time frame as well, but do not assume that the ads belong in the arts or entertainment section. Try to reach out to people where they are, not where you hope they will be. This use of *response compression,* whereby multiple media are deployed within a tightly defined time frame, increases message awareness and impact. Multiple media are used because different individuals respond to different media and because people in general are more likely to respond when they have had multiple exposures to a message.

CONSIDER MANY MARKETING COSTS AS INVESTMENTS, NOT EXPENDITURES

Many marketing costs, such as those dedicated to developing a branding campaign or building young audiences, are undertaken with the understanding that they will not provide immediate returns but are investments in the arts organization's future. When budgets are tight, these expenses are often eliminated or at least cut back. Similarly, costs for advertising, direct mail, and other current audience development activities are often viewed as expenditures that can be cut when revenues fall below expectations. They are an easy target for budget-minded managers because their costs are variable whereas many of an organization's other expenses are fixed. Arts managers must realize, however, that slashes in the marketing budget not only compromise the marketing department's ability to meet capacity goals but also lead to cutbacks in communication and service and compromise the organization's ability to provide value and satisfaction to its target customers. Marketing needs to be seen as an investment center whose expenditures create long-lasting customers and revenue flows.

6

Delivering Value Through Pricing Strategies

Price is what you pay. Value is what you get.

—Warren Buffet

I N THE PERFORMING ARTS PRICING IS AN ESPECIALLY COMPLEX issue. In the business sector success is evaluated primarily by the bottom line, and the company's efforts are directed to ensure profitability. In the nonprofit sector income generation is a means of fulfilling the organization's mission, rather than an end in itself. In nonprofit arts organizations, which prioritize artistic vision, attracting broad audiences, and education, monetary costs are only one of myriad factors that contribute to pricing decisions. Furthermore, arts organizations face unique costs that put them in a disadvantageous position relative to the business sector.

ANALYZING COSTS AND VALUE

Arts marketers need to consider the costs incurred not only by the arts organization presenting a production but also by the consumers attending a performance.

Costs to the Arts Organization

Performing arts organizations do not benefit from the productivity gains experienced by the rest of society. Since the early twentieth century, increases in efficiency in our technology-oriented, for-profit economy have been continuous and cumulative. Output per man-hour has doubled approximately every twenty-nine years, so that wages and productivity have risen in tandem. In contrast, productivity in the arts has actually decreased relative to the rest of the economy. A Shakespearean play will always require the same amount of time for casting, rehearsals, set-building, and performances as it did a century ago; a live performance of a forty-five-minute Schubert quartet will take the same three man-hours to produce as it always has. Yet artists' wages have risen over time, even if their productivity has not, so that their income can keep pace with incomes in the rest of society. This is what economists William Baumol and William Bowen call an inevitable *cost disease* of growing financial pressures and an ever-widening gap between income and expenses.[1]

Also, arts organizations are typically guided by their artistic directors, who often value innovation and risk, resulting in relatively narrow audience appeal and therefore relatively high cost to the organization per audience member. Furthermore, many arts organizations incur substantial expenses for fixed costs—primarily for institutional overhead—costs that must be met no matter how many tickets are sold.

Typically, a central part of the performing arts mission is to attract as broad an audience as possible, which by definition means setting some ticket prices at a level that is affordable for virtually anyone who would like to attend. This calls for pricing strategies that are focused on customer segments rather than on the organization and its costs. Organizations depend on contributed income to compensate for the difference between the organization's expenses and its earned income, yet garnering adequate donations is a perpetual struggle. As a result of all these factors, nonprofit performing arts organizations, no matter how successful artistically, often operate under constant financial strain.

Consumer Costs and Value

As arts marketers seek new approaches for broadening their audience base and building frequency of attendance among current
audiences, they often express concern that their organizations' already
high ticket prices, not to mention likely price increases, act as a barrier to successful audience development. So it is essential to ask, How
important is price to the customer? And for exactly which customers
is price important?

Intangible Costs

Customers have many costs in addition to the price of the ticket
when attending a performance. There are the psychic costs some people
have in not wanting to feel ignorant about the art form, in not knowing
if they will enjoy the experience, or in not knowing if there will be other
people "like them" in the audience. Some people may avoid going to a
theater in what they perceive to be an unsafe neighborhood. Others
may not have a babysitter available or may not want to fight traffic.

In the performing arts we are competing on *value for time* as much
as on *value for money.* Clearly, there are people for whom disposable income is a deciding factor in whether or not to attend an arts event. But
for the majority of people *predisposed* to attend the arts, especially in
metropolitan areas with varied cultural offerings, price is much less of
a factor than time. This issue is highlighted in Arts Council England's
forecasting report *Towards 2010,* which identifies *time poverty* as a key
barrier to arts attendance across almost all social segments. In 1998,
63 percent of the population surveyed agreed that "I never seem to
have enough time to get things done." High-income groups were particularly affected, but a third of the respondents said they were "willing
to spend money to save time."[2]

Perceived Value

Different audience members are at different stages of the life cycle
of arts attendance and therefore have different perceptions of value for
money and the equilibrium point at which they are comfortable with

purchasing a ticket of a particular price for a specific show. Committed arts attenders are generally comfortable paying a high ticket price, as their past experience has shown that the benefits they receive offset the financial investment they have made. At the other end of the spectrum, first-time attenders may be less inclined to purchase an expensive ticket because they are unsure whether the personal benefits they will receive will justify the financial cost.

For the purpose of analyzing the impact of price among nonattenders, it is important to draw a distinction between the *nonintenders,* those for whom pricing is not an issue because they do not intend to purchase a ticket for other reasons, and the *intender-rejectors,* those who would like to attend but become alienated as a result of pricing policy. For the vast majority of people, the nonintenders, rejection has set in before price becomes a consideration, because for these people there is probably an irreversible barrier: lack of interest. Therefore one can conclude that there is little point in trying to use major price cuts to access the mass market; price cutting will not generate full houses and will work against the organization's best interest in other ways because revenue will be greatly reduced from the current patrons willing to pay higher prices.

Many performing arts companies offer low ticket prices in an attempt to attract audiences who could not otherwise afford to go, the intender-rejectors. A ticket to see the English National Opera at the coliseum can be obtained for as little as £5 ($9), and the Royal Opera offers one hundred top-price Monday night tickets for £10 for those willing to turn up and try their luck ninety minutes before the performance.

A report by the U.K.-based Institute for Public Policy Research (IPPR), issued in April 2004, claims that cut-price tickets encourage existing fans to attend more often but do not attract new audiences. Says Ian Kearns, associate director of IPPR, "Research shows that cost is not the major limiting factor."[3]

Yet, it takes time and multiple exposures for someone to develop an attachment to an art form. On the premise that newcomers and occasional attenders need an affordable and gradual way in, New York City Center offered a Fall for Dance Festival in 2004 and 2005— six different programs over the course of a week for only $10 per ticket. "Performances sold out almost immediately, and long lines of people waited for returns every night, providing heartwarming evidence of a serious hunger for dance performances at the right price," said Roslyn Sulcas of the *New York Times*.[4] However, organizations must enlist the support of generous donors or sponsors in order to afford to sell tickets at such a low price. This festival was discontinued after two years.

Effect of Price on Ticket Purchase

As costs continue to spiral upward and as audience size and contributed income levels remain relatively stagnant, performing arts organizations face an ever-increasing need to raise their ticket prices. Often, performing arts managers base ticket price increases on an analysis of the earned revenue needed to meet internal costs, without a thorough understanding of the market viability of these pricing decisions. However, there are serious concerns that as ticket prices increase, the subscriber base will erode, single ticket buyers will attend less frequently, and it will become continually more difficult to attract new attenders. There are also concerns that at higher prices people will select seats in less expensive seating areas of the venue and decrease their levels of contributed support.

In response to concern over these issues the marketing directors of four major performing arts organizations in San Francisco collaborated on an in-depth investigative market research study to quantify and analyze the factors that influence ticket purchases and, specifically, the effect ticket price has on the purchasing behavior of current audience segments. The performing arts organizations participating in this 1996 study were the San Francisco Symphony, San Francisco Opera, San Francisco Ballet, and American Conservatory Theater (A.C.T.). I was engaged as the market researcher to manage this project.

Among the four organizations' audience members who were surveyed, the study found that 41 to 65 percent of respondents claimed that interest in a performance is the most important factor in their purchase decision; about 25 to 60 percent said that scheduling issues prevail, and only 8 to 29 percent said that ticket price drove their decision. (The percentages varied by organization and by whether the respondents were subscribers or single ticket buyers. Please see Table

10.2 for a breakdown of the responses.) Among those who cited price as a primary factor, just as many people stated they were *unwilling* to pay a stated ticket price as said they were *unable* to pay. This distinction highlights the fact that for many people, interest is the barrier to attendance, not price. For those *unable* to pay, low-price strategies can be highly effective. Only current attenders—those who already showed significant interest in the organizations and their offerings—were surveyed in this research, but marketers should investigate the barriers affecting those *unwilling* to attend and design strategies that might be effective in attracting this segment. Ticket pricing cannot be determined irrespective of the other aspects of the marketing mix; rather, all factors must be coordinated and integrated into an overall strategy.

One series of survey questions was designed to learn about people's pricing decisions relative to seat location. We asked whether people planned to stay in seating areas of the same price when making their selections for next season. If they were shifting seats, we asked what their new location would be. Although for each organization we noted movement out of and into certain seating locations depending on price changes, this movement was minimal, and for the most part was statistically insignificant. Also, given that people may value different performances differently, we asked symphony patrons if they would purchase tickets to six individually described concerts and, if so, in which seating location they would purchase their tickets. We thought that people might choose to sit closer to the stage when a soloist was performing and choose a less expensive seat for purely orchestral concerts. But the responses demonstrated that the majority of people choose the same seating area for each performance they attend. Seat switching from concert to concert averages 3 to 5 percent of ticket buyers, and never exceeds 10 percent. Therefore we can reasonably conclude that once people value attending a concert, they do not put different price values on their seating choices concert by concert.

The survey found that programming is by far the most important variable in people's decisions to attend, and their interest in specific productions is what determines the success of a season. Following programming in importance is the fact that with patrons' changing lifestyles and more competition for their leisure time, people find it increasingly difficult to schedule in advance. Although many of the single ticket buyers who responded to this study were once subscribers but are no longer, price does not appear to have played a major role in this shift. Rather, the primary motives for this behavioral change are that many people prefer to select which programs to attend and many have difficulty scheduling in advance.

The survey verified what has long been assumed by performing arts marketing managers: that most current attenders—except those who purchase budget-priced tickets—have little sensitivity to price increases. Price increase has little or no effect on their ticket purchasing behavior. This does not mean that there is no limit to the amount that ticket prices can be raised. We did observe slightly more sensitivity to ticket prices among the respondents who received surveys with higher stated ticket prices than among those who received lower stated ticket prices. In general, price sensitivity seems likely to occur at higher prices than those tested in this survey, but because of limitations in its design, this survey produced no information about where that price point is.

The marketing directors of the four organizations participating in this study were concerned about finding their patrons' breaking point: the point at which prices are so high that attendees reduce their frequency of attendance or discontinue attending performances altogether. There was no evidence of either of these situations occurring in the near future. Prices can comfortably be raised annually at moderate levels.

In conjunction with the written audience survey, the American Conservatory Theatre's box office personnel recorded information as people called for tickets. We were interested in knowing whether customers received their first-choice seat location, and if not, what their second choice was. For example, if people preferred midpriced tickets and those were sold out, did they choose lower- or higher-priced seats? The survey found that on average, 77 percent of single ticket buyers were able to purchase tickets for the date and price they preferred. For the 23 percent who did not get their first choice of seating location, the great majority moved *up* in price, rather than down, indicating that a good seat location is far more important to them than a lower price. These responses suggest that attenders want the best experience possible and appreciate the value of good seat locations more than a lower-priced ticket.

Again, it is important to note that these studies surveyed current attenders only. Therefore they did not capture information about the price sensitivity of people who are not currently attending but who are potential future attenders.

Other market research verifies our findings in San Francisco. In a British study of infrequent attenders, price was found to play a role in consumers' ticket purchase decisions. But programming choice, value, and enjoyment were reported to be as important as price in motivating ticket purchase.[5] In another British study of people interested in theater, 76 percent of respondents rated price in the second tier of issues for potential attendance, well below their first-tier rating of quality of performance, entertainment value, and subject matter.[6] In a survey of lapsed subscribers at the Writers' Theatre in Glencoe, Illinois, play selection was cited as the most important reason for not renewing (47% of respondents). Ticket price was a distant second reason (12% of respondents).[7]

PRICING STRATEGIES

Many arts attenders are not price sensitive; they want the best seats and are willing to pay for them. However, there are also many people who enjoy attending the arts but can do so only if inexpensive tickets are available. There are two basic objectives an arts organization may attempt to realize through pricing strategies: *revenue (or cost recovery) maximization* and *audience (size and diversity) maximization.* These objectives are not mutually exclusive, and savvy arts managers often find they can meet both goals simultaneously.

Competition-Oriented Pricing

Simply by stating their prices, organizations position themselves in comparison to other arts organizations in terms of such factors as quality, size, image, reputation, and location. It is *perceived* value that determines worth in the eyes of the customer, and price is a strong indicator of the experience people expect. The community theaters in an area will all price their tickets similarly, and that price will be significantly lower than the price at major regional theaters downtown. In the arts world, where ticket prices do not typically cover costs, pricing is largely a function of industry wisdom concerning the price that will both yield a fair return and elicit reasonable demand, which in turn is based on the price-value equation. The crucial factor is that people must believe they are getting appropriate value for their money. In fact, lower ticket prices sometimes do not realize a greater audience, as people may expect that they will have a lesser experience.

Product Form Pricing

In product form pricing different offerings are priced differently. A presenting organization will charge more for a famous star than for a rising star. A theater may charge more for a full-scale musical production than for a two-actor drama with minimal sets. However, most organizations that offer subscriptions price all the productions in a subscription series the same, no matter what their appeal or cost. Single ticket prices may reflect differences in cost, as it is easier to sell musicals at a higher price. Yet it is important for arts managers to maintain the perceived value of different events consistently across a season. One strategy they can employ is to vary the number of seats in each price category by performance, so that when Renée Fleming is singing a recital, there may be many more higher-priced tickets, and when an unknown conductor is performing twentieth-century repertoire, there may be more lower-priced seats. This strategy is commonly employed by organizations that do not offer packages of programs. But heavily subscribed organizations are likely to find this strategy impossible to implement.

Location, Time, and Special Event Pricing

Different seat locations and days of performances are often priced differently even though the cost of offering each seat is the same. Many patrons will pay a steep premium for the best seats, and higher prices are often charged for the more desirable weekend performances.

People are also willing to pay significantly higher prices for special events, such as opening night, which may include a complimentary glass of champagne and an opportunity to mingle with the artists after the show. The operative word for this pricing strategy is *special;* people must feel they are receiving benefits in terms of such features as exclusivity and excitement. When they do, they are not only willing but eager to pay a premium price.

Location pricing may also be a function of where the performance is taking place. For example, an orchestra may offer summer concerts in a park for free or for one low price.

Special pricing strategies may be effective in selling tickets for performances that are offered at unattractive times, such as perfor-

---

Pricing Neighborhood Concerts in Saint Paul

As an experiment, to help combat a decline in ticket sales, in February 2005 the Saint Paul Chamber Orchestra (SPCO) announced a dramatic reduction in subscription prices for its 2005–2006 Neighborhood Series concerts, performed at four metro-area venues. Tickets that were normally priced from $11 to $47 were lowered to $10 and $25 for adults and $5 for kids under seventeen. Six months later the SPCO reported a 43 percent increase in subscription ticket sales for that series, or 950 additional subscribers. Of total subscription sales, 135 were for children. A news release on the SPCO Web site stated:

> The decision to lower prices stems from SPCO's commitment to serve the broader community. "We want to serve more people, especially younger people and families," said Bruce Coppock, President and Managing Director of the SPCO. "Our mission is to bring classical music to the community, and we want to make it as easy as possible for people to come."
>
> Lower price of admission is consistent with the renewed emphasis on a true neighborhood concert experience—an informal, family-friendly place to hear world-class music within a short distance of one's home. "You can put on a sweater, grab your kids and come hear a world-class orchestra in your neighborhood for a price comparable to what you'd spend at the movies," said Coppock.[8]

mances of holiday shows offered between Christmas and New Year's Eve, as most people prefer to attend holiday performances before Christmas Day.

Christmas Carol on Sale in Milwaukee

Since 2000, the Milwaukee Repertory Theater has been holding a one-day sale—a buy-one, get-one-at-half-price offer—for after-Christmas performances of *A Christmas Carol*, about three months in advance of the performances. In 2003, the Rep sold $190,000 worth of tickets in that one day, $95,000 of which came from online sales.

The sale is marketed through direct-mail, print, and online advertising. The organization distributes 20,000 brochures, places full-page four-color ads in the major newspapers the Friday and Sunday before the sale, sends e-mails to 20,000 Rep patrons, and places online ads on major Milwaukee Web sites.

David Anderson, marketing director of the Milwaukee Repertory Theater, has found that a majority of people taking advantage of the discount are new patrons. In addition to selling tickets that would not have been likely to sell otherwise, the added benefit of holding a sale of this nature is that all these early ticket holders have about three months to tell all their friends that they are going to the show![9]

Capacity Utilization Pricing

In the past a Jewel Food Stores market typically ordered ten cases of extra-large eggs per week to stock its dairy cases. Dairy department personnel never had reason to question whether this quantity was adequately serving customers, because if the extra-large eggs sold out, people substituted other sizes without complaint. But then the company noticed that customers of its online store, PeaPod, order extra-large eggs almost exclusively. This clear display of customer intent has changed in-store ordering. Now Jewel orders—and sells—more extra-large eggs in its stores, increasing customer satisfaction.

Arts marketers often analyze how many seats in each price cate-gory in their house have sold for various performances. But for the seating areas that do tend to sell out—usually the prime seats—do marketers know how many more tickets they *could* have sold had more been available? Such information is an important key to pricing strat-egy and to rescaling the pricing structure of the house, when possible. In order to optimize both attendance and revenue, marketers need to match supply and demand at each level as much as possible.

A *capacity utilization analysis*—counting the number of tickets sold in each section for each performance—will tell you whether 100 percent of the seats in a section are sold out; a box office tally record-ing whether each customer received his or her first choice of date and seat location will inform you if you could have sold 105 or 125 per-cent of those seats. Such data are extremely useful when there is an op-portunity to rescale the pricing sections in the hall or when repricing according to supply and demand.

Revenue Management

Revenue management is the act and the art of progressive pricing, or changing the ticket price over time based on the anticipated or ac-tual supply and demand, as is commonly done by some airlines. Such price discrimination is a complex activity that must be strategized with great care. The "right" answer is different for each organization and for each discrete situation.

Sometimes, lower ticket prices are offered far in advance of the performance (for certain seating locations or for the entire hall) to stimulate advance purchases. If the discount is great, say half price, people may take a chance on an event they are not sure they will like. If the discount is smaller, as it usually is, the price is not likely to drive the purchase for people who would not have purchased at full price either. Early discounts appeal primarily to regular patrons who would otherwise have paid the full price and who are eager to guarantee good seats. As a result some organizations reduce their revenue when they offer discounts unnecessarily.

Some organizations have experimented with raising or lowering prices twenty-four hours to one week or more before the perfor-mance, depending on how ticket sales are going. The idea of offering two tickets for the price of one shortly before the curtain rises on a show that is not selling well has been around for decades. (Current industry wisdom says that marketers should offer "buy one, get one free" instead of "two for the price of one" because the word "free" is a significant lure. Marketers should also consider offering half-price tickets to attract people attending alone or in odd-numbered groups.) The reduced-price strategies of offering rush and standby tickets will be described later in this chapter.

Some organizations have borrowed the airline model of raising prices just before a popular production begins or toward the end of a run. However, there are several reasons why this is not a good idea. First, people have busy schedules and should not be financially punished for waiting until shortly before the performance to buy their tickets. People should be motivated by the potential scarcity of tickets for a show they really want to attend, not by price hikes. This mindset is better not only for a current show but for future ticket sales as well. When a future production is of interest to people who have just seen a current show's price rise, they may assume that prices are rising for the future show also, even if this is not the case. The result is that fewer tickets will sell.

In the airline industry, where ticket price increases close to the travel time are the rule, people typically do not travel on late notice by choice, especially for leisure travel. Similarly, no one *has* to attend a concert. People are likely to choose not to attend rather than pay more. People may be accustomed to airline pricing, but for other scarce items such as the hot children's toy of the season or a table at a popular restaurant, prices do not go up as availability becomes scarce. When arts marketers do charge a premium price for an event, they should ascertain that they are offering a product and benefits of premium value to the customer. Marketers must be sure that customers leave with both the tickets that they wanted and the sense that they were treated fairly.

A practical problem from the organization's perspective is that with revenue management, managers are unable to publish their ticket prices in their season brochures. Without even a range of prices offered in advertisements, some people are not likely to take the next step and call the box office or check the Web site for more information. Besides, variability leads to uncertainty; uncertainty may reduce interest.

For the most part a focus on changing ticket prices over time for the same seats and same shows is a distraction for the marketing manager from what really matters to the patron: not price, but value. The marketing manager must create a total experience that the customer finds attractive. Customer segment pricing is a common and effective approach for varying ticket prices.

Customer Segment Pricing

Each customer segment may have a different ability and willingness to pay for tickets. Organizations can maximize their audience and their revenue by responding to these differences. For the sake of developing pricing strategies, the audience can be segmented by loyalty to the organization (subscribers, multiple single ticket buyers, and first-time buyers, for example); by age and life cycle stage (students, adults with children, and seniors, for example); by groups (as discounts are usually given to customer groups purchasing a bloc of tickets for a single performance); and by myriad other segments that can be identified by managers as significant and viable and that can be offered special pricing (either high or low) without causing other segments to feel they are being discriminated against.

Arts marketers have many variables to consider when setting pricing strategies: the number of different prices, the price ranges, the difference between prices, the number of seats at each price, the location in the hall of the variously priced seats, promotional discounting, premium pricing with special benefits, revenue management, and surcharges. Managers should take advantage of as many pricing strategies as possible, without creating confusion for the customers.

Matching the number of tickets offered at different prices to demand can be just as important as what those prices are. Some people tend to book in price ranges—low-price bargain hunters, mid-price value seekers, or top-price quality seekers—almost irrespective of what the actual prices are. It is therefore important to offer a set of price ranges to meet the needs of those different segments. Of course there are certain special events for which a one-price policy makes sense, such as a concert in the park (if there is any charge at all) or certain general admission, first-come, first-served events. These are the exception rather than the rule, however.

HIGHER HIGHS AND LOWER LOWS One strategy that helps achieve both revenue maximization and audience size maximization is to have *higher highs* and *lower lows:* set prices as high as the market will bear for those eager and willing to have a premium experience, offer low-priced tickets for interested patrons who could not attend otherwise, and offer a range of prices in between, depending on the size and configuration of seating areas and on audience demand.

Because patrons who buy high-priced seats are relatively *price inelastic,* meaning that price increases have relatively little effect on their willingness to buy a ticket, arts marketers can often increase the price of their most costly seats by a much greater percentage than they can increase the price of the least costly seats.

Marketing managers can be easily misled by the fact that many subscribers are willing—even eager—to pay top prices for tickets. However, frequent ticket buyers, the subscribers, who often account for as much as 80 percent of sales (including extra tickets purchased for special events and for other people) account for only 20 to 25 percent of ticket buyers. Managers must keep in mind the attitudes of infrequent attenders and those purchasing a ticket to an organization's performances for the first time.

SUBSCRIBER DISCOUNTS People pay for what they value, and people place a high value on quality experiences. For the best possible experience, people are not only willing but even eager to pay a premium. So why do arts organizations habitually offer discounts to their subscribers, those who prove by committing to an entire season of performances months in advance that they highly value the experiences they will have with an organization? Says Penn Trevella, former marketing coordinator of the Royal New Zealand Ballet:

> Our research showed that discounting tickets was not the key motivator for subscribers, but rather people subscribed because they wanted to secure the best possible seats and they also wanted to feel as though they were involved and contributing to our organization. As a result of the findings, we overhauled our subscription offering and shifted the emphasis from price discounts to securing the best seats and to the other benefits they receive as subscribers that they would not

receive if they just purchased tickets on a show by show basis, such as complimentary programs, opportunities to be more involved with the company, complete flexibility to change their tickets should the need arise, and so on. The end result was that we doubled our numbers in the first year. I think the offer of discounted prices is a motivator to first time subscribers but it becomes less important over time as individuals' level of commitment changes and they begin to seek out other benefits such as the opportunity to have more involvement with the company and to develop their knowledge of the art form.[10]

Marketers must realize that enticing first-time subscribers with very low one-time prices will result in a lower renewal rate. The more price breaks and gimmicks used to attract people initially, the less likely they are to renew at regular rates.

Offering a caveat to this position against subscriber discounts, some arts managers have told me that their audiences value the *idea* of a discount and seek a special price even if the reduction is only one or two dollars per ticket. Situations such as these highlight the importance of market research to learn what truly matters to the customer and the numbers of customers that would be meaningfully affected if the discount were to be dropped.

REDUCED-PRICE STRATEGIES Arts marketers often find it beneficial to adopt certain low-price strategies to target broader audiences and increase frequency of attendance among current audiences. Most often, low prices are offered as part of a range of prices for programs, so that the organization's incremental costs for selling these seats is extremely low. Box office personnel are already on hand, tickets and program booklets are preprinted, and marketing communications have for the most part been paid for.

When price acts as a barrier, whether for first-time attenders or for those who would like to attend more frequently than they are financially able to do, a variety of strategies can be employed. Typically, these strategies appeal to those who are highly flexible in terms of taking a chance on getting seats and indifferent as to where they sit in the hall but who make price the prime determinant of their attendance at a performance they would like to see. Among the most common of these strategies are rush tickets and standby tickets. Special promotional pricing strategies are frequently used also.

RUSH TICKETS Rush tickets are deeply discounted tickets offered shortly before a performance, typically either two hours before the show or any time the day of the show, according to the preference of the organization. Seats lose all their value the minute the curtain rises, so many organizations use this strategy to sell excess capacity because receiving a low price is better than receiving nothing at all. Rush tickets are not advisable of course for organizations that enjoy a fair amount of day-of-performance ticket sales.

Rush tickets typically vary in cost from half to less than half price. One U.S. orchestra, whose ticket prices range from about $30 to $90 (even more for box seats), charges $30 for all rush tickets, and this price may get the ticket buyer seats worth $90, thanks to turnbacks from subscribers unable to attend.

Many cities offer ticket booths where people can purchase half-price tickets on the day of a performance. However, people who take advantage of the discount face the inconveniences of going to the booth and often waiting in long lines. The New Jersey Theatre Alliance offers discount tickets online for forty-three participating companies, an approach that not only accommodates contemporary lifestyles but has been successful in attracting new audiences.

STANDBY TICKETS Standby tickets are offered for the seats of no-show patrons at sold-out shows. Some organizations report that often 5 to 10 percent of patrons do not show up for a performance, leaving seats empty that could be resold. Typically, standby tickets are sold for half price starting two hours before the performance. Patrons wait in line until show time or are given numbers that reflect the order in which they arrived. The primary difference between rush and standby is that with rush tickets, patrons are given a specific seat location at the time of purchase. With standby tickets, at about two minutes before the curtain, the standby patrons are invited to take any empty seats in the hall, with the understanding that if the people who purchased those seats show up at intermission, the standby ticket holder will have to move. It rarely happens, luckily, that no other seats in the hall are available for them to move to. (If this were to happen, the organization would refund the standby ticket price.)

SPECIAL PRICE PROMOTIONS Performing arts organizations will often offer a discount to people who respond to a certain advertisement or who purchase tickets by a certain date or for select performances. A small discount for responding to a marketing communication is an inexpensive way for a marketing manager to track an ad's effectiveness. Time-limited price offers may stimulate ticket purchases, as many people like a bargain even if the savings doesn't amount to much. Reduced prices for certain dates may be a good way to stimulate attendance for performances that are not expected to sell well.

One small theater company near Chicago sends an e-mail message to people who have already seen the show currently running, saying, "If you loved this show, forward this message to your friends." The message includes a description of the show and what people are saying about it. Unfortunately, the message also includes a $5 ticket discount offer—not enough of a savings to serve as an incentive for people who want to take their friends' recommendation. More important, this discount may be viewed by readers as an act of desperation by an organization trying to fill seats for a production with a lukewarm reception. Generally speaking, if a discount is offered, make it more substantial—such as 50 percent off Tuesday and Wednesday evenings—or do not discount at all.

Controlling Other Direct Costs

Marketers should take into account not only the price of the ticket but also other direct costs the consumer faces that are in the organization's control. The marketing manager may be able to collaborate with nearby parking facilities to arrange a preferred parking fee for the organization's patrons. Also, and importantly, marketing managers should not accept without analysis and negotiation whatever surcharges third-party ticket providers charge the customer. Marketers are typically very cautious about each dollar increase in the ticket price, yet customers may be subject to handling fees of $5 or more per ticket. Arts managers should do everything in their control to limit "convenience" fees charged by third-party ticketing services. Of course marketers should also evaluate their own service fees charged through the box office or online sales. If people are hanging up the phone or leaving the Web site without making a purchase, how much of that is due to what they may consider exorbitant surcharges? It is worthwhile for managers to investigate the answer to this question.

Modifying Prices

Typically, marketing managers set new prices based on a percentage increase from the previous year, or they make an intuitive decision loosely based on past and anticipated demand. As we will see in the Chicago Opera Theater example that follows this section, capacity utilization analysis is a more scientific approach that will generate far better results.

RESEARCH ON PRICING STRATEGIES When marketing managers express concern that their ticket prices are too high, I suggest they review their capacity utilization data over a period of time. As long as the organization provides consistently high-quality performances and fine customer service, high-priced tickets are rarely the problem they are assumed to be. Marketers often find that the most expensive seats sell best and that the midpriced tickets are the hardest to sell. In such cases marketers should consider rescaling the house, if possible, to add more A-level or C-level seats. Also, creative strategies can be developed to sell the midpriced seats. Highly targeted group sales and special promotions are among the tactics that can be used to accomplish this goal.

It is often useful to interview or survey current and potential patrons to see what the market will bear in terms of price increases and to learn what new pricing strategies are likely to attract broader audiences and more frequent attendance. Be aware, though, that people do not typically accurately report the prices they would be willing to pay; rather they often understate the amount. Designing questions that will elicit as realistic a response as possible is tricky. Marketers would do well to engage the services of an experienced marketing researcher for this purpose.

PRICE DISCRIMINATION STRATEGIES When planning price discrimination strategies, marketers must consider several conditions.

First, be very careful that different segments show different intensities of demand. For example, offer a discount to senior citizens for a weekday matinee if there is already demand from this segment for that performance and if more potential demand is identified. Do not offer senior discounts for Saturday evening performances if you are able to meet your capacity goals with full-price ticket buyers. Alternatively, offer a senior discount in the mid- and low-priced seating sections only, as many seniors are able and happy to pay full price for the best seats.

Make sure that those not eligible for a particular price advantage do not feel discriminated against. People who buy tickets well in advance at full price like knowing they have tickets and have good seats. It is not bothersome to those people that some people stand in line a couple of hours before the show and hope to get tickets at half-price in whatever seats are still available.

Members of the lower-price segment must not be able to resell the product to the higher-price segment. So, for example, a deeply discounted student ticket must be clearly identified as such and students may be required to show their school identification card to the ticket taker.

Pricing Strategies at Chicago Opera Theater

In 2002, Chicago Opera Theater (COT) began to plan for its move in 2004 from the aging Athenaeum Theater, which was inconveniently located and had inadequate facilities and parking, to the new Harris Theater for Music and Dance, a state-of-the-art facility in downtown Chicago's new Millennium Park. Unquestionably, the market would bear higher ticket prices in the new venue, which features many amenities and adjacent underground parking. With its greatly increased costs for performing there, COT was eager to maximize ticket revenue.

As the marketing consultant to COT, I suggested that in developing ticket price strategies, we first evaluate what modifications could be made to prices for the 2003 season, COT's last season at the Athenaeum. COT had been offering an early-bird subscriber discount, which was thought to be helpful in increasing renewals during a traditionally slow cash flow period. We eliminated this discount and, instead, gave patrons an incentive to renew early, a chance to win restaurant coupons, which were donated to the organization in exchange for the marketing benefits to the businesses. This strategy was highly effective as early renewals remained consistent with previous years' rates.

Also, for the 2003 season the regular subscriber discount was reduced so that subscriber ticket prices more closely approximated single ticket prices. As I have discussed, subscriber discounts are, in effect, price breaks offered to the patrons who are the most interested, most loyal, and most willing to pay. Research results show repeatedly that elimination or reduction of this discount does not have a negative impact on renewals. In fact, no COT patrons failed to renew in 2003 because of the reduced discount. COT realized thousands of dollars of increased income from these strategies, not counting the additional income realized from a modest price increase in each section of the hall.

For the 2004 season, COT had the opportunity to scale the new hall into seating sections according to anticipated capacity utilization and to price tickets according to what the organization expected the market would bear. Given the extremely high quality of COT performances in recent years, the excitement over the new performance space, and the fact that a large percentage of COT patrons also attend Chicago's Lyric Opera, where ticket prices are high, COT planned to institute moderate to significant price increases in various seating areas for 2004. (Chapter Nine offers a more extensive discussion of COT's brand identity issues.)

COT offers five performances each of three operas per season. In the past COT had offered lower-priced tickets for weekday evenings and Sunday matinees than for weekend evenings. However, a capacity utilization analysis of the three previous seasons showed that opening night performances (which are on Wednesday evenings), Thursday evening performances, and Sunday matinees were popular and well attended, especially in the higher-priced seats, so it was decided to eliminate day-of-week price differentials altogether.

In Tables 6.1 to 6.4, ticket sales data are given for one opera in the 2003 season and one in the 2004 season. In each case the opera analyzed is the one that sold the median number of tickets: Benjamin Britten's *The Turn of the Screw,* performed in 2003 at the Athenaeum, and Monteverdi's *L'incoronazione di Poppea,* performed in 2004 at the

TABLE 6.1.   *Single Tickets Versus Subscription Sales:*
Turn of the Screw *at the Athenaeum, 2003.*

Seating Section	Available Seats for 5 Performances	Single Ticket Price	Subscription Price per Performance	Single Tickets Sold for 5 Performances	Subscriptions Sold for 5 Performances	Single Tickets as a Percentage of Subscriptions
A	2,750	$65	$58	977	999	98%
B	700	$45	$40	234	110	213%
C	1,350	$35	$30	513	295	174%

TABLE 6.2.   *Section Seats Sold by Totals and Percentages:*
Turn of the Screw *at the Athenaeum, 2003.*

Seating Section	Available Seats per Performance	Available Seats for 5 Performances	Total Seats Sold	Percentage of Seats Sold	Seats Sold as Percentage of Total Sold
Entire hall	960	4,800	3,128	69.5%	100%
A	550	2,750	1,976	72.0%	63%
B	140	700	344	49.0%	11%
C	270	1,350	808	60.0%	26%

Harris Theater. As can be seen in Table 6.2, 69.5 percent of the available seats for all five performances of *The Turn of the Screw* were sold overall. In the three seating sections in the Athenaeum (Table 6.1 lists the number of seats in each section), 72 percent of Section A seats sold (the highest-priced section), 49 percent of Section B, and 60 percent of Section C. Of the total tickets purchased for the five performances of this opera, 63 percent were purchased in Section A, 11 percent in Section B, and 26 percent in Section C. Clearly, *the greatest number of patrons prefer the best and most expensive seats.* In evaluating the ticket purchasing behavior of subscribers and single ticket buyers (Table 6.1), we found that the numbers of Section A tickets

TABLE 6.3. *Single Tickets Versus Subscription Sales:*
Poppea at the Harris Theater, 2004.

Seating Section	Available Seats for 5 Performances	Ticket Price: Subscriber or Single Ticket	Single Tickets Sold for 5 Performances	Subscriptions Sold for 5 Performances	Single Tickets as Percentage of Subscriptions
A+	1,120	$97	256	922	28%
A	2,080	$85	840	482	174%
B	1,010	$60	471	274	172%
C	2,255	$45	910	668	136%
D	495	$30	305	99	308%

TABLE 6.4. *Section Seats Sold by Totals and Percentages:*
Poppea at the Harris Theater, 2004.

Seating Section	Available Seats per Performance	Available Seats for 5 Performances	Total Seats Sold	Percentage of Seats Sold	Seats Sold as Percentage of Total Sold
Entire hall	1,392	6,960	5,227	75.1%	100%
A+	224	1,120	1,178	105.0%	23%
A	416	2,080	1,322	64.0%	25%
B	202	1,010	745	74.0%	14%
C	451	2,255	1,578	70.0%	30%
D	99	495	404	82.0%	8%

sold to subscribers and to single ticket buyers were nearly equivalent;
however more than twice as many single ticket buyers as subscribers
purchased tickets in Section B, and there were nearly twice as many
single ticket buyers in Section C. A careful analysis of all these data
helped us decide how to scale seating sections and devise pricing levels for the new hall.

COT managers were planning to raise ticket prices in Section C
from $30 to $45, but in keeping with COT's mission of having some

ticket prices that are affordable for virtually anyone who wishes to attend, we decided to create a fourth section, Section D, in the back half of the balcony, with a ticket price of $30. Furthermore, students are eligible to pay half price for tickets, so they can attend in Section D for only $15. It is interesting to note that significantly more students purchased seats in Section C than in D in 2004, showing that they want the best experience they can afford, not necessarily the cheapest price.

For the loyal subscribers and donors who are willing to pay high prices for the best seats, we created a new section, Section A+, in the center of the main floor. Section A ticket prices had been increased from $65 at the Athenaeum to $85 at the new Harris Theater with no subscriber discount—a significant increase—but we recognized the opportunity to offer A+ seats at an even higher price of $97. Before renewals went out to all COT subscribers, a letter was sent to current Section A subscribers, saying in part:

> We understand that as a dedicated COT patron, you value an excellent seating location for our performances. We are pleased to announce that the new Music and Dance Theater Chicago has a seating section with such a premium view that we are able to offer a new seating category, "A+" seats, a level higher than the "A" level "best" seats that you currently enjoy at the Athenaeum Theatre.
>
> The general renewal letter will go out in May to all of COT's patrons. Until that time, you, as a loyal subscriber, have priority to reserve your seats in the "A+" section for next season and into the future. Once these seats are filled, patrons have the right to renew them as long as they wish. The quantity of "A+" seats is limited and we may not be able to accommodate all the people who would like to reserve these seats.

COT began to receive orders for Section A+ subscriptions the day after this mailing was sent, and when the season began, that section was nearly sold out. By the end of the season, 105 percent of A+ seats had been sold (see Table 6.4). This number is higher than 100 percent due to the fact that as some A+ subscribers exchanged their tickets for another performance or turned tickets back as a donation, single ticket buyers eagerly purchased them.

Integrating the Marketing Mix Elements

In developing pricing strategies, always keep in mind the principles of integrated marketing management. All elements of the marketing mix—product, price, promotion, place, and people—should be congruent for each offering. The ticket prices must be harmonious with the organization's reputation, the stature of the artists, the quality of the hall, and the communicated messages themselves.

Furthermore, it is important for the marketing manager to carefully evaluate sales in terms not only of price but also of all the marketing communications undertaken (newspaper, magazine, and radio ads; public relations; direct mail; e-mail; the organization's Web site; and so on) to see how effective each medium was. Sometimes the weakness is in the message (or lack thereof), not in the production or the pricing strategy. In other words, price should never be considered exclusive of the other elements of the marketing mix. It is how price works in conjunction with the core product and all the communication efforts that creates the magic.

Says Merryn Carter, marketing and development director of the Melbourne Theatre Company in Australia, "What is important to arts attenders is 'value for money.' The more exciting their experience while they're with us, the less important price is likely to be."[11]

Conducting and Using Marketing Research

What we call results are beginnings.

—Ralph Waldo Emerson

RESEARCH IS THE STARTING POINT FOR MARKETING. Marketing research plays a critical role in understanding customer attitudes and behavior and in planning marketing strategy. As important as research has always been, the need for marketing research information is greater now than at any time in the past. As consumers have become more selective and demanding in their purchasing behavior, marketers find it more difficult to predict people's responses to different features, benefits, packaging options, information sources, ticket purchase outlets, pricing, and other attributes unless they turn to marketing research. Also, as market segments become smaller and as marketers attempt to reach out to new segments, organizations need to learn more about the needs and wants of all these varied target markets. Market research also empowers marketers to effectively improve their customer service strategies.

There is concern among some managers and artistic directors that audience research will compromise the artistic mission and integrity of the organization. But it is up to the organization to determine how the information gleaned from the research will be used, so these directors are missing an opportunity to use market research information to their advantage.

BUDGETING FOR MARKET RESEARCH

Although research provides a critical resource, information, marketing managers have limited budgets and assign higher priority to other expenditures. Marketers are also constrained because their knowledge of the correct use of marketing research and its technical aspects is typically limited. Furthermore, marketers are often discouraged from conducting research by the arts organization's top-level managers and board members who do not adequately understand the uses and value of marketing research.

However, marketing research need not be expensive. The extensive information already available to most organizations in their databases allows detailed analysis of ticket sales by production, performer, time of year, day of week, time of day, seat location, ticket price, audience segment, individual audience member, and so on. Focus group discussions with eight to twelve participants can yield rich information, often for only the cost of offering light refreshments and complimentary tickets. Even when more broadly based and more structured information is needed, there are ways to modify the typically high cost of extensive surveys. Surveys administered by e-mail and the Internet or inserted in programs at performances eliminate high mailing costs, and arts organizations can often get assistance from marketing students, professors, and consulting firms eager to do low-cost or pro bono work for nonprofits. Furthermore, if arts marketers would adjust their budgets by slightly reducing their advertising and promotion expenditures and increasing their research expenditures, they would gain information that would help them better target and fine-tune their efforts and get more results from the advertising and promotion money they do spend.

Once managers begin to realize the benefits gained by regularly administered, well-planned, and well-executed marketing research, they will not only value but come to depend on the process, and they will provide for it in their budget allocations. When a specific decision is important enough, significant expenditure for research on the decision issues is well justified.

Supertitles at Chicago Opera Theater

Chicago Opera Theater (COT) began offering supertitles in 2000 for the foreign language operas it presented. However, many people find it difficult to understand the words in English language operas as well. During the telemarketing campaign for 2003 subscription renewals, several patrons refused to purchase tickets for COT performances in English unless supertitles would be offered. It has become routine for the Metropolitan Opera and Chicago's Lyric Opera, among others, to offer supertitles with all their operas, but COT's general director, Brian Dickie, was personally opposed to supertitles for English language operas.

Brian Dickie is not alone in holding this attitude, as numerous "purists" are vehement about their opposition to titles. Director Graham Vick once vowed to bomb the English National Opera should it let supertitles into the house, describing them as something that will "make audiences passive and castrated and anesthetize the art form."[1]

Says *New York Times* music critic Anthony Tommasini, "In my passions and my ideals, I side with the purists about the threat titles represent to opera in English . . . audiences will look to the screens rather than pay attention to the singers; singers, knowing that audiences are relying on the projected texts, will cut corners on diction so that they can linger on a luscious sustained tone. Yet the pragmatist in me understands the frustrations of sitting through an opera in English when you cannot make out the words. Nothing induces passivity, even hostility, to opera more than that."[2]

Despite his strong personal opposition, Dickie willingly allowed questions about supertitles to be included in an audience survey conducted in the spring of 2002 to test the extent of audience dissatisfaction. Survey results showed that 69 percent of respondents preferred that supertitles be offered for all productions; 19 percent said they should be offered sometimes; and 12 percent said supertitles should never be offered. Many respondents volunteered personal comments on this issue in the margins of their survey, and those in favor of supertitles were far more outspoken

Supertitles at Chicago Opera Theater, *continued*

than those against. Several people reported that they would not return to COT at all without supertitles offered at all operas. This result indicated more than a preference for supertitles; it indicated a strong demand. In light of the compelling survey results and after consulting with three of his key conductors and directors, Dickie decided to offer supertitles for all productions.

Once the supertitles decision was finalized, marketing personnel phoned the disgruntled former patrons with the news. These patrons renewed their subscriptions and were delighted not only with the information that their dissatisfaction had been addressed but with the personal attention they received. The brochure for the upcoming season boldly featured the message: "Supertitles for all Productions" to attract new audience members.

In a similar response to audience preferences, the English National Opera announced that beginning in 2006, it would employ supertitles for all its productions. Apparently, its house is still standing, despite Graham Vick's threat.

PREPARING TO CONDUCT RESEARCH

Arts marketers planning to undertake research programs should acquaint themselves with various approaches to marketing research; the marketing research process; and the rudimentary principles of probability sampling, questionnaire design, and interpretation of results. Arts marketers need not be focus group leaders, survey designers, or statisticians. They should be familiar enough with market research methods and processes, however, to facilitate communication with the researcher and to guarantee that the organization's research needs are fulfilled.

Unfortunately, it is not uncommon for marketers to "borrow" a survey designed by another organization and use it after making only minor adaptations, with the outcome that the survey questions do not address the issues pertinent to the organization. This results in doing research just for the sake of the process, without adequately considering the desired resulting information. Furthermore, many surveys developed by arts organizations are improperly designed, resulting in unreliable responses. If questions are worded incorrectly or are placed in the wrong order, responses are likely to be invalid. For example, questions about people's attendance habits and preferences should be at the beginning so that the respondents are immediately drawn to the primary importance of their opinions, preferences, and attendance behavior. Personal questions, which typically are more sensitive, should be included at the end, as people may not complete the survey if they are asked first about their age and income. Another example of design failure regards the question of the respondent's gender. When a survey is conducted at a performance, the percentage of women among the respondents is often higher than the percentage among the audience. One logical explanation for this is that when a man and woman attend together, typically the woman fills out the survey and responds for both, except when the gender question appears. Then the woman responds for herself. This anomaly can be rectified by asking a series of gender questions: (1) What is your gender? (2) On behalf of how many patrons—including yourself—are you completing this survey? (3) Please indicate the gender(s) of your companion(s). In this way marketers can get a better idea of the gender breakdown in their audience.

Many excellent books have been written on marketing research methodology, and arts marketers wishing to conduct their own research should familiarize themselves with proven approaches.[3]

Processes for Gathering Information

A wide range of marketing research techniques are available. Here are some of the most popular and useful techniques.

Observation

Marketers can learn a great deal by knowing what customers are thinking and feeling during the ticket purchasing process and while attending performances. Observation techniques are simple, informative, and inexpensive approaches for learning more about audiences and their reactions to offerings. Marketing personnel can simply listen to comments expressed by patrons in the lobby and can listen in on conversations over the phone or in person at the box office. Box office personnel and ushers should be asked to report their observations as well. More formal techniques involve mystery shopping and transactional surveys administered by box office personnel and customer service managers who receive e-mail messages from patrons.

MYSTERY SHOPPING Organizations can make use of *mystery shoppers,* people who pose as customers and rate the performance of personnel such as ticket sellers or ushers. These mystery shoppers can also attend competitors' performances to observe their offerings and procedures firsthand and listen to consumers' reactions. Researchers use mystery shopping to evaluate directly the quality of service delivered. This means standing in line at the box office, waiting on hold on the phone, searching the Web site for information, ordering tickets online, being seated by an usher—going through the entire patron experience.

It is not necessary that this type of research always be done anonymously, that is, by a person unknown to organization staff. In fact it is revealing for marketing directors to observe encounters with patrons and listen in on phone conversations in the box office, during telemarketing sessions, usher training, and so on. No matter what the size of the organization, the chief marketing officer should not only be aware of but should orchestrate all customer contacts.

Leonard Berry, in his book *On Great Service,* advises that "researchers use a rating form to systematically and comprehensively record their evaluations." With this method the organization can reveal systemic deficiencies and rate the performance of individual service providers. "Keys to proper usage," says Berry, "include educating employees on why and how mystery shopping will be used and using the research in positive, constructive ways, such as rewarding servers who receive outstanding scores and helping those with poor scores to improve. It is necessary to shop individual service providers multiple times during a performance appraisal period" to get a true picture of how they communicate with patrons and to minimize potential bias.[4]

TRANSACTIONAL SURVEYS Transactional surveys are conducted at the time a person contacts an organization to purchase tickets, to request information, or for any other reason. Through these surveys people provide ongoing feedback on the quality of customer service while the experience is still fresh. This technique also facilitates corrective actions with dissatisfied customers. When the contact is by phone or in person, patrons can simply be asked if they have been satisfied with the encounter, if their needs and preferences have been met, and if they have any further questions or concerns they would like to share. When the contact is via the Internet or e-mail, a response mechanism should be built in, asking people to share their questions or concerns. Employees should share with a manager, as quickly as possible, any comments requiring a response. And whenever possible the marketing director or even the executive director should respond to the customer, demonstrating that people at the highest level of the organization care about each patron.

Transactional surveys are also useful for tracking people's ticket purchasing behavior. For example, knowing the amount of time between a ticket purchase and the performance helps marketers select the most advantageous timing for their advertising efforts. Knowing how many calls came in just after an ad, promotion, public relations article, or other communication helps marketers determine the effectiveness of the strategy. Knowing whether a seating area that sold 100 percent of capacity could have sold 105 percent or 150 percent is important information for the marketing directors as they develop pricing structures. It is also important to record whether or not people purchase tickets when they phone and, if not, whether they were able to get the performance date or price they wanted.

A simple one-page survey can be composed for box office personnel to fill in for each patron who phones for tickets, except when the box office is so busy that customer service will suffer if time is taken to complete the surveys. Because demand varies by production throughout the season, it is best to conduct this study over a full season of performances and to repeat it several years later to test changes in consumer behavior.

The rapid growth of online ticket sales makes it relatively easy to track the timing of purchases relative to performance dates but creates new challenges for marketers who want to capture other information suggested here. For example, when a person does not complete a transaction, a dialogue box can appear or the person can be sent an e-mail message saying, "You stopped at Step Three of your ticket purchase transaction. Please tell us why." Several options and a blank space can be offered for people's responses. For example, the options might be, "No seats available for my preferred date/seating area/ticket price," "I had to answer an important phone call just then," "I needed to check with companions about the date and time," and so on.

Focus Group Research

Focus group research involves bringing together eight to twelve persons for a one-time meeting of two to three hours to respond to questions posed by a skilled moderator. It is typically a good practice to hold several focus group meetings, each consisting of people representing a single segment. For example, one focus group might consist of frequent attenders and another might have infrequent attenders or members of some other special segment the organization would like to understand better. At times the marketing director may find it valuable to place people from different segments in the same focus group so each subject can be exposed to varied perspectives. Focus groups are also a useful step in developing a brand campaign for the organization as participants can share their perspectives on the organization and help managers decide which characteristics should be emphasized and which should be repositioned.

Trained moderators have special techniques for getting beneath the surface of issues and for eliciting in-depth responses. The interaction among respondents may stimulate richer responses or newer and more valuable thoughts than subjects would have on their own.

Sometimes the organization's director or marketing manager sits in on focus group sessions and responds to questions that may arise. Focus group sessions are often videotaped and discussed later by a management team. However, even though focus groups are an important preliminary step in exploring a subject, their results should be used cautiously as they cannot always be projected to the general population. Marketers often use information gleaned from these groups in designing surveys to be administered to a larger sample. Focus groups are complementary to quantitative research, and most of the time they should not stand alone.

Customer Advisory Panels

Customer advisory panels involve using meetings, phone interviews, or mail questionnaires with customer sample groups so they can provide periodic feedback and advice. It is necessary to recruit highly cooperative respondents because of the importance of having continuity of membership in these groups. This approach allows for in-depth questioning and for fast access to customer viewpoints when decisions affecting customers must be made quickly. The organization can create several panels differentiated by loyalty status, with members such as long-term subscribers, new subscribers, and infrequent attenders; by demographic characteristics, with members divided by age, gender, or ethnicity; or by life cycle status or certain lifestyle characteristics, with members such as people with children in the home or snowbirds who go to warmer climates for the winter. Panel members need to be rewarded in some way, such as with gift certificates or a special event.

Individual In-Depth Interviewing

Individual in-depth interviews involve lengthy questioning of a small number of respondents, one at a time, often using disguised questions and minimal interviewer prompting so the respondents will not be influenced by possible question or interviewer bias. A primary objective of this approach is to get beyond the parameters by which market researchers and the organization's marketing manager define the problem being investigated.

Individual interviews are used instead of focus groups when a greater depth of response per individual is desirable, when the subject matter is so sensitive that respondents would be unwilling to talk openly in a group, and when it will be helpful to understand how attitudes and behaviors link together on an individual pattern basis.

Service reviews are periodic, in-depth personal interviews with customers to discuss all aspects of the service relationship. It is helpful both to bring back the same customers from time to time to observe changes in their attitudes and experiences and to bring in new people with fresh perspectives.

Gerald Zaltman, author of *How Customers Think,* claims that marketers can misuse surveys and focus groups in an effort to get consumers to explain or even predict their responses to products. "Standard questioning," says Zaltman, "can sometimes reveal consumers' thinking about familiar goods and services *if* those thoughts and feelings are readily accessible and easily articulated. Yet, these occasions occur infrequently. Fixed-response questions, in particular, won't get at consumers' most important thoughts and feelings if the manager or researcher has not first identified them by penetrating consumers' unconscious thoughts. Most fixed-response questions and focus group moderator questions address at a surface level *what consumers think about what managers think consumers are thinking about.*"[5] One important benefit of individual in-depth interviews is that they help marketers avoid this trap.

Marketing Experiments

The most scientific way to research customers is to present different offerings to matched customer groups and analyze differences in their responses. By controlling the variables, the organization can measure response variations. For example, an organization can test the most effective subject heading, special offer, and/or priority of information in an e-mail newsletter, at no cost whatsoever, by sending each possible format of the newsletter to a different sample group of its customers. Then the marketer evaluates the responses and sends the most effective format to the bulk of the e-mail list.

Survey Questionnaires

The survey is the most popular and widely used device for investigating, describing, and measuring people's knowledge, beliefs, product and media preferences, satisfaction levels, demographics, competitive choices, and decision-making processes. Marketers seeking extensive information or desiring to survey nonattenders should administer the surveys by mail, e-mail, or telephone interviews. To quickly survey current attenders, questionnaires can be stuffed into programs. It is important to keep in mind that those who respond to either e-mail or snail mail surveys are likely to be self-selecting groups with different characteristics.

Total market surveys are more comprehensive in detail than transactional surveys as they seek to investigate an overall assessment of a company's service and offers. Also, they usually seek demographic customer information, which must be done in a situation that allows anonymity. Staff and consultants should brainstorm to identify all aspects of the customer's experience that they can evaluate. In addition to closed-ended questions, space should be provided for patrons to write comments about other issues they have in mind. Because experiences change over time, these surveys should be repeated every few years.

Special surveys should be administered with new, nonrenewing, and former customers. Asking new customers why they came is a powerful question. The organization may find that poor service or other factors under the marketer's control are the cause of customer defections. When this is the case, the organization may be able to win people back and keep others from defecting.

Survey questions are typically designed to be codable and countable, so as to yield a quantitative picture of customer opinions, attitudes, and behavior. By including personal questions the researcher can correlate the answers with the different demographic and psychographic characteristics of the respondents. In using the findings, the organizations should be aware of possible biases resulting from a low response rate, poorly worded questions, or other flaws.

THE MARKETING RESEARCH PROCESS

Effective marketing research involves several steps.

Defining the Problem and Setting Objectives

The first step calls for the managers and the marketing researcher to define the problem carefully and agree on the research objectives. Unless the problem is well defined, the findings are not likely to be valuable to the organization. The manager should make clear to the researcher what the decision alternatives are and then the two can work together to determine what additional information is required to make those decisions. Also, the manager should share with the researcher the financial, political, and other constraints under which the organization operates that may affect the way the research is approached and evaluated.

Developing the Plan

The second step of the process calls for developing the most efficient plan for gathering the needed information. Designing a research plan calls for decisions about the research method to be used, the sampling plan, contact methods, questionnaire design, and management of research biases.

Collecting and Analyzing Data

The next steps are to collect and analyze the data. The data collection phase is generally the most susceptible to error, and research biases should be controlled for as best as possible. Once an adequate sample has been obtained, pertinent findings are extracted from the data. The researcher tabulates the data and develops frequency distributions, averages, and measures of dispersion. Using this information the researcher analyzes the results in terms of the managerial decisions to be made and forms a series of recommendations, in effect transforming research data into marketing insights.

Creating Reports and Disseminating Findings and Recommendations

The researcher then creates reports to submit to management and the board. An executive summary of the findings reports and analyzes the results and makes recommendations in a few succinct pages. The executive summary should not include a multitude of numbers and descriptions of complex statistical techniques; it should present the major findings that are relevant to the marketing decisions facing management. Often the researcher will make a presentation about the major findings at a meeting of the board of directors.

Generally, the researcher will also submit an extensive, detailed report of the findings and analyses of each part of the questionnaire. Such detailed information is useful to the marketing manager and sometimes to the executive director or a marketing professional on the board; these are possibly the only people who have the patience and the necessary skills to wade through all the data.

Implementing Recommendations and Evaluating the Process

The most important thing about planning is the process itself, not the plan. Says Philip Kotler, "Planning forces you to think deeply and futuristically in a more systematic manner."[6] Yet too often the final report is shelved before the organization acts on most of the recommendations. One way this shortsighted approach can be avoided is by keeping the researcher involved during the implementation phase. He or she understands the data and their nuances and has already thought hard about what the results should mean to the manager. Continued teamwork by the manager and researcher will increase the likelihood of good decisions being made and followed through.

The research process just undertaken should also be thoroughly evaluated to see if it could have been carried out more effectively, to see if further research is needed in certain subject areas or with other segments, and to decide if and how often similar research should be repeated.

The following section describes some of the processes used in the San Francisco survey research project in which I participated. (I discussed some of the findings of this survey in Chapter Six and will present more findings in Chapters Ten and Eleven.)

Survey Research in San Francisco

Concerned over both spiraling costs and the possible negative effect on ticket sales of price increases, the marketing directors of four major performing arts organizations in San Francisco collaborated on an in-depth investigative market research study to quantify the effect ticket price was having on the purchasing behavior of their current audiences. The organizations participating in this 1996 study were the San Francisco Symphony, San Francisco Ballet, San Francisco Opera, and American Conservatory Theater (A.C.T.). A local foundation was eager to fund this project because of its collaborative nature. I was engaged as the market researcher to manage the project.

Identifying Research Objectives

The project had three primary objectives.

Because ticket price is a function not only of *ability* to pay but of *willingness* to pay—based on the person's interest level—the first objective was to explore the attitudes, interests, and preferences of current attenders: what factors attracted them to attend, what factors might serve to increase their frequency of attendance, and what barriers were limiting or preventing their ticket purchases.

Historically, pricing decisions have generally been based on the educated guess of marketing personnel as to what the market response would be under various pricing scenarios and for various programs. So the second objective was to quantify pricing sensitivity levels of key consumer groups in order to significantly reduce uncertainty in the pricing decision-making process.

The third objective was to compare audience behavior and attitudes across the four participating organizations to identify similarities and differences among the organizations. This would help us determine whether the responses from audience members at specific organizations could be generalized to a broad population of arts attenders.

Developing the Plan

To meet all of these objectives and to guarantee that our results would be statistically significant required numerous questions, quantifiable results, and a large number of respondents. Therefore we readily determined that a mail survey sent to a broad range of current attenders at the four participating organizations would best meet our needs. Although much of the survey would be the same for each organization, certain questions would have to be customized to accommodate the differences among the organizations, especially in their pricing structures.

Before the pricing levels to be included in the questionnaires could be determined, we wanted to know how well or poorly tickets had been selling in recent years in each pricing section at the four organizations' venues.

USING INTERNAL DATA A professor of statistics and economics from the Kellogg School of Management joined our team to conduct a capacity utilization analysis that would quantify ticket purchasing behavior. Using data provided by the marketing directors, he analyzed the percentage of capacity sold by each organization over the past three years, breaking it down into categories of production and price. Price categories included such factors as seat location in the hall, day of week, and time of day. Thus the capacity utilization analysis identified the price categories that were selling at or near full capacity, where it was likely that prices could comfortably be increased more than average, and those categories that were selling well below capacity, where price reductions might be indicated.

Through the capacity utilization study, we found that the marketing directors had been adjusting prices extremely well to market demand and that dramatic pricing changes were indicated in only one case: the second balcony at A.C.T., where seats were selling at only a small percentage of capacity. We used the results of this capacity utilization study to help determine the price levels that would be tested in the part of the survey where subjects were asked about their anticipated future ticket purchases. Our resulting pricing recommendations would be based on both the responses to a wide range of questions asked in the survey and the results of the capacity utilization study.

DETERMINING THE SURVEY PROCESS AND CONTENT Next, the research process was developed. We decided to mail surveys to 8,000 households (2,000 per organization), random samplings of the audience members of the four participating arts organizations. The samples were chosen from equal numbers of long-term subscribers (five years or more), short-term subscribers (one to two years), and single ticket buyers. The resulting four lists of subjects were merged and purged, so that no one would receive surveys from two or more of the organizations. Surveys were color-coded by organization to help us organize the responses as they were returned for analysis.

We created two sets of surveys for each organization, each with one price structure to which people would respond. One-half (1,000 people for each organization) of the sample population received version one of the survey, with lower prices for each offering, and one-half received version two, with higher prices. This strategy of offering each respondent one set of prices, rather than price options for each offer, was used to avoid a response bias, because when given a choice people naturally select lower prices. The differential between the high and low prices offered in the two versions varied by organization and was determined by the marketing director of each organization in collaboration with the researchers. On average there was a 15 percent differential between version one and version two prices. These versions were also color-coded so we could readily identify which version a subject had received.

Questions were crafted to ask respondents about their ticket purchasing behavior for the current season (1996–1997) and anticipated purchases for the following season (1997–1998). We asked specifically about programming choices; various pricing structures; preferred seat location, day, and time for a performance; and packages preferred. The survey also questioned respondents about their interest in special offers we had designed to break down barriers assumed to inhibit ticket purchases. These special offers included a ticket exchange option for single ticket purchases and extended payment plans for subscription purchases.

Respondents were also questioned about their reasons for attending performances, their reasons for attending less frequently than in the past or for letting their subscriptions lapse (when applicable), and their demographic information, so we could clearly understand the relative importance of price in their decision making.

The survey's scope was so extensive that it required several pages of questions. We offered incentives to help ascertain that a viable percentage of the subjects would respond.

OFFERING INCENTIVES A typical response rate for a mail survey administered to arts patrons is 20 to 25 percent (a much higher response rate than surveys for most goods and services). But we wanted an even higher response rate to provide the basis for a richer analysis. We did not have money in the budget to mail surveys to twice as many people, so we offered incentives to increase the response rate. Two free tickets to select performances were offered by the symphony, the ballet, and the theater. The opera offered a one-time 10 percent discount at the Opera Shop.

The value of a desirable incentive was clear. The response rates for the symphony, the ballet, and the theater averaged 46 percent, approximately double the usual rate. The response rate from opera patrons, who obviously did not value their weak incentive, was 23 percent. Incentives are an extremely effective way to increase the quantity of responses, and these incentives were also low cost because the free tickets were for programs that had anticipated excess capacity. The organizations also benefited by getting more people in the hall for programs that were not likely to sell at capacity. The only real cost to the organizations was the effort of handling the ticket vouchers.

Although it was important for us to offer survey respondents anonymity to encourage them to share personal information, we needed contact information in order to provide the ticket vouchers. We managed this by having a voucher form separate from the survey, and we promised patrons that we would separate this voucher from their responses as soon as we opened their envelope and verified they had completed the survey.

Analyzing the Data

The marketing research firm we engaged to input and tabulate the responses, analyze them statistically, and cross-tabulate various categories provided us with five bound books—one for each organization and one comparing results among the organizations—each with one hundred pages or more filled with statistics. I carefully studied this data to find the information that would guide us in decision making on the issues we had identified at the beginning of the process and to identify any other data that might be useful to us in other ways. I developed reports for each organization that summarized the objectives, processes, and findings and that described my recommendations for ticket pricing and other programs and strategies that would leverage the responses we received. I discussed these findings and recommendations with the marketing directors and then made presentations at board meetings, so that board members could discuss what they read in the report and have their questions answered.

In general we found that prices could comfortably be raised annually at moderate levels. However, when setting new prices, marketing managers would have to carefully analyze their capacity utilization in all seating locations and for all price-related offers. To accommodate both the people who were not price sensitive and those for whom price was a significant barrier, the policy of *higher highs* and *lower lows* should be central to pricing decisions. The organizations should capitalize on their opportunity to increase frequency of ticket purchase among current attenders, increase customer satisfaction, and build new audiences by offering a ticket exchange option to single ticket buyers. Similarly, an extended payment plan for subscriptions should be offered as survey results indicated that this strategy would be likely to increase the number of tickets sold to current single ticket buyers who were interested in subscribing but needed to pay over a period of several months.[7]

Although the results of the survey questionnaire varied somewhat among the participating organizations, overall the responses were sufficiently congruent that they can be considered generalizable, especially to other cities with an audience base economically, educationally, and culturally similar to the audience base in San Francisco.

Project Evaluation

Our extensive research yielded rich results, which have been helpful in guiding not only the participating organizations in their marketing strategies but also other organizations that have become aware of the findings.

Our process highlighted the importance of capacity utilization analysis in setting ticket prices and for scaling the appropriate number of seats in each pricing section of the hall, when feasible. Marketing managers should carefully analyze their capacity utilization in all seating locations and for all price-related offers annually or when setting new prices, whether or not they conduct audience research.

It is advisable to survey audiences every three to five years, using past surveys as benchmarks, to detect changing attitudes about the importance of pricing in people's decision to attend and any changes in reactions to various pricing levels.

As before, it is important to note that this survey, as extensive as it was, researched current attenders only. It offers no way to determine what pricing strategies would be attractive to intender-rejectors, those who would like to attend but cannot afford to do so. Many organizations do offer low-priced tickets for upper-balcony seats, rush tickets the day of the performance, and other promotions. If people are not taking advantage of these offers, is it because they are not aware of the offers or because they do not want to attend if it means sitting far from the stage or taking a chance on obtaining seats at the last minute? These are communications challenges for the marketer, who could better publicize special prices, explain that there are no really "bad" seats in the hall, suggest that rush ticket buyers are usually successful in obtaining tickets at the box office the day of the performance, and offer rush tickets online so people can have the convenience of knowing whether seats are available without leaving their home or office. Research into these and other pricing factors as they affect intender-rejectors would be valuable to the arts community as a whole.

The Power of Marketing Research

Marketing research provides managers with powerful information that dramatically increases their effectiveness in appealing to and satisfying customers. Customer expertise also provides marketers with the courage of conviction they need to promote their point of view to the leaders within the organization.

Arts marketing directors need to identify a few key, high-level marketing priorities and to link these priorities to the organization's mission and growth objectives. Marketing research provides the insights and proof arts managers need to move forward with marketing strategies and tactics.

Leveraging the Internet and E-Mail Marketing

*If you make a product good enough, even though you live in the
depths of the forest, the public will make a path to your door,
says the philosopher. But if you want the public in sufficient numbers,
you would better construct a highway.*

—William Randolph Hearst

THE INTERNET AND E-MAIL HAVE IRREVOCABLY CHANGED
the daily lives of consumers. They have also irrevocably changed
the work of marketers. It is crucial for arts managers and marketers to
understand how to use these means of communication effectively and
to be sure to capitalize on their many benefits.

INTERNET MARKETING

How important is the Internet to people's lives? Researchers investigating how people would react to not having access to the Internet had a challenging time getting started as it was incredibly difficult
to recruit participants willing to be without the Internet for two
weeks. Those who finally participated in the study had withdrawal
symptoms and a sense of loss, frustration, and discontentedness.[1]

In a few short years the Internet has become a mass market medium. In 2005, according to Jupiter Research, approximately 66 percent of American adults were online in the United States, spending on average more than thirteen hours a month surfing the Web. By 2010, the number of adults online is expected to grow to 74 percent. In 2004, 85 percent of people with household incomes of $75,000 or more had Internet access. By 2010, it is expected that 98 percent of this segment will be online. Although only about 28 percent of seniors sixty-five or older (11.5 million individuals) in the United States and 20 percent of seniors in Europe were online in 2005, their numbers will continue to soar as more seniors become comfortable with computers and as the population of computer users continues to age.[2] Seniors are among the fastest-growing Internet user groups, their ranks having increased 47 percent from 2000 to 2004. The Pew Internet and American Life Project has found, from random telephone surveys conducted in 2004 and 2005, that Internet users tend to have a larger network of close and significant contacts than nonusers do—a median of thirty-seven compared with thirty for nonusers—and they are more likely to receive help or advice from someone within that social network.[3]

To learn about the demographics, habits, and preferences of online arts audiences, CultureFinder.com, an online information source for arts events across the United States, surveyed its newsletter subscribers. The 2003 survey found that among subscribers thirty-five to fifty-four years old, 74 percent are online. Forty-six percent of subscribers aged fifty-five or older are online, a much higher percentage than many arts managers would estimate. Among the findings was a relatively high average income level, consistent with the income level of arts audiences in general. The average household income of CultureFinder.com newsletter subscribers is $75,000, which is about 50 percent higher than the average U.S. online household income of $49,000.[4] Among the households surveyed, 83 percent of those with incomes over $70,000 are online, which is an important statistic for arts managers to consider.

Results of a *Fast Company*–Roper Starch Worldwide online survey of U.S. Internet users demonstrate why people are spending so much time online: the Internet adds real value to their lives. Presented with a series of statements about the Internet, 94 percent of respondents agree that the Net makes communication easier, 96 percent agree that it lets people get information quickly, 82 percent agree that it empowers consumers, and 67 percent say that the Internet makes shopping easier and more enjoyable.[5]

The days when people used the Internet solely for information search and were afraid to enter their credit card information online are rapidly disappearing. Mintel, a research company, reports that 32 percent of adults surveyed purchased products over the Web in 2003, up from 9 percent in 2000.[6] According to McKinsey & Company, in 2004 U.S. Internet retailing totaled $90 billion, a dramatic growth from $8 billion in 1997. E-Business Express, an online development firm, forecasts that online sales growth will continue at the same explosive pace. Jupiter Research reports that although online sales are still a relatively small component of overall U.S. retail sales, a large percentage of offline purchases are influenced by research performed online.[7] Clearly, electronic commerce is no longer just for tech-savvy shoppers, but has moved into the mainstream as people are more confident using the Internet. In an informal survey of arts managers who offer ticket purchase online, I found that it is common for them to sell at least 30 percent of their tickets online, even if their online sales option has been in existence only for a year or two.

New uses for the Internet continue to be developed. Surveys show that more than 70 percent of all travelers get to their destinations before making final decisions about their entertainment options. Boeing is building Internet connections for travelers on its planes, and one of the online services to be offered will be information on cultural events at the passenger's destination. Because approximately half of all travelers include at least one cultural event as part of their trip, this "captive audience" provides a great opportunity for arts organizations to market to potential attenders.[8]

"The Internet," say 85 percent of respondents to the *Fast Company*–Roper Starch survey, "will fundamentally change the way we live and the way we work—an overwhelming endorsement of the view that the Web changes everything. We will do more online research, get more news from the Web, send and receive more e-mail, and make more purchases online—all because the Net allows us to do these things faster, cheaper, and better than we have ever been able to do them before." Because the Web "addresses inefficiencies in traditional business models, it threatens the existing order. Its most threatening feature is this: We want all of this to happen. And that is the most powerful force for change that there is."[9]

New Marketing Paradigms

The new information age has changed perspectives on how and when people make their choices and their purchases. Before the high-tech information age, all contacts between a business and a customer were initiated and controlled by the marketer. Because of the re-

Downloading Concerts in Scotland

The Royal Scottish National Orchestra (RSNO), in partnership with Scottish TV, offered audience members at the RSNO's popular Classic Bites concerts in Glasgow and Edinburgh a free download of music they had heard at the concert. Audience members were given a password and instructions, allowing them to download the performance for future enjoyment immediately after the concert. The music was made available for download in MP3 format from a specially designed Web site hosted by Scottish TV. The concerts featured selected extracts from the 2005–2006 season's performances. With each classic bite lasting four to twelve minutes, the concerts were designed to make live orchestral music more accessible to the public. More than 6,700 music files were downloaded from two concerts. Bobby Hain, managing director of broadcasting, SMG Television, commented, "We have received fantastic feedback from concertgoers who were able to enjoy the performance again and again in their own homes." RSNO chief executive Simon Woods said, "As the global market for music evolves in new and exciting ways, it is vital that orchestras are always on the cutting edge. Classic Bites is designed to appeal to audiences who may be new to classical music, so we can take the fantastic response to the download offer as a sign that the great repertoire we play continues to have an appeal to people which goes beyond the first listening."[10]

sponse mechanisms built into Internet marketing with e-mail, marketing has become a two-way exchange. Along with these advances come certain service expectations that customers never had before. With traditional methods, marketing is driven by the marketer; the marketer chooses what information to disseminate and when, where, how, and to whom it is distributed. Traditionally, customers know only what marketers choose to tell them. In the new information age paradigm, customers choose to enter the engagement process and define the rules of the engagement. They want to be in control of the process—when and how they buy. They want to be able to browse and have access to information and choice without having to contact many resources, wait in line, or be put on hold on the telephone. As people become more accustomed to the many benefits accrued by doing business online, they are likely to become increasingly intolerant of inefficient offline searching for performing arts information and of impatiently waiting on hold to order tickets by phone during limited box office hours.

Because online patrons can define the features and options they want on many products and readily access a world of information on virtually any topic, they are naturally impatient with organizations and marketers who do not offer a wide range of information and who are not flexible and responsive to their needs and preferences. Customers also expect marketers to remember all the information they have provided to the organization and to use this information in all future dealings so it doesn't need to be repeated with each new contact.

Web Site Benefits

Web sites present myriad benefits to both the organization and the customer.

BENEFITS TO THE ORGANIZATION Although Web site and e-mail marketing place much new responsibility on the shoulders of arts managers, the organization receives many benefits that more than compensate. First of all, the Web presents everyone's site equally. On the Web the smallest arts organizations can do many things as well as multimillion-dollar companies. Highly detailed information can be presented without concern for printing costs and mailing weight. The

Web is colorful, easily updateable, and is ideal for spreading news. The Web makes frequent general and personalized communication with patrons easy. An online presence is important in raising the company's profile locally, nationally, and internationally. It is cost effective, both in terms of reducing costs and increasing revenues. Effective Web site and e-mail marketing can be highly valuable for developing new audiences and for improving interaction with current customers.

Writing about the advantages of a Web site for large corporations, Jack Welch, former chief executive officer and chairman of the board of General Electric, said that "digitizing a company does more than just create unlimited business opportunities; it puts a small company soul into that big company body and gives it the transparency, excitement and buzz of a start-up."[11] One can just as well say on behalf of financially constrained arts organizations that digitizing a company does more than create unlimited business opportunities; it puts big company strength into that small company body and gives it the resources, reach, and buzz of a major corporation. This means, of course, that arts organizations must develop and maintain their Web sites to the highest possible standards.

BENEFITS TO THE CUSTOMER The Internet offers arts patrons an opportunity to browse in a relaxed setting, quickly obtain virtually any information desired, decide at leisure when and what to attend, and act instantly—at any time of day or night—to order tickets—in other words, the conveniences not available through any other media. The ease of online ticket purchasing twenty-four hours a day, seven days a week, has made traditional box office hours obsolete for many patrons. In fact many arts organizations are finding that the most popular time frame for ticket purchasing and surfing for information on their sites is from 9 P.M. to 2 A.M.

Patrons can also "try before they buy" with video and audio clips or photos, features that help break down barriers inherent in traditional media. The Web site can help patrons plan their visit with transportation, parking, and restaurant information. Patrons can e-mail their questions and requests to the organization and, one hopes, receive a timely, personal response. These features are of course major benefits to the organization as well.

Site Design, Content, and Evaluation

The e-user is looking to be engaged in cyber experiences. The e-marketer's goal is to encourage customers to go beyond visiting a site just to check out the organization's hours or to purchase a ticket. The marketer wants users to put the site among their personal bookmarks and check it frequently. This means that the marketer should review the effectiveness of promotional campaigns used to bring people to the site and should review how often the site is updated with compelling content. Marketers should be sure to budget for updating the site frequently, not just for the initial design and technology. Consider the creative way the London Symphony Orchestra is attracting people to its site.

Ringtones for Sale at the
London Symphony Orchestra Web Site

The London Symphony Orchestra (LSO) offers for sale a vast array of LSO recorded ringtones that people can download for their cell phones. This idea resulted from the orchestra's use of text messaging to alert students to late availability of concert seats. Socializing at pubs has stimulated huge numbers of ringtone downloads; when people hear their friends' phones ring, they want classy ringtones also.[12]

The site should have a marketing focus with technical know-how, meaning that the marketing department should have ownership of Web site management. Web sites developed and maintained by a "techie" in the back room or off site are often more of a detriment to the organization's image and relationship-building efforts than they are an advantage. As always in marketing, think from the perspective of the customer, not the product; focus both on reaching out to new visitors and on building relationships with customers, and adhere to a consistent style that clearly demonstrates and celebrates your brand image.

When designing a Web site, marketers should think in terms of what online patrons want and need. It is important to keep in mind that the technical sophistication of online users varies greatly. To accommodate people with low-powered computers or dial-up service, Webmasters should make sure that sites are as uncomplicated as possible, without add-ons like Flash or Shockwave.[13] For users who have built high-speed Internet services into their lifestyles, it is crucial to provide easy access to up-to-date information and clear navigation of the site.

Make sure that all sections can be used by all browsers, and that the links work across the site. The site must download quickly; if it takes ten seconds to download, you may lose visitors before they get to the home page. Once there, can they quickly find what they are looking for? With one click, visitors should be able to access schedules, the ticket purchase page, and any special promotions; everything else on the site should be no more than two or three clicks away.

An effective performing arts Web site generates interest and excitement. The site should be attractive and eye-catching and should visually represent the organization well. However, designing a Web site is not just about having the best-looking site possible; it is primarily about getting information across in a clear, concise manner.

Be sure that you do not just reproduce text from one medium to another. Write especially for the Web, adding more content than is practical in brochures and advertisements. Include detailed information about the organization, the productions, the artists—anything that will add value to the visitors' experience. Arts patrons are willing—sometimes even eager—to read more than the standard seventy-five- to one-hundred-word descriptions about productions. Companies can engage patrons by providing more background, study guides, and photos and by posting the program content online. Quality information fosters investment by patrons in the organization and its offerings.

Arts managers can stimulate people's interest in the organization and greatly enhance their experience with the performances and their understanding of the art form by writing regular *blogs* (Web logs) and posting them on their Web site. Brian Dickie makes entries almost daily into his blog, titled "Life as General Director of Chicago Opera Theater." He comments on wide-ranging topics, including what is going on behind the scenes at rehearsals and performances at Chicago

Opera Theater, his travels to other opera companies, his auditions of young opera singers for the international competition he judges, his interviews and speaking engagements, and even some personal experiences, such as the birth of his daughter. He includes illustrative photographs and links to other sites of possible interest and provides an opportunity for people to respond to his comments online. Dickie's blog presents an interesting perspective that is usually available only to people working in the field.

A major challenge in online marketing is to attract people to your site. Whenever possible, use the organization's name as its Web address (URL) so people can easily guess where to find it. Consider having multiple URL addresses, all of which drive the patron to the same site, especially if your organization's name presents users with a spelling choice, such as *theatre* versus *theater*.

Ask relevant organizations to set up a link to your site in exchange for links to them from your site. Possible *link partners* are other performing companies, arts councils, tourist information agencies, and corporate sponsors. Put your Web site address on everything you produce: print and radio ads, direct mail, programs, posters, and so on. Send regular e-mail bulletins that encourage a click-through to your site.

Once people have come to your site, make sure they want to stay, browse, and return for future visits. Take advantage of the opportunities Internet marketing provides to update frequently—even daily—so that the site is continually fresh and encourages frequent visits. The Web should offer the visitor an experience that compared to other media (brochures, ads, and so on) is more thorough, more personal, more involving, faster, and easier. As soon as performance reviews come out, the best quotes can be excerpted and posted at the top of the home page. The organization can also include entire reviews on the Web site or provide a link to review sources. Digital photos can be uploaded to the Web site to give visitors an idea of what the production and its performers look like. The Web site should offer current ticket availability and special offers for particular performances or for special market segments, such as students or seniors. Keep people engaged with such items as a brief interview with an artist, event programs, site-related quizzes, and interactive activities, examples of which are described in the online education section of this chapter. Offer a daily or weekly blog of commentary by the artistic director, artists, or others who can bring alive the creation and analysis of the production for site visitors.

Of course the Web site should also feature a full complement of basic, rarely changing information: the organization's mission, history, and people (artistic and administrative personnel); full descriptions of each of the season's offerings, along with schedules, venue information, maps, driving directions, parking, and local restaurant information; donor and volunteer information; a learning center; and a FAQ (frequently asked questions) section. The Web site should also offer links to useful resources such as in-depth information about the works the organization presents or produces and sites for purchasing specific books, CDs, DVDs, or videotapes that relate to the organization's offerings.

The organization's Web site and e-mail messages should provide contact information for each relevant department in the organization. Someone in each department should respond to these contacts with a personal message in a timely manner and all customer comments and complaints should be carefully considered.

Arts marketers should test the usability of their site by inviting ten to fifteen people of different ages and different comfort levels with using the Internet to purchase tickets and seek other information online. Watch these subjects as they go through the process to identify gaps in navigation, misunderstanding of buttons and functionality, and problematic descriptions or jargon. When you ask these people for feedback, you may find, for example, that when they click on the "Literature" button, they expect to find books on featured composers, not the offer to send a brochure that they actually find.

By tracking how many pages general users view on your site per visit, you can test the site's *stickiness.* Julie Aldridge, executive director of the Arts Marketing Association of Great Britain, and consultant Roger Tomlinson suggest that if many people visit fewer than three pages, you should ask yourself if the home page is confusing and if it provides the right information and links. If people are viewing six to ten pages, check the conversion rate to see if people are doing what you want them to and are not just spending a lot of time because they are lost. Also, check the site's effectiveness at bringing people back for more visits, and actively employ methods to increase that percentage.[14]

Online Ticketing

Organizations are finding that people who purchase tickets online are those who have been the most difficult to reach with traditional marketing messages. It is fairly common that online ticket buyers are significantly younger than the average audience member, live farther from the venue, and are first-time buyers.

Online Ticket Sales: San Francisco Opera

In early 1999, after two years of developing its Web site to include online ticket sales for single tickets and subscriptions and after hiring two full-time Webmasters, the San Francisco Opera launched a promotion for the site. Freeway billboard ads for the operas invited people to "Visit a Web site that sings: www.sfopera.com." The Web site address was listed on all the company's collateral materials, and banner ads were purchased on several other Web sites. In the first year the opera's Web site generated approximately twenty million hits and online ticket sales were strong. An impressive 60 percent of the online ticket sales came from first-time buyers, who had a very different profile from that of traditional box office purchasers. The median age of an online purchaser was thirty-five years, versus fifty-one years for traditional box office users, and most online buyers lived south of the city in San Mateo and Santa Clara Counties, rather than in San Francisco where most traditional tickets buyers live.[15]

Online Ticket Sales: Chicago Symphony Orchestra

In September 2000, the Chicago Symphony Orchestra (CSO), whose Web site had been garnering a modest response, introduced a vastly expanded, upgraded site. By the end of the 2000–2001 season the orchestra had quadrupled its online ticket sales to more than $880,000, up from $220,000 in 1999–2000, the first year online sales were offered.[16] By the end of the 2004–2005 season,

Online Ticket Sales: Chicago Symphony, *continued*

online ticket sales totaled $2.5 million, representing 12.8 percent of total sales and 30 percent of single ticket sales. Significantly, the CSO sold 42 percent of its online orders during times when the box office was not open. The most encouraging aspect of this success is that 47 percent of online buyers are new to the symphony's database, and some of them are as young as high school students.[17]

Online Ticket Sales: Ravinia Festival

At the Ravinia Music Festival, a summer concert venue outside Chicago, Internet sales accounted for 1.7 percent of total tickets sold in 1995. Then each year Ravinia's sales online doubled, reaching 49 percent of all tickets sold in 2003. Twenty three percent of the reserved seats in Ravinia's pavilion were purchased online. Of the less expensive tickets for the lawn, where patrons can picnic on blankets or folding chairs while listening to the concert, 66 percent were sold online. In the 2004 and 2005 seasons, online ticket sales stayed at the same level, primarily because more events are selling out in advance, according to ticketing manager Angus Watson. Even people who traditionally purchase tickets at the box office or over the telephone are purchasing online as well.[18]

Online Ticket Sales: Florida Grand Opera

In the 2004–2005 season, total ticket sales at the Florida Grand Opera increased 3 percent over the previous season, while online ticket sales increased 14 percent.[19]

These examples offer clear evidence that it is not the art itself that is at issue for many nonattenders or infrequent attenders, but how and when information and tickets are made available. Clearly, arts organizations that still resist offering online ticket sales are not only seriously limiting their audience growth, but may be risking the loss of some of their current audience as well.

APPROACHES TO ONLINE TICKETING Ideally, the organization will offer real-time ticket sales online. With real-time sales, patrons can select their seats and get immediate feedback on the sale. If it is not feasible to offer real-time sales online, arts groups can provide an order form to be printed out and submitted by fax, e-mail, or mail; however, credit card information should not be accepted by e-mail because this method is not secure. Patrons ordering tickets via e-mail are later phoned by box office personnel for their payment information. Although it is not as simple and smooth a process as ordering online, a downloadable form allows patrons to act on their ticket purchase decision immediately and at any time of day. If they must wait to phone during box office hours, this inconvenience may serve as a deterrent.

In the United States many arts organizations provide a real-time ticketing contract with a third-party ticketing service. Some services, like Ticketmaster, require that the visitor navigate through a wide variety of offerings from multiple organizations on their site. They also charge fees to both the patron and the organization. Sometimes these fees are so high that they either deter people from buying tickets or, at the least, decrease the patron's satisfaction level with the experience. Furthermore, services like Ticketmaster use and promote their own logo on their Web site, are not integrated with the organization's own database, and do not provide the organization with comprehensive patron information, so the organization cannot readily access all-important patron data. Often these ticketing services are not set up to take any payments other than for single tickets, so if a patron would like to subscribe or make a contribution, that must be done as a separate transaction directly with the arts organization.

Although contracting with Ticketmaster or its competitors is an easy way for arts organizations to make tickets available online, arts organizations are far better off in the long run if they invest in other ticketing services that are designed to coordinate with the organization's own software and serve its marketing and fundraising strategies. These systems typically appear to the customer to be part of the arts organization's own Web site. The ticket provider uses the organization's home page design template so that the transition is seamless and patrons are unaware that they are going to another site when they click on "Buy tickets." In addition to the upfront costs of installing these systems, which vary depending on the sophistication of the organization's hardware and software, the organization is usually billed a reasonable per ticket fee, which is typically passed on to the patron as a handling fee. The patron does not pay any fees directly to the ticketing service, and the arts organization has complete control over all charges to the patron. Ideally, the ticketing service is integrated with the organization's database so that the organization captures full patron information on every transaction.

FEATURES OF ONLINE TICKETING Every arts organization's Web site should have one-click access to ticket purchasing information highly visible on the home page and easily accessible from every other page. The ticket information should also be one click away from information about each production, schedules, layout of the venue, reviews, and other performance-related news.

With most ticketing systems, patrons can view a diagram of the hall and sometimes view the stage from various seating sections. Purchasers select a preferred section or price category and are then offered the best available seats or a selection of available seats. They are also given the option to reselect if acceptable seats are not available on the chosen date. In the United States, Great Britain, and some other countries, the customer provides credit card information (sites are guaranteed to be secure), and tickets are mailed to them if the performance date is at least ten days away. If the performance is closer to the purchase date, tickets are held at the box office to be picked up by the customer arriving for the performance.

Other features that are rarely if ever found on arts organizations' Web sites but that would greatly enhance the customer experience and build the quantity of tickets sold are ticket exchanges online, discounted tickets "authorized" by a key code or access number, group sales with an automatic discount or perks for volume purchases, subscription ordering and renewal, and even a special code for concierges to receive a commission for tickets purchased on behalf of a guest.

Building E-Loyalty

Web sites are far more than just publishing tools; they are communication tools, offering opportunities for two-way dialogues with customers and automated personal relationships.

Superbly designed sites like Amazon.com and bbc.co.uk have given customers high expectations for their online experiences. People expect easy navigation, up-to-date information, easy purchasing options, fast service, and fast responses. However, many Web sites frequently disappoint, frustrate, and anger customers as a result of being too slow, difficult to navigate, or unresponsive. Says Laurie Windham, in her book *The Soul of the New Consumer,* "The Web has created an impatient customer with a short attention span and a low tolerance for mistakes."[20] Furthermore, marketers must deliver not only fundamental benefits but new motivating features as well, features that in a short period of time often become expected. Another factor complicating online marketing is that with the inroads the Internet has made into consumer buying patterns, companies must now target consumers online based on their activity and shopping habits, which can also change rapidly. Constant research and investigation are key to tapping into consumers' needs and wants.

Julie Aldridge and Roger Tomlinson suggest that arts marketers design their Web sites to appeal to people at each level on the *loyalty ladder,* both to speak to their current interests and needs and to encourage them to continue their relationship with the organization.[21]

Suspects, new visitors to your site, are on the lowest rung of the loyalty ladder. Research shows that once a new visitor has clicked on your site, you have about three seconds to convince him or her to stay. To capture the new visitor's attention, make sure that your organization's *Internet value proposition* is immediately clear. In other words, have a clear primary purpose and communicate it on the home page. Can visitors quickly understand what the organization is, what it represents, and what the Web site will offer them? Does the design reflect the organization's core branding values? To begin to develop a relationship, consider offering a pop-up window that appears for new visitors only, asking them to sign up for your e-mail list. At the least, clearly offer on the home page a button for people to click to sign up for e-mails.

Prospects are people who have contacted you for information, so they have demonstrated an interest in the organization but have not yet acted on it. These people need to be persuaded to make a purchase. Features that may be effective are strong images, awards, customer recommendations, and reviews. Make it easy for people to try out the organization and its offerings with money-back guarantees and trial subscriptions or memberships. Don't intimidate newcomers with a home page that features invitations to attend events like a $500 per person gala fundraiser.

Customers are people who have attended the organization's offerings at least once. If your site is database driven, ask visitors about certain preferences and request their permission to use this information when they visit your site in the future. To capitalize on this information, create dynamic Web pages, showing different content to different people, according to their stated (and purchased) interests, so the messages will deliver the benefits of interest. Also, each time someone offers you information, reward him or her with a relevant, personal reply.

Clients are frequent attenders. To build profiles of the best customers, request more in-depth information. Customers will continue to give you information if you use their responses to improve the communication they receive from you and if you respect and guard their privacy. Relevant, timely, and personal updates can be managed by e-mail and with links to the Web site. Customers can receive advance notice of performances, the opportunity to book tickets before they go on sale in the box office, regular newsletters, and special offers.

Advocates are the people most loyal to the organization. Advocates should be given plenty of opportunities to spread the word (add a "forward this page to a friend" button) and should be encouraged to donate online.

Loyalty marketing, which focuses on building relationships through trust and personal communication, follows the same principles online as off. With suspects, the key aim for the Web site is to gain permission for future contact. With prospects, those who have visited your Web site but have not as yet purchased tickets, make it easy for them to attend their first performance at your venue and do not ask for too much too soon. With customers, those who have purchased tickets at least once, start to get to know them, anticipate their needs, and understand and exceed their expectations. With clients, regular attenders, focus on retention and increasing frequency; use dynamic dialogue to make relevant and timely recommendations. With advocates, loyal customers, make it easy for them to promote your organization and its offerings with viral marketing options.

Online Education

Web sites offer arts organizations myriad opportunities for educating their publics, whether novice or knowledgeable, young or old. The organization can offer in-depth information about each production, biographies of performers, program notes, and even a basic course in the particular art form, such as describing the instruments in an orchestra or opera styles through recent centuries. An organization can recommend a discography and a reading list for patrons interested in educating themselves further about the organization's offerings. Over time, each organization can continually add more value and more information for its Web site visitors. The only cost for enriching a Web site is the time, creativity, and knowledge of the staff.

Dsokids.com at the Dallas Symphony Orchestra

The Dallas Symphony Orchestra (DSO) Web site features an extraordinarily creative and playful yet highly educational learning center for children at www.DSOkids.com. There are enough colorful, graphically exciting, and fun games and material here to keep even an adult involved for hours at a time. In Beethoven's Baseball the site visitor can make a "hit" by answering a question and identifying the correct composer. This game builds familiarity with composers and shares interesting, humanizing anecdotes about their lives. Clues help the player both succeed and learn. In the Time Machine game the player scores by placing composers in the correct time period. Composers' names pop out of the machine at the click of a mouse, and the player is entitled to three hints for each composer. Another option on the site provides information about musical instruments. One can click on the name of any instrument in the orchestra and hear it play. Young musicians have their own section on the site. One pop-up page says: "Should you practice your instrument every day? Not necessarily. Dr. Suzuki says you should only practice on the days you eat." There is also an extensive, cleverly designed section for teachers, filled with information that is also of interest to parents and any adult who wants to learn more about orchestras, orchestral music, and the DSO and to access links to other informative Web sites.

Many arts organizations bemoan the lack of arts education in the schools and are deeply concerned about whether today's young generations and their progeny will have enough interest in the arts to sustain symphonies, theaters, opera companies, and dance companies for the future. Fortunately, some arts organizations are taking arts education into their own hands. They are capitalizing on the power of the Internet to present the performing arts in an entertaining and wonderfully absorbing yet highly educational way.

E-Mail Marketing

E-mail has become a highly effective and efficient communications tool for arts organizations. It is used for motivating ticket sales among a wide variety of market segments, for enriching the experience of people who already have tickets, and for sharing all kinds of information in a timely and nearly cost-free manner.

Permission Marketing

People want e-mail from the companies that interest them. When patrons sign up to be part of an organization's e-mail list, they are engaging in a transaction even though no money is changing hands. They are trading something they value—their privacy and personal information—in return for the marketer's promises, first and foremost, to protect this information by not selling it to others, and then to send them valuable, relevant, and timely messages. As a result, when consumers receive opt-in e-mail, messages they have given the marketer permission to send, their reaction to these messages differs dramatically from their response to junk mail. In the CultureFinder. com survey of its newsletter subscribers mentioned earlier, 83 percent of patrons responded that they were curious or eager to read the organization's e-mail messages; only 2 percent said that they deleted the messages without reading them. In contrast, 84 percent of patrons said that they deleted spam—e-mail to which they had not opted-in—without ever reading it.[22] It is important to know that people tend to exhibit a personal relationship with individual arts organizations, as demonstrated by the fact that 51 percent of CultureFinder.com arts

Motivating Ticket Sales by E-Mailing Cambridge Students

Due to the mobility and seasonality of students at the two universities in Cambridge, England, direct mail is an ineffective method for informing and attracting students to performances at the Cambridge Drama Center. E-mail seemed an obvious alternative, as both universities offer the theater the students' e-mail addresses. In 2003, upon receiving an initial e-mail contact, more than 350 students opted in to receive the theater's e-mail communications. The messages were text-based (not attachments), which is what the great majority of respondents preferred, and included hyperlinks, which have been extremely effective in encouraging Web site traffic. More than 80 percent of e-mail subscribers have booked tickets for an event as a direct result of receiving an e-mail from the theater.[23]

Fastnotes at the Los Angeles Philharmonic

The Los Angeles Philharmonic has devised a solution to the problem experienced by many audience members of trying to scan program notes in the few moments between the members' arrival and the start of the concert. FastNotes is a brief set of program notes e-mailed free to interested parties a week or so before a concert. The notes include links to iTunes or similar Web sites that will allow FastNotes subscribers to hear a brief passage from the music to be played. Deborah Borda, the Philharmonic's president, hopes that in addition to providing information about the composer and the work being performed, the notes will give audiences a sense of how concert programs take shape and why she and music director Esa-Pekka Salonen decide to juxtapose certain works and composers during the same evening. Just one day after FastNotes was announced, the service had already enrolled about 2,000 subscribers.[24]

patrons claim that they read opt-in arts e-mail as carefully as they read mail from their friends.[25] Says Seth Godin, in his book *Permission Marketing,* "the most important part of the permission troika—anticipated, personal, and relevant—is anticipated."[26]

Godin describes how the marketing process can be overhauled to get the benefits of both broad exposure and targeted messages. Instead of forcing a message on large numbers of people, whether or not they are candidates for a given product, Godin wants to entice consumers to grant their permission to enter into a dialogue about the product. As these consumers get more information about the product—information that can be customized according to their interests—they are likely to become loyal and profitable customers. Although this process sounds expensive, Godin say it can pay off in fewer wasted messages and higher customer loyalty. Godin, head of direct marketing at Yahoo!, dismisses traditional advertising practices as *interruption marketing.* He concedes that permission marketers also rely on interruptions to introduce themselves to a broad base of customers. But the introductory ads can be quite simple because they do not need to sell the product. All they need to do is ask permission to say more. From that point on, all participation is voluntary.

Permission marketing can work in a number of media, but it is tailor-made for the Internet and e-mail marketing, where easy interactivity promises to facilitate marketing dialogues. Messages that do not initiate or sustain dialogue can be quickly identified and changed or dropped, minimizing wasted ads. Traditional marketing relies on disparate media for advertising, research, sales, promotional activities, coupon distribution, and customer support. The Internet, in contrast, permits companies to put these separate channels of customer communication into a single, focused, coherent response mechanism. Marketers can create awareness, educate, generate trials, reward loyalty, provide customer support, and generally simplify the customer's life. E-mail marketing cannot replace other marketing media, but it does eliminate the need for certain costly marketing efforts and greatly enhances the marketing department's total communication plan.

Nick Usborne, frequent contributor to *ClickZ,* takes Godin's concept one step further. He says, "If you really want to practice permission marketing, change the name to 'trust marketing.' If you have to earn and maintain the trust of your customers, you have an ongoing task. You can't assume it. You have to earn it, again and again . . . with each visit, every transaction, every customer service call, every outbound promotional e-mail. Because if you don't have your customer's trust, their permission is worthless."[27]

E-Mail Benefits

E-mail provides several important benefits over other forms of direct marketing.

E-mail is nearly cost free. If the e-mail message is created in-house, it costs only staff time for writing copy, uploading images, and formatting. If an organization contracts with a professional e-mail service, such as Patron Technology, it costs only pennies per patron. Printed and mailed marketing materials, in contrast, can easily cost thousands of dollars, averaging up to as much as one dollar per patron.

E-mail is an important vehicle for stimulating visits to the organization's Web site.

E-mail allows the organization to create mass customization—to communicate with many people at the same time but in a personalized way. By generating regular, direct, two-way communication with key customers, the organization can develop an understanding of customer needs—and respond to them. Such response develops a sense of involvement and trust in the organization on the part of the customers.[28]

E-mail messages can be and frequently are forwarded to other prospects. More than 60 percent of CultureFinder.com arts patrons reported that they had forwarded e-mail to their friends in the previous month.[29] And the forwarding does not necessarily stop there: friends often forward to other friends. This is what is known as *viral* marketing—what is commonly a word with negative connotations becomes a happy consequence for arts marketers who know that their best resource for spreading news is their interested and loyal patrons and that e-mail is the ideal medium for accomplishing this.

E-mail is an immediate vehicle. As with all media the messages need to be strategized and crafted, but e-mail delivery is instantaneous, whereas marketing pieces sent by regular mail require time for printing, stuffing, labeling, stamping, sorting, and mail delivery.

Timely E-Mail at Chicago Opera Theater

Chicago Opera Theater (COT) was informed by the *Chicago Tribune* in December 2002 that General Director Brian Dickie would receive the newspaper's annual Chicagoan in the Arts award, to be announced in the forthcoming Sunday edition. The day before the public announcement, COT sent a message to all its e-mail patrons sharing the exciting news and telling them that the organization wanted them to be among the first to know. This gave message recipients a sense of feeling special and being an insider, even though Sunday papers are on newsstands Saturday afternoon.

Patrons respond more often and much more quickly to e-mail messages than to mailed material. On average, people respond to regular mail marketing pieces in three weeks; they respond to e-mail messages within forty-eight hours. This means that marketing managers can more rapidly evaluate the effectiveness of their messages and design new messages and offers for the various marketing segments, thereby leveraging more opportunities to spread news and sell tickets.

E-mail tends to generate a much higher response rate than regular mail marketing. An average response rate for mailed pieces is 1.5 percent. (However, this response rate does vary widely with the quality of the list. One can expect a significantly higher response from a well-targeted mailing list.) CultureFinder.com has reported that 10 percent of its e-mail recipients click through, and 25 percent of those patrons purchase tickets. The Florida Grand Opera tracked response rates to an e-mail request for updated patron information. Less than two days after the message was sent, 27 percent of recipients opened the message, and 37 percent of those people responded with the requested information.

It is also easy for the marketing manager to track which and how many recipients opened the e-mail message and how many clicked through to the organization's Web site and to garner other valuable information.

People's desire to receive e-mail messages is not limited to the arts organizations that they have attended in the past. Eighty-seven percent of CultureFinder.com survey respondents said they would be likely to join the e-mail list of an organization to which they subscribe, 76 percent would join the list of an organization from which they have bought tickets in the past, 60 percent are interested in e-mails from organizations in cities to which they frequently travel, and 58 percent would like to receive e-mails from organizations whose performances they have never attended but would like to know more about.[30]

When one considers the higher response rate, the tendency of people to forward messages to others, and the dramatically lower price to create and send messages, it is clear that e-mail marketing is a highly effective and efficient marketing vehicle.

E-Mail Strategy

E-mail, like all other marketing tools, requires strategic and creative planning. Sending out an occasional e-mail message or blasting patrons with a series of frequent e-mail promotions when, for example, the organization wants to announce a special program or sell a large number of tickets to a production that has not sold well to date will not sustain interest and loyalty for very long. Each organization should develop an overall plan for e-mail marketing, just as it does for advertising, regular mailings, public relations, and other marketing efforts.

The marketer should always keep in mind the recipient's perspective. Why would people want to receive this information? How will they benefit? Furthermore, the marketer needs to consider how the benefits provided dovetail with other marketing offers, such as those contained in subscription brochures and advertisements.

"At the heart of all e-mail marketing," says Eugene Carr, "is relevance and value."[31] The success of e-mail campaigns is dependent on the nature and quality of the offer itself. E-mail communications can offer value by providing more detailed information than is available to the general public, early notice of events or offers, timely reminders of special programs, and private offers or discounts. E-mail recipients want to feel special. It is up to the marketer to deliver something of special value to the customer in each e-mail message.

Godin's ideal situation is *intravenous* marketing, in which organizations continually resupply their products after getting initial permission.[32] Not only will opt-in customers grant providers permission to send additional information, they'll actively solicit information. They'll engage in dialogue with marketers, will take the lead in satisfying their own needs, will be eager to buy when they've found the right match, and will forward the e-mail to others they think will be interested.

Building E-Mail Lists

A successful e-mail program depends on building and maintaining a high-quality list. Quality, of course, means having as extensive as possible a list of current addresses of those who opt-in to receive messages from your organization. The organization needs to plan the staff time to regularly update the e-mail list as new names are added, people's addresses change, or people choose to opt out. Recruiting people to subscribe to online e-mail services is not unlike selling a performance. The marketer must promote the e-mail service and communicate its benefits at every possible opportunity the organization has—and creates—for this purpose with current and potential patrons.

At the Mark Taper Forum and its sister theater, the Ahmanson, roughly 85 percent of the e-mail addresses on the theaters' list are collected through online transactions or by box office and phone staff at the time of sale. The remainder come from people as they sign up on the Web site or enter the theaters' online Win Tickets promotions.

E-mail addresses can also be collected through all ticket order forms for renewals, new subscriptions, or single tickets. When taking a ticket order, box office staff should request this information. If the box office personnel are very busy, such as during the hour or two before a performance, they can ask patrons to fill out a simple form and give it to an usher when showing their ticket for entry. A program booklet insert can be headlined with a request that patrons provide their name and e-mail addresses and drop the form in a box specially provided for this purpose in the lobby. Forms may also be distributed in the lobby for those who do not have program books or who have left them at their seats. To encourage people to fill in the forms, the organization may offer a drawing for a ticket giveaway, a compact disc recording, dinner for two at a local restaurant, or other gift of value to the patrons.

E-mail addresses should be collected at all special events in which the organization participates, such as festivals, readings, or lectures, and at local bookstores and libraries, usually accompanied by a ticket give-away promotion for which people must fill out an entry form.

All mailings and advertisements should encourage people to visit the organization's Web site, where a version of "Join our e-mail list" should be boldly visible on the home page and accessible with one click from other Web site pages. An effective approach is to have a sign-up pop-up screen appear the first time a patron visits the site. Culture-Finder.com increased its daily sign-ups fivefold when it adopted this approach. Anyone in contact with an organization and its staff via regular mail, phone, or e-mail should be asked if he or she would like to be included in the e-mail list.

Many organizations (and some countries) have a policy that prohibits the sale or trade of e-mail lists. Whether or not you have a policy forbidding such sale or trade, it is a good practice to follow. It will ensure that you do not erode the trust you have developed with your e-mail patrons, which may happen if they begin receiving unwelcome messages from another arts organization. Instead, your organization can collaborate with another arts organization by creating a special e-mail to your audience about the other organization's event or by including this information within a regular e-mail from your organization; then the other organization returns the favor. Make sure you are providing value for your patrons by making an offer they couldn't get elsewhere, and make sure the offering is congruent with your patron profile. If people respond to the partner organization about the offer, then the partner organization can request their permission to add their e-mail addresses to their own list.

Shortly after people sign up for your e-mail list, they should be sent a message welcoming them. If they have signed up via the Web site, the welcome message should go out automatically, within seconds if possible. On the Web site sign-up page, patrons should be asked about what interests them. The more data the marketer has about the patrons and their interests, the more the organization can segment mailings. In this way patrons will be sure to receive the information of interest to them and will not be bothered with what does not apply to them, such as renewal reminder notices for people who have already subscribed or information about popular music concerts for those who like only classical.

The Messages

The e-mail marketing plan involves the selection and timing of various types of messages. The content, style, and frequency of the messages should be driven by what the marketer hopes to achieve. The two primary types of messages in use by many arts organizations are information-oriented e-newsletters and action-oriented e-postcards. In his book *Wired for Culture,* Eugene Carr says that "regular communication from an institution to its members is at the heart of a long-term loyalty building strategy."[33] Depending on the length of the organization's season and the number of productions it performs, an e-newsletter can be sent weekly, monthly, or every two months. But whatever the frequency, these newsletters should be regularly scheduled and consistent in look and type of content. An organization might produce several versions of each newsletter, sending different versions to groups targeted by interest or by category, such as subscribers and nonsubscribers. If a version is intended for a youth audience, for example, the language and style might be changed to appeal to this target group.

These newsletters are typically filled with information designed to educate the recipients; to reinforce their relationship with the organization; and to promote the organization, its activities, and its mission. Each newsletter should consist of a series of short articles of fifty to one hundred words, with photos (when appropriate) and links that direct traffic to the organization's Web site for more information. Says Carr, "The simpler and more direct these articles are, the better they work."[34] The articles may include notifications about free pre-performance lectures, free lunchtime concerts or lectures, other educational events, fundraisers, symphony broadcasts, or interviews with the musical director on television or radio. Announcements may be made of the forthcoming season of performances ("Visit the Web site for information about next season's productions and reserve your seats now!"), and there may be brief features or human interest stories about performers, designers, or directors for an upcoming production. The newsletter, or at least one article, may be signed by the artistic or executive director, giving the recipients the good feeling of being contacted by an important person in the organization.

E-postcards are used to supplement e-newsletters, targeting segments of the organization's list with specific offers. The goal of the e-postcard should be to motivate an action—typically to purchase tickets in response to a limited-time special offer, an announcement of a renewal deadline approaching, or a performance that is nearly sold out. The postcard may also be used to announce such things as an upcoming educational program, a free lunchtime concert at the library, or special parking arrangements while an area near the concert hall is under construction. It may provide a link to special information on the Web site, such as a recent review or an interview with a key performer. It may link the patron to information that will facilitate a greater understanding of the art form in general or of a particular production, composer, playwright, or choreographer. It may provide an opportunity for patrons to give the organization feedback on their experience at a recent performance or it may be used for market research—so the organization can learn more about its e-patrons and their attitudes and preferences. The postcard should be highly focused, with a limited amount of copy, and should have a simple and direct visual approach. If the marketer tries to accomplish multiple goals in one e-postcard, most likely the main goal will not be achieved.

Arts organizations that enjoy extended runs of a production should send e-mails to people who have seen the show asking them to forward the message. For example, an e-mail might say, "If you loved this show, please share this message with five friends!" Include in the message not only reviews and awards but also information that will enrich the experience, perhaps some of the information that is included in the press kit and other background information and photos that will bring the show alive for people. For example, a message about Pulitzer prize–winner Paula Vogel's *The Long Christmas Ride Home* can make it clear that this play is anything *but* holiday entertainment, even though it is being offered during the holiday season. People who might be put off by the title can learn that the play is provocative and operates on many levels. Potential attenders may greatly benefit from knowing about the story, the playwrights it honors, the history of

Japanese puppetry (puppets are central to the play), and other factors at the discretion of the marketer and the dramaturge. In this way the organization can help people who have seen the show to provide a comprehensive and valued recommendation to people they think will enjoy it.

Eugene Carr points out that there is a real art to subject lines, as the marketer has much to accomplish in only eight to ten words.[35] First, identify yourself; be sure your organization's name or "brand" is unmistakable. Make the purpose of the message clear. For example: "Seattle Opera Single Tickets on Sale Today," or "Symphony Holiday Tickets: Special Web Offer." Make the format of your subject lines and body content consistent so that readers will instantly recognize your organization's messages.

Every e-mail communication should be "short, sharp and relevant," says Judith James in her section on e-mail marketing at fuel4arts.com, the Australian Council for the Arts Web site, which is replete with useful information for arts marketers. The content should be compelling and its meaning must be clear to the reader, who may give the message only a cursory glance before deciding to read or delete it. Avoid using attachments as people often will not open them because of concern about viruses or because of the inconvenience. Instead, provide links to key pages on your Web site where viewers can investigate in-depth information.[36]

Arts marketers should be aware of the policies that constitute good e-mail etiquette. If you are sending an e-mail to a small number of people, make sure the e-mail program has a *blind carbon copy* (bcc) feature so the list of e-mail addresses is hidden from the recipient's view. If this feature is not used, patrons could receive an e-mail with all the other recipients' e-mail addresses at the top. However, use the bcc feature cautiously as your server could malfunction if you try to send a message to too many people at once. In one case customers received 200 copies of the same message as the server kept trying to re-send overnight. When sending e-mails to large numbers of people, use an e-mail program capable of merging the database of recipients with individual e-mail messages.

The organization's privacy policy should be published at the bottom of each e-mail message and on the organization's Web site. Each e-mail message should include an option to "unsubscribe," with instructions for simple and quick execution. Once a person opts out of receiving further e-mails from your organization, the only e-mail that person should receive from you is the unsubscribe confirmation.

Tracking and Evaluation

Among the outstanding benefits of both Internet and e-mail marketing is the ability to readily track a wide range of information about patron behavior. Many Web hosts provide the hosted organization with a site where managers can check at will such information as how many people visited the Web site by day or by the hour, the patrons' host server addresses, how many pages on the Web site each patron visited, and how long the patron spent there. Managers can also view the page at which each patron entered the organization's Web site and at what page he or she exited, which is especially helpful in evaluating the effectiveness of special marketing tactics, such as an e-mail message that encourages people to link to a particular page on the site or a mail or radio promotion that offers a special price for on-line ticket purchasers. Managers can track the number of people who opened the message, the number of click-throughs to the Web site, the numbers of new e-mail subscribers and of people who are opting out of their e-mail subscriptions, and even the number of destinations to which an e-mail is forwarded.

Marketing managers can easily measure the success of e-mail messages by determining increased sales or inquiries around the time a particular e-mail was sent; by counting the number of sales at a unique price or the sales or inquiries going through a unique telephone number or e-mail address, one available only to e-mail subscribers; and by asking callers how they heard about an offering or event.

The organization may decide to promote an offer in two different ways to small groups of recipients on its e-mail list, then test to see which promotion received the best response rate. The best performing offer can then be sent to the rest of the e-mail list.

Organizations may also e-mail short surveys to their patrons to monitor whether e-mails are read and valued. The survey might ask patrons how frequently they read the messages, check their level of satisfaction with the content, and request or test ideas to improve the e-mail communications.

To gather information that is not readily available to the marketing director, organizations can hire specialists who collect and analyze data about e-mail and Web site visits. Some Web analysts are willing to work for arts organizations on a pro bono basis to develop contacts with the organization's supporters.

INTEGRATING ONLINE MARKETING WITH OFFLINE MARKETING

As powerful as Internet and e-mail marketing are, they cannot replace traditional marketing methods. Just as it is important to integrate direct mail with telemarketing, public relations, and advertisements, it is essential to integrate online marketing with all other marketing methods as well. Timing of e-mail messages should be appropriate for the target audience and should complement ads, direct mail, and public relations efforts. Special Web and e-mail pricing offers should be strategically integrated with the overall pricing plan.

A rule of thumb in marketing is that people need three exposures before they act on an offer. Online marketing adds variety to those exposures and touches many people in ways that are likely to be far more compelling than just seeing a newspaper ad or direct-mail brochure repeatedly.

Crucial to the success of online marketing and the integration of all marketing tools is the investment by marketing staff, artistic personnel, development staff, and the education department in the development and updating of Web site content. Too many arts organizations recruit people to work on the Web site alone—people who often are tech-savvy but are not aware of how the site fits in with other communication tools or strategies.

Online marketing is proving its effectiveness every day; it is the primary source of growth in direct marketing at the current time, and it is the way of the future. This medium is a gift for the arts. How arts marketers use it and what they use it for will determine their success.

Identifying and Capitalizing on Brand Identity

It's not who you are that holds you back, it's who you think you're not.

—Anonymous

It's hard to read the label when you're inside the bottle.

—Roy Williams

A BRAND IS TO MARKETING WHAT THE MISSION IS TO THE entire organization. The brand drives the entire marketing function. Because marketing is an organization-wide function, not something to be left to the marketing department, the brand, in an important sense, drives the entire organization.

Branding has been a key marketing buzz word of recent years. But branding is not something that will disappear when new marketing tactics come into practice to attract and retain customers. In fact branding is not a tactic at all; it is an organizing principle so broad and so defining that it can shape and direct just about anything an organization does. During the brand-building process, every aspect of the organization should be investigated, including all its business practices. This does not mean that branding will interfere with the organization's mission or artistic vision. On the contrary, a thorough brand development and implementation process guarantees that the organization's mission and artistic vision will remain in clear focus and central to all activities. Of course a great brand requires a great product. The organization must have a distinctive offering, not simply a distinctive image.

A brand is not a logo; it is not a label. A brand carries meaning and associations. It taps into emotions. It is a symbol of trust between the organization and the customer. The brand is an indication of quality and features to expect and services that will be rendered.

Says Philip Kotler in his book *Marketing Insights from A to Z,* "Don't advertise a brand; live it."[1] Live it through every method with which you communicate with your publics, from your advertising to the style and quality of your direct-mail pieces and Web sites, to the way ushers and box office personnel relate to your customers, and of course, to the quality and consistency of the work on your stages.

Brands are social, as they represent ideas that people have in common. The power of a brand is demonstrated in the extent to which it brings people together for a common purpose—to share in an experience or to buy the same thing—while being personally relevant.

Brands are powerful because they work psychologically. They can enhance our sense of self-identity; articulate and confirm beliefs; change or endorse attitudes and values; influence perceptions, associations, and opinions; and when they act as the deciding factor in purchase choices, influence behavior. Brands also influence our use of language—how we articulate our attitudes and opinions about the organization, its offerings, and other related topics. In order to influence behavior, marketers must often first face the challenge of changing attitudes, which tend to be deep-seated and knee-jerk, having become automatic after extensive or compelling experiences.

Brand awareness may be the traditional measure of brand strength, but brand relevance and brand resonance are far more valuable aspects of the branding package.[2] Says Scott Bedbury, author of *A New Brand World,* "Top-of-mind awareness and other surface-level viewpoints of a brand reveal little about a brand's real strength or weakness. To fully understand a brand you have to look much deeper. You have to strip everything away and get to its core and understand how it is viewed and *felt* by people inside the company and the world outside."[3] The overall goal is to create a brand image that is compelling

ARS Viva Symphony Orchestra:
Communicating the Experience

Ars Viva, an orchestra whose core members are gifted Chicago Symphony Orchestra musicians and that is conducted by its founder and highly respected music director, Alan Heatherington, offers two performances each of five programs over the course of a season at the North Shore Center for the Performing Arts in Skokie, Illinois. *Ars Viva* means "living art."

The organization discusses its name on its Web site: "Our commitment to variety is embodied in our name. Ars Viva: something old and something new, something tested and true from the treasures of musical art (*Ars*), juxtaposed with fresh creative statements of living composers (*Viva*). Our seasons have featured works from the standard orchestral repertoire side by side with new and interesting contemporary music."[4]

Ars Viva emphasizes living art in another sense as well. Its slogan, featured on the back cover of the 2006–2007 season brochure as well as in other materials, is "Making music come to life!" The season brochure entices the reader to look beyond the front cover, which features a dramatic photo of Maestro Heatherington conducting, and says, "You're not just attending a concert . . ." The reader turns to the second page and the thought continues, ". . . You're experiencing life." Also on this second page, Heatherington discusses Oscar Wilde's remark that "life imitates art far more than art imitates life." Says Heatherington, in part, "The Ars Viva experience is all about integrating art and life. . . . We like to think that Ars Viva musicians and audiences come together with an immediacy of communication that connects our art to our daily lives, so that the cares of the day melt into the music of the evening. . . . We all become involved in processing our deepest joys and sorrows in a life-affirming context shared by young and old alike, professionals and armchair aficionados gathered in the same space to discover something of inestimable value, inextricably linked to real life. *Ars Viva: making music come to life!*"

Rather than excerpting comments from music critics' reviews of past performances, the brochure brings alive the nature of the

ARS Viva Symphony Orchestra:
Communicating the Experience, *continued*

experience to come through Heatherington's vivid, informative, and sometimes humorous descriptions. For example, on the page that gives information about the program titled *Celebrating the Mozart Year,* Heatherington says: "Concertmaster David Taylor always thrills audiences with his impeccable performances, and the 'Mozart Factor' is certain to lift your spirits while actually making you more intelligent!" About the program titled *Americana,* Heatherington says: "Here is the *perfect* program for those fence-dwellers who remain unconvinced that American composers of the past 100 years have had something worthwhile and enduring to say. The Ives symphony was completed in 1904, while Polifrone's *Ballad* was among his final works completed earlier this year. Patrick Blackwell is a dazzling vocal communicator, and the orchestral musicians themselves have an astonishing surprise you must not miss!" (The surprise, I was told privately, is that the musicians will sing the hymns on which the Ives symphony is based.)

The brochure includes a two-page spread dedicated to families, featuring comments from parents and grandparents about the joys of sharing the Ars Viva experience with their children and grandchildren, and showing their two- or three-generation photos, taken in the lobby after a performance. Ars Viva says: "Give your children and grandchildren the gift of *music.* . . . Instill a *love* of music. . . . *Share* a special time together. . . . It just might change their lives." This page also presents a poignant and appropriately placed observation once made by Hans Christian Andersen: "When words fail, music speaks."

Alan Heatherington has been lauded by audiences and critics alike for his informative comments from the stage before each piece, which create an atmosphere of anticipation, excitement, and true enjoyment for the audience.

The Ars Viva brand is strong and clear in the hearts and minds of its artists, its managers, and its audiences, and is carried through in every message on and off the stage.

in its creativity, relevance, and dynamism in relation to various market segments. To build the brand, marketers must develop rich associations and promises for the brand name and manage all the customers' brand contacts so that they meet or exceed customers' expectations associated with the brand.[5]

According to British consultant Morris Hargreaves McIntyre, a brand's identity is supported by several component parts: namely, brand value, brand personality, brand attributes, brand benefits, and finally, brand perception. Says Hargreaves, "the battleground for the customer takes place in the sphere of brand perception: will it fulfill my needs or not?"[6]

It is important to make clear to people the true nature of the experience they will have so that their expectations will not differ from reality. Misleading communications often lead to disappointment and to a feeling of being manipulated; honesty builds trust. It is also important to present an emotional appeal. According to Bedbury, "The near-universal desire for greater personal freedom, and the more particular American quest for rugged individuality, are what we might call *cultural emotions. . . .* Effective brand building requires making relevant and compelling connections to deeply rooted human emotions or profound cultural forces."[7]

Organizations must create their brand value proposition carefully, strategically, and analytically. Then the brand value proposition must be used as the key driver of the company's strategy, operations, services, and product development.[8]

Following are two case studies. The first shows how Tiffany & Company changed people's perceptions of the company and dramatically broadened its customer base without changing its products. You will readily see how Tiffany's issues are applicable to performing arts managers. The second is a more extensive and detailed presentation and analysis of the branding process undertaken at Chicago Opera Theater in anticipation of its move to a new venue.

Rebranding at Tiffany & Company

Tiffany & Company has historically been the place for royalty and the wealthy to purchase special pieces of jewelry, china, and silver. But when the company went public in the late 1980s, management undertook a strategic transformation to broaden Tiffany's customer opportunity without negatively affecting the company's loyal, traditional customer base. Tiffany accomplished this by changing its positioning from, in effect, "baubles for the world's elite" to "timeless gifts for the truly special occasion"; in other words, by making a dramatic shift from *demographic* to *behavioral* targeting. The philosophy behind this shift is that *everyone* has special days—a birthday, anniversary, graduation, and so on—and a person can feel special every day while wearing Tiffany jewelry.

In an annual report Tiffany states, "A Tiffany product exists not for the moment, but to bring beauty, excitement, and glamour to the *ceremonies of daily life* for generations to come" (emphasis added). A gift from Tiffany may be given on a special occasion, but the result is that the Tiffany wearer feels special every day when checking the time on her Tiffany Tesoro watch or when donning Tiffany signature earrings. One newspaper ad shows a strand of Tiffany pearls and says only: "Some days matter." It is significant to note that no person is shown wearing the pearls; Tiffany wants readers to imagine themselves or their loved ones in that picture.

To address the concerns of those who say they would be delighted to purchase a Tiffany piece but cannot imagine affording one, a Tiffany ad states: "We believe that the true value of an object is not expressed by price. When you look at objects produced by great designers, you will recognize the value of timeless design." When an object is timeless, finely crafted, and lasts for generations, its high value reduces the impact of its price.

Upon seeing Tiffany's signature robin's egg blue box, people from all walks of life say that it resonates with excitement, mystery, uniqueness, and a sense of being beloved and, most of all, special. These words encapsulate the essence of Tiffany's brand, demonstrating how clearly and powerfully the brand identity has been communicated over the years.

There is much value for arts marketers to glean from this case study. Celebrations internal to the organization and its offerings—a composer's birthday, a director's anniversary with the organization, or a new performance hall—are unlikely to be attractive to many attenders, especially those who attend infrequently. A concert, dance, or play is something that many people cannot afford regularly but will readily pay for on their *own* special occasions. Furthermore, Tiffany's emotional appeal, pervasive throughout its communications, and the design quality and consistency of Tiffany's marketing materials are exemplary. It does not take great imagination or a large budget to create branded and enticing tickets, ticket envelopes, and gift certificates, making tangible the nature of the intangible experience to come. Not only is Tiffany's gift box robin's egg blue, but every catalogue arrives in an envelope of that color, immediately identifying the sender. Catalogue recipients report that this envelope alone stimulates in their mind brand characteristics such as "special" and "exciting."

The arts, like Tiffany, have historically been viewed as elitist in content and as intended for the privileged and those who are highly cultured. By focusing on the *special* rather than the elite aspects of attending the arts, arts organizations can help *all* people feel comfortable that the arts are for them. And by communicating that art enriches us, broadens us, and becomes a part of us, arts organizations can suggest the same "timeless" quality that greatly enhances Tiffany's offerings.

BRANDING AT CHICAGO OPERA THEATER

In 2002, anticipating a forthcoming move to a much larger and more expensive venue, the board and staff of Chicago Opera Theater (COT) undertook a strategic brand analysis, a project that I was engaged to facilitate.

Historical Overview

Chicago Opera Theater, founded in 1974, is a midsize opera company performing repertoire drawn from seventeenth-, eighteenth-, and twentieth-century chamber operas. COT's mission is to provide first-class productions of the small- to midscale opera repertoire; to advance opera as a vital, living art form; to develop young artists; to expand and diversify its audience; and to be one of the best small opera companies in the country and an integral part of Chicago's cultural landscape. COT fulfills this mission through affordable tickets, unique repertoire, performances in intimate venues, and in-depth arts education and outreach programs.

Over much of its history the quality of COT's productions was inconsistent, and this was a major cause of the serious financial setbacks the company suffered several times.

In 1999, COT underwent a major internal reorganization, resulting in the appointment of Brian Dickie as general director. Dickie has extensive experience in the opera field, and since his arrival in Chicago, the quality of the performances has been consistently high. COT has been enjoying rave reviews, not only locally but from New York City critics and, more important, from audiences who have been enthusiastic about the quality and great style of the productions.

For most of its existence, COT performed at the aging 960-seat Athenaeum Theatre, located in the heart of one of the city's Near North neighborhoods and a significant distance, both physically and psychologically, from the downtown venues of the city's major cultural organizations. The Athenaeum, whose age had not been burnished to charm, lacked important amenities such as handicapped accessibility, convenient parking, entertainment lounges, and adequate bathroom facilities.

In November 2003, construction was completed on the new, well-located, state-of-the-art, 1,500-seat Joan W. and Irving B. Harris Theater for Music and Dance, named for its major donors. COT planned to begin having its performances there in February 2004. COT knew it would incur dramatically increased rental costs in this new venue, which would require a significant increase in both ticket sales and contributed income. To accomplish this, COT needed to build awareness of the organization, its offerings, its dramatically improved quality in recent years, and its new home; build increased interest and involvement among infrequent attenders; and build commitment and loyalty among subscribers and donors.

Brand Development

We began the brand identity analysis in the spring of 2002. The purpose of the analysis was to guide COT in developing and implementing strategies to strengthen its brand presence in the Chicago area as well as to capitalize on the citywide excitement over the new facility. We planned to put some elements of the new brand positioning in place for the 2003 season, in order to build a strong base for further growth with the move to the new venue in 2004.

AUDIENCE SURVEY The first step of the analysis was to conduct an audience survey. Brand building is more intuitive than analytical, but tools such as audience surveys can be invaluable in learning how patrons view the organization, its offerings, and those of its competitors. A well-designed survey can help the organization's managers determine which features of the organization's offerings the patrons value, indicating effective positioning strategies, and what concerns patrons have, indicating possible changes and modifications. Understanding how patrons view the organization helps managers determine which characteristics of the current image to retain and build and which to dispel. In order for a survey to be well designed, the managers and marketing researcher must carefully define the issues and agree on the research objectives.

The survey we designed was inserted in the program book for all performances of COT's third and last opera of the 2002 season. Patrons were asked questions regarding their satisfaction with the programming, artists, seating, scheduling, ticket price, performance location, and quality of the current venue; their interest in the new venue; the factors that encouraged subscription; their preferences regarding the use of supertitles; their information source for the present performance; the other arts organizations they attended; and their personal demographic information. Responses from 753 patrons (21 percent of the subscribers present; 19 percent of the single ticket buyers) were tabulated and all personal comments were recorded.

The survey found that 61 percent of subscribers were aged fifty-five or older; 64 percent of single ticket buyers were under fifty-five. As is typical in the performing arts industry, subscriptions were less common among younger attenders.

An important finding that affected the brand-building effort was that 89 percent of respondents also attended the Lyric Opera of Chicago, one of the largest and finest opera companies in the world. A great majority of these people both subscribed and contributed to the Lyric. This huge crossover audience made it abundantly clear that COT was appealing to opera lovers, that many opera lovers were not satiated by their season of experiences at the Lyric Opera, and that COT had carved a strong and viable niche in performing high-quality, smaller-scale opera. Given that Lyric patrons form the base of COT's loyal if comparatively small audience, we realized that the Lyric should not be seen as a competitor to COT but rather that the Lyric's audience should be viewed as a great resource for our audience-building efforts.

Some survey respondents reported that they especially liked the intimacy of the current venue and its neighborhood location. Few respondents complained about difficulty with finding street parking at the current venue, but many were concerned about ticket prices and parking fees in the new location. Some people were waiting impatiently for the new venue to open; others were enjoying the older atmosphere of the current venue. It is important to note here, however, that only current patrons, people who accept the Athenaeum's limitations, participated in the survey.

BOARD OF DIRECTORS AND STAFF BRAINSTORMING SESSION   Once the results of the audience survey were tabulated, analyzed, and prepared for presentation, key members of the board and staff participated in a lengthy brainstorming session about the organization's image and identity. The agenda was to address perceptions of COT, of its competition, and of opera in general; to identify the ways the session participants viewed COT's audiences; and to review the audiences' views of COT and its offerings, as revealed in the survey results. The analysis of these factors led the group to determine how COT was currently perceived and what image COT desired to project, to identify current and potential market segments, and to identify opportunities for building COT's image and identity.

Perceptions of opera in general. The participants in the brainstorming session employed a wide range of adjectives, both positive and negative, to describe opera in general. The negative comments may derive from how they know or imagine others to feel about opera, because in their roles at COT they are naturally dedicated to this art form. However, the negative terms may also describe their honest opinions of opera in general and may reflect why these people are dedicated to COT, which they believe offers a better experience.

Intimidating
Snobby
Difficult
Long
Expensive
Absurd
Elitist
For old people
Impersonal
Stimulating
Exciting/thrilling
Challenging
Tuneful
Dramatic
Romantic
Socially rewarding (status)
Visually stimulating
Glamorous
Complex

Arts marketers must select descriptive words carefully when communicating aspects of their offering to various market segments. For example, some people find *challenging* to be a positive attribute; others prefer familiar works and traditional styles of presentation and do not want to be challenged. The word *elitist* also has both positive and negative connotations, depending on the individual's perspective. In a similar vein *status* is an important positive factor to some people but meaningless or negative to others.

Participants' views of COT. It is clear from the descriptions that follow that session participants had not only an exclusively positive but also an enthusiastic view of the experience of attending opera at COT.

Exciting
Refreshing
Fresh and immediate
Intimate and personal

Engaging
Creative
Adventurous
Theatrical
Musical
Humorous
Young

Perceptions of the audience experience at COT compared to the experience at the Lyric Opera. Next, participants described the nature of the COT experience compared to that of attending performances at the Lyric Opera. The resulting descriptions and comparisons were extremely useful in developing positioning statements for attracting both Lyric attenders and people who are not opera aficionados.

COT	*Lyric Opera*
Unpredictable	Predictable
Adventurous	Dependable
Unique repertory	Familiar repertory
Unfamiliar cast	Famous name performers
Hip, authentic, revelatory	High social status value
Intimate, engaging, theatrical	Distant view, nontheatrical
Lower price (lower perceived value or good value?)	Expensive, but good value for money

Of course these descriptions are broad generalizations; for example, the Lyric Opera presents new works too and features some young, little-known artists.

Most COT board members and managers had estimated that 50 percent of COT's audience also attended the Lyric. They were surprised to hear that in actuality 89 percent of COT patrons attended the Lyric. COT board members and managers also viewed the COT audience as much younger than the Lyric audience. So they were surprised to hear that the audience survey showed that on average COT audience members were the same age as Lyric attenders. This information became centrally important in later planning for positioning statements and selecting highly targeted advertising media.

Opportunities

Members of the brainstorming session then focused on identifying COT's best opportunities for building its brand. Key factors centered around awareness of COT's quality and the enticing nature of its productions, the new venue, and high-potential target segments.

Participants agreed that COT must build awareness and a general *buzz* about its consistently high-quality, hip, engaging, theatrical productions of rarely seen operas by famous composers.

Next in importance was building on the excitement of the new venue. Board and staff members delighted in the great potential for attracting new patrons to the Harris Theater. Its location provides greatly increased convenience and stature for most potential patrons, as it is part of the city's new and highly publicized Millennium Park. The hall is larger than the Athenaeum but maintains the sense of intimacy that is so important to COT's identity. The Harris boasts great sight lines; fine acoustics; modern amenities, facilities, and comforts; and safety features. There is a surplus of indoor parking spaces adjacent to the venue's lower lobby, and public transportation is easily accessible.

The board and staff members identified several market segments that they considered viable opportunities for the 2003 season at the Athenaeum. The plan was to bring in as many new audience members as possible in 2003, especially subscribers, with the promise of offering them priority seating at the new venue in 2004. (Details of this plan were presented in Chapter Six.) Due to constraints in both financial and human resources, it was not possible for COT to target all the segments identified, so it was decided the primary focus would be on Lyric Opera audiences. The Lyric, with approximately 3,500 seats and eight to twelve performances of each of eight operas over its season, has a huge audience base. COT, with a 1,400 seat hall and only five performances of three operas each season, needed only to attract a small percentage of the Lyric's audience to be successful in audience growth. Although many Lyric attenders prefer the familiar, COT would be attractive to those among them who are interested in adventuresome programming and productions.

Other viable segments to target included audiences of the Chicago Symphony Orchestra, Music of the Baroque, Chicago Shakespeare, and other select theaters; the arts-aware public aged eighteen to thirty-five, a market segment that is important to nurture to create long-term sustainability for the organization; the general public over age thirty-six; suburbanites from areas that have a high percentage of cultural attenders; and various groups (candidates for group sales).

For the 2004 season in the new venue, additional segments were added to this list, including arts tourists; people who work near the Harris Theater; more groups, including continuing education groups, clubs, alumni groups, and businesses located near the venue; people celebrating special occasions; and students.

Implementation of the Brand Campaign

In conjunction with the COT staff, I further analyzed the rich material gleaned from the audience survey and the brainstorming session. Results were used to select strategies and tactics and were translated into copy for season brochures, postcards, the Web site, print and radio advertisements, and press releases.

Given available resources, it was decided that COT would continue to reach the general public through traditional means such as newspaper advertisements, radio ads on Chicago's classical music station, and advertisements screened at select "artsy" movie houses in the city and suburbs. Group sales efforts would be made by box office personnel during their available time. The policy of half-price tickets for students would be stated in all advertising material, but efforts to work with local universities in developing collaborations that would result in attendance at COT performances were not possible given current staffing levels.

In the 2003 season, for the first time, each advertisement and direct-mail piece was professionally designed, following the themes of the brand campaign and assuring design consistency. Images were selected for the promotional copy for each opera that reflect the quality and nature of the COT experience as a whole and the nature of each opera. E-mail messages to patrons were also designed to be consistent with messages in other communication media, even though they were done in-house and with readily available fonts.

Positioning statements were selected for emphasis with targeted segments. The wholly redesigned Web site, the season brochure, and various printed and radio advertisements featured words and phrases that highlight appealing aspects of the experience of attending opera at COT and reinforce its brand identity: *unique repertory, innovative, witty, intimate, theatrical, engaging,* and *stimulating.*

For Lyric Opera attenders, COT emphasized that it carries on the tradition of great opera in Chicago. COT ads in the Lyric program featured an excerpt from a column by Wynne Delacoma, music critic of the *Chicago Sun Times,* who succinctly and dynamically wrote: "Rabid opera fans grieve when Lyric's season is over, and no doubt they're beginning to feel the same about COT."

To appeal specifically to theater lovers and others who appreciate a visual, dynamic, interactive element in their performing arts experiences, COT used the phrases "Opera that's real theater!" and "Thrilling music; stunning theater." The latter became the slogan for use on letterheads, mugs, and the like.

Significant funds were earmarked for a full-page ad in the Lyric Opera program book throughout the Lyric's entire season and for sending brochures to mailing lists obtained from the marketing managers of eight area performing arts organizations whose audiences matched the profile of COT attenders, with a special focus on Lyric Opera attenders.

Two Years Later

COT's first season in the new Harris Theater ran March through May 2004, to significantly larger audiences than in the previous venue. In 2005, attendance growth slowed, as is often the case the second year in a new home, even though reviews remained consistently stellar. Due to exciting programming and intense marketing efforts, by midway through the 2006 season, subscription volume was up over 10 percent and total ticket revenue exceeded the budgeted amount by nearly $130,000, passing the $1 million mark for the first time.

COT has a clear niche of presenting consistently high-quality, hip, engaging theatrical productions of rarely seen operas by famous composers in an intimate state-of-the-art venue. So that Chicago Opera Theater can continue to expand its audiences and its role as a leader in Chicago culture, it must continue to deepen and refresh its brand identity.

INSTITUTIONAL MARKETING

A brand campaign is not a plan to be implemented with the next season's marketing materials; it is a long-term investment in the organization. Each individual event, program, communication strategy, and customer service encounter is a crucial element of the branding process. The brand is a symbol of the trust between the organization and its publics, and trust is something that must be developed and nurtured over time. A brand develops strength through consistency, yet because a brand must be relevant to its customers, aspects of the organization's brand identity must be regularly reviewed. Like the mission, brand identity has long-range implications, but it must be ascertained that the brand continually resonates with audiences in a dynamic environment replete with changing tastes and values.

Building Loyalty
Subscriptions and Beyond

A business is worth no more than the lifetime value of its customers.

—Philip Kotler

FOR DECADES, SUCCESSFUL AUDIENCE DEVELOPMENT activities have focused on intensive subscription campaigns at a majority of performing arts organizations. The full-season subscriber is the ideal ticket buyer, guaranteeing an audience and an expected revenue source. However, since the mid-1990s, increasingly more audience segments find subscribing unattractive. Not only are many arts marketers less successful at attracting new subscribers, but each year fewer current subscribers are likely to renew. Furthermore, some artistic directors and arts managers have come to realize the limitations that having a heavily subscribed audience places on them.

In this chapter I present the pros and cons of subscriptions from both the organization's and the customer's perspectives, suggest a new mind-set for the arts marketer to adopt concerning the meaning of a valuable customer, and recommend ways to build the subscriber base. I also offer alternatives to full-season subscriptions as ways to build loyalty among current and potential audiences.

SUBSCRIPTIONS

In the 1960s, the introduction of public relations expert Danny New-man's *dynamic subscription promotion* (DSP) campaign launched an audience development boom in the arts that lasted nearly thirty years. Historically, claims Newman, hundreds of stage companies closed quickly because their economies were based on the hope of selling most of their capacity to the general public through single ticket sales. Consistently strong single ticket sales could only happen if all the shows produced were commercial hits—obviously an impossibility for any theater producer and especially so for a nonprofit organization with a mission of artistic exploration.

In the 1960s and 1970s, backed by the Ford Foundation and its creation, the Theatre Communications Group, Mr. Newman helped more than four hundred performing arts organizations thrive by rooting them in the subscription concept—selling tickets not to one show but to a full season of performances—and by teaching managers how to attract subscribers in significant numbers. The momentum gained by early successes with subscription campaigns encouraged the inception of numerous new professional theaters, dance companies, symphonies, and opera companies, and before long subscription drives became the backbone of most every performing arts audience development campaign. The New York City Ballet entered its first subscription drive in 1966 and in its first season, attracted 28,000 subscribers. Largely thanks to subscription promotions, the Alabama Shakespeare Festival witnessed growth in attendance from 3,000 in 1972 to more than 300,000 in 1989. In the United States many organizations large and small rely on subscribers to guarantee an ongoing audience for their programs, and focus a huge percentage of their marketing efforts and resources on building and retaining subscriptions.

The Rationale for Subscriptions

In his popular book *Subscribe Now!* Danny Newman presents several compelling explanations for the value of a strong subscriber base.[1]

SINGLE TICKET BUYER ATTITUDES AND BEHAVIOR Single ticket buyers typically attend only the biggest hits of the season. For the more esoteric shows with limited appeal, for productions without big-name performers, and during bad weather, reliance on single ticket buyers often means playing to halls with too many empty seats. Not only does this hurt the organization financially and morally, but it deprives the organization of the opportunity to inspire and educate. Through repeated exposure to a variety of offerings, people develop a rising threshold of repertoire acceptance, says Newman.

ARTISTIC BENEFITS A strong subscriber base gives artistic directors more latitude to experiment than they have when dependent on single ticket buyers. With a subscription package, people are buying tickets for some programs they would not have attended otherwise, guaranteeing an audience for unfamiliar or unpopular repertoire. Even if there are one or two programs in a season that the subscriber does not like, typically he or she takes it in good spirit and renews the following season.

ECONOMIC BENEFITS Subscribers offer arts organizations significant economic benefits. Subscribers provide the organization with guaranteed revenue, which is often paid many months in advance of the season. This helps the organization to maintain a cash flow during the off-season, to reduce interest expense on loans, or to earn interest through short-term investments.

Overall, subscribers require much lower marketing expenditures than single ticket buyers do. The Theatre Communications Group (TCG), in its annual survey of its member theaters, reported in 2005 that over the previous several years, single ticket marketing expense as a percentage of single ticket income averaged 22 percent, whereas subscription marketing expense to subscription income has averaged 14 percent.[2]

These numbers do not tell the whole story. The marketing costs for attracting a new subscriber may be very high—in some cases they total as much as 50 to 100 percent of the first year's subscription revenue. However, one must consider the *lifetime value* of the subscriber. The cost of renewing subscribers is minimal, so over time those patrons who continue to renew provide the organization with significant earned revenue garnered at relatively low cost. Also, many subscribers bring in other new subscribers and single ticket buyers from among family and friends.

Furthermore, subscribers, motivated by their sense of commitment to the organization, become prime resources for contributions. Respondents to the San Francisco audience survey, discussed at length in Chapter Seven, made contributions as shown in Table 10.1.

INFLUENCE OF CRITICS   For organizations without a strong subscriber base, especially smaller, grassroots companies without big-name productions or star performers, critical acclaim can be a matter of life and death. Large subscription audiences greatly reduce the power of the critics to close a play with bad reviews. When an organization enjoys a large subscriber base, the real power belongs to the subscribers, who spread the word about the shows they like and who cast their vote at renewal time each year on the basis of their reaction to the entire season.

Limitations of Subscriptions from the Organization's Perspective

Despite their many benefits to the organizations, subscriptions present some significant limitations. Although subscribers give the organization some freedom to experiment, regular attenders come to expect certain styles and balk when the artistic director goes too far afield. One of the major factors contributing to people's willingness to subscribe is the avoidance of risk. Subscribers expect the work to fall within a certain stylistic range; they don't want their avant-garde theater to perform traditional productions of the classics and vice versa. The thought that "I might not enjoy this" undermines the per-

---

TABLE 10.1.   *Percentages of Attenders Donating to Four San Francisco Organizations.*

	Subscribers	Single Ticket Buyers
San Francisco Symphony	67%	29%
American Conservatory Theater	50	14
San Francisco Ballet	62	40
San Francisco Opera	88	21

ceived value of a subscription. As a result, a subscription program tends to work best with "safe" repertoire—repertoire that is within the range of people's expectations.

Orchestras in particular, with their high fixed costs, are constrained by a financial model that is largely dependent on subscription sales. Therefore they have little room to experiment—they have no R&D capacity like other industries—and even less room to fail. "Until this equation fundamentally changes," says consultant Alan Brown, "subscription marketing will continue to be the sweet honey that sustains orchestras and a slow-acting poison that impedes their long-term sustainability."[3]

In the performing arts, demand differs by core product offering, so it is extremely helpful to be able to set different capacities for different productions. Financially, it doesn't make sense to offer the same number of performances of every concert or play when the marketing director knows that some productions will be a hard sell and others could sell out more performances. Also, both the audience and the performers have a far better experience when the hall is full than when it is half empty. The structure of a subscription-based season, however, makes variations in the quantity of performances of each production difficult to arrange. Furthermore, differing demand suggests that marketers can charge more for some productions and should charge less for others. However, in most organizations with a large subscriber base, the ticket price for an esoteric two-person play is the same as for a popular musical.

Critics do not appear to have either the positive or the negative effect that Newman claims they do. In the San Francisco study, *review by the media* was rarely cited as an influence for or against attendance; it was mentioned by only 2 percent of respondents from the symphony, opera, and ballet audiences. This low level of influence by critics is a function of the fact that these organizations have relatively short runs of each production so that readers of the reviews have little time to plan to attend a critically acclaimed program. At the American Conservatory Theater, where each play runs for several weeks, short-term single ticket buyers (one to two years of attending performances at A.C.T.) were the most highly influenced by the media (36.4%), whereas 9 percent of attendees of five years or more claimed to be influenced by reviews. This indicates that people familiar with

A.C.T. over time are less dependent on "expert" opinions for attendance decisions. Word-of-mouth recommendations from acquaintances are far more influential than critics are.

At a session titled "Are Subscriptions the Past, Present or Future of Opera?" directors attending the 2004 Opera Europa conference summarized the varying attitudes of European performing arts managers. Some companies still rely heavily on subscriptions; some, like Théâtre Royal de la Monnaie in Brussels, believe that having more than 50 percent of the house subscribed is "dangerous," whereas others have experimented with changing or eliminating subscriptions in order to avoid bringing in the same old audiences time and again. At twenty-three opera companies surveyed at the conference, subscription tickets as a percentage of total tickets sold ranged from 3 percent to 93 percent.

Hanover Opera lost 5,000 people—half its annual audience—when it boldly dropped subscriptions. "But," said artistic director Oliver Kretschmer, "we continued to do work we believed in and began to make more contact with the audiences, and after two years our audiences started to change. The old types never came back but new ones started coming in." Hanover's dramatic policy change was driven by its managers' opinion that, according to Kretschmer, "the subscription system is not the system of our time. We are always sold out now, but younger people do not necessarily want to subscribe. The old idea of eight or nine operas is dying." Andreas Homoki of Berlin's Komische Oper said that the advantage of having no subscription system is that the audiences are less conservative and dull. However, he added, the risk is that "you can have a perfectly good production that ends up with only 300 people in the audience." Yet, some companies prioritize the high level of income they can consistently depend on from subscriptions. Says Ulrike Hessler, director of public relations and development at the Bavarian State Opera, "Subscribers are not our favorite audiences; they like 'easy art.' But they bring in money."[4]

Subscriptions from the Audience Perspective

People are willing to pay well in advance, to risk some artistic exploration, and to eliminate the role of the critic and other opinion leaders from their ticket purchase decision. But these factors, which constitute Newman's rationale for subscriptions, are actually costs from the customer perspective—costs people are willing to pay as long as they receive benefits of value to them.

Subscribers believe in an organization and its leaders and trust that most of the time they will want to experience what the organization offers on its stage. Beyond this, in survey after survey, subscribers report that their reasons for subscribing are primarily to guarantee their seats—the same preferred seats—for every show and secondarily to make sure they see all the shows in the season (or in the package, for companies with a wide range of offerings). Fortunately for performing arts organizations, many people value these benefits and continue to subscribe, and many organizations are successful at continuing to attract new subscribers. Many organizations offer other subscriber benefits, but most often these are additional perks, not reasons to subscribe.

Yet it is more challenging than ever for arts marketers to persuade people to renew and to attract new subscribers. In the San Francisco audience survey, 50 percent of former subscribers said that their primary reason for no longer subscribing was that they preferred to select specific programs to attend. For them, this preference has come to take precedence over guaranteed seats. And as more people lapse their subscriptions and more seats become available, guaranteeing one's seats in advance becomes less urgent. This is an advantage for ticket buyers even though it is a worry for marketing managers.

People who subscribe report that they *like* to plan in advance. But the reduction in frequency of attendance is due to the fact that many people have become more spontaneous in their lifestyles and have difficulty scheduling in advance, the reason given by about 37 percent of both subscribers and single ticket buyers for reduced frequency.

A significant percentage of both subscribers and single ticket buyers report they are attending less frequently because of their dissatisfaction with the programs offered. Most productions appeal differently to different audience segments. A production may have great appeal for certain segments, but other segments will find it not to their taste and will not want to spend their time and money on it. Or people may have seen a production already and have no interest in seeing it again. This latter issue creates problems for artistic directors in planning a season of performances; for each person in the audience who has seen *Swan Lake* many times, there are many new or potential audience members who have never seen it. In our modern society, people have become accustomed to products designed to appeal to micro-segments, and are less tolerant of products and services that do not meet their needs and interests.

Many managers fear that their tickets prices are keeping people away, and in an effort to lure more subscribers, theaters surveyed by TCG offered 20 percent greater subscription discounts in 2003 than in 1999. Despite these special price offers, these theaters' average sub-scription renewal rate dropped 8 percent over the five-year period from 1999 through 2003.[5] Clearly, this discounting strategy has not been effective. In the San Francisco study, we found that discounts are low on the list of reasons why people subscribe; price was the fourth rea-son in importance for attending less frequently. Together, those un-willing and those unable to pay current ticket prices made up only 16 percent of subscriber respondents and 20 percent of single ticket buyer respondents. As further evidence of the relative unimportance of ticket price to subscribers, many organizations have eliminated their sub-scriber discounts without affecting their renewal numbers. People often like to get a bargain, but it can take the form of special privi-leges or treatment rather than ticket price discounts.

Detailed responses by subscribers and single ticket buyers for each of the four organizations whose audiences we surveyed in San Fran-cisco are found in Table 10.2.

Changing Values and Behavior

Subscriptions continued to increase in the industry as a whole until the early 1990s, at which time the first signs of a dramatic shift in audience behavior and attitudes appeared. This shift is a factor of lifestyle changes, of ever-increasing competition for leisure time ac-tivities, of the relationship marketing and strong customer service per-spective that has come to permeate much of the rest of society, and of people's growing desire to make purchases far more spontaneously than in the past.

Furthermore, the recession that began in 2000 and the tragic events of September 11, 2001, served as catalysts for people to act on their growing reluctance to purchase subscriptions or even single tick-ets as far in advance as they often did in the past. "More people are

TABLE 10.2.   *Why Attenders at Four San Francisco Organizations Are Attending Fewer Performances or Have Stopped Subscribing.*

Reason	Symphony		Theater		Opera		Ballet	
	Sub*	S.T.*	Sub.	S.T.	Sub.	S.T.	Sub.	S.T.
Prefer to select own programs to attend rather than a series	15%	65%	16%	53%	17%	42%	18%	41%
Difficulty scheduling in advance	31	42	60	37	25	35	32	36
Unwilling to pay ticket prices	21	21	8	23	22	29	17	19
Dissatisfaction with programs offered	12	23	36	37	22	12	17	19
Unable to pay ticket prices	21	16	4	16	17	20	20	15
Less recreational time	17	17	28	27	11	20	19	17
Increased involvement with other arts orgs.	15	16	20	28	8	13	11	15
Inadequate value for the money	6	15	8	14	17	22	11	10
Available seats too expensive	6	15	4	16	8	18	7	13
Preferred seats unavailable	2	12	16	9	3	13	6	10
Preferred dates sold out	4	12	8	4	8	12	—	5
Loss of interest in this type of performance	4	10	8	8	6	3	1	4
Presence of small children in household	2	9	8	11	11	6	8	8

(continued on next page)

TABLE 10.2.   *Why Attenders at Four San Francisco Organizations Are Attending Fewer Performances or Have Stopped Subscribing.*

	Symphony		Theater		Opera		Ballet	
Reason	*Sub*	*S.T.*	*Sub.*	*S.T.*	*Sub.*	*S.T.*	*Sub.*	*S.T.*
Inconvenient location of performances	8	6	8	4	6	5	35**	33**
Age/illness	15	2	—	1	—	2	—	1
Travel time/hassle	8	3	—	4	3	5	1	2
Other	8	7	4	8	28	12	13	10

Note: Sub. = subscriber; S.T. = single ticket buyer.

**While the War Memorial Opera House, the Ballet's traditional home, was being renovated, the Ballet performed temporarily in other locations.

attending than ever before, but they're buying in different ways," said Jack McAuliffe, former chief operating officer of the American Symphony Orchestra League. Increasingly, patrons are putting off ticket buying until the last minute. "Everyone is waiting longer to buy tickets than five years ago," said Ed Cambron, the Philadelphia Orchestra's vice president of marketing, in 2004. "It used to be, you had a window that started six weeks out. Now, that's shrunk to three or four weeks, and you see a lot of sales in the week before the concert occurs."[6]

A shift from early subscription purchases to later and later single ticket purchases creates several problems for performing arts groups. Revenue comes in later, single ticket sales require significantly more marketing expenses and a different tactical focus, and financial planning and cash flow projections are more difficult.

In looking at the results of the John S. and James L. Knight Foundation's Classical Music Consumer Segmentation Study in 2001, the largest discipline-specific arts-consumer study ever undertaken in the United States, with nearly 25,000 completed surveys and interviews, researchers became acutely aware of changing attitudes toward subscribing, especially among younger audiences. Among ticket buyers in the eighteen to thirty-four age cohort, 15 percent are highly inclined to subscribe, compared to 56 percent of those aged seventy-five and older. About half of performing arts subscribers are now sixty-five years old or older. Among single ticket buyers, 36 percent are former subscribers who have opted out of subscription packages but who remain in the audience. A survey of 4,421 audience members of the Chicago Symphony Orchestra (CSO) during the 1996–1997 season showed that 61 percent of CSO subscribers were aged fifty-five or older, and 63 percent of single ticket buyers were aged fifty-five or younger.[7]

Furthermore, the traditionally accepted concept that people who enjoy attending an organization can gradually be encouraged to subscribe has not generally proved to hold true. For example, the CSO study showed that 47 percent of single ticket buyers had been attending for eight years or more; another 21 percent had been attending for two to seven years.

Clearly, says consultant Alan Brown, "subscription marketing is becoming an increasingly dysfunctional marketing paradigm."[8]

The change in buying patterns is primarily a generational shift, part of a seismic shift in how people spend their leisure time and dollars. Many in the arts express concern that younger people are not interested in arts offerings and will not attend, but in fact members of the younger generation eagerly attend when marketers make available offers that match their lifestyles.

These changing attitudes and behaviors do not mean that performing arts organizations should abandon their subscription marketing programs. What they do mean is that arts marketers should develop strategies for retaining the people who do subscribe and for attracting those who are likely to subscribe while they also devote significant human and financial resources to attract those who are interested in attending on a less frequent and more spontaneous basis. Arts marketers still tend to focus the majority of their messages and benefits on subscribers, thereby cutting themselves off from attracting other potential attenders. In the rest of this chapter, I will discuss strategies for attracting and retaining subscribers and alternative package buyers. In the next chapter I will address approaches for building sales and loyalty among single ticket buyers.

Attracting Subscribers

The marketing director must carefully consider which benefits prospective subscribers will value and prioritize aspects of the offer around these benefits. For example, given current customer attitudes and behavior at most organizations, it makes sense to make an emotional appeal on the front cover of the season brochure and offer subscriber discounts, if any, in the back of the brochure near the order form. Tactical benefits like discounts and complimentary ticket exchange privileges are typically not reasons for people to subscribe. These benefits do, however, make the offer more attractive once people have the *desire* to see a series of performances. Of course each marketer must get to know his own audience and prioritize the benefits and their placement in the brochure accordingly. Writers' Theatre in Glencoe, Illinois, is one arts organization that has designed a new benefit to appeal to its many patrons who cannot or prefer not to attend all the shows in the season.

Trade-A-Show Benefit at Writers' Theatre

Managers at Writers' Theatre in Glencoe, Illinois, have been listening to their audience. For the 2006–2007 season, in addition to traditional subscriber benefits such as guaranteed seats and flexible ticket exchanges, they are offering a new Trade-A-Show benefit. Typically, arts organizations allow their subscribers to exchange tickets to one performance for tickets to another performance of the same production. Writers' Theatre's Trade-A-Show benefit allows patrons to trade their subscription tickets to one show for tickets to a different show one time during the season. This allows them to do such things as skip one show entirely and then take family or friends with them to another show. This offer accommodates people who may dislike a certain playwright or theme as well as the snowbirds, people who spend the winter in a warmer climate.

In response to some people's concern that they may not like some of the shows in a series, the Mark Taper Forum, part of the Center Theatre Group in Los Angeles, offers new subscribers this money-back guarantee: "It's simple. Just attend your first performance. If you're not satisfied with your subscription, we'll refund your money for the balance of the season." Says Director of Marketing and Communications Jim Royce, "It makes a lot of people feel much more comfortable about buying subscriptions. And it works. We have had fewer than 500 out of 67,000 cancel." Since the low year of 1996, subscriptions at the Mark Taper Forum have grown by about 20 percent and are now expected to remain stable. Royce attributes his organization's success in selling and retaining subscriptions to a focus on building long-term relationships with single ticket buyers, reengaging former subscribers, upgrading donors, gaining referrals from current subscribers, and providing patrons with superior service.[9]

DESIGNING THE OFFER The target market for each offer should be clearly identified so that the right messages and language are used to attract the audience. Like every marketing communication, the brochure must speak to the customers it is attempting to attract. The marketing manager may choose to develop more than one season brochure with different positioning in each. For budgetary reasons, when this strategy is employed, many companies choose to change only the cover. One dance company's brochure targeting young women twenty to forty years of age displays photos of attractive male dancers; another brochure targeting men celebrates the athleticism of the dancers.

Designing a subscription offering is a relatively straightforward task for an organization that offers only a few productions a year. Organizations such as large orchestras, which may offer dozens of different concerts in a single season, need to divide their season into different packages of balanced offerings, creating combinations of concerts that will appeal to the various subscriber segments. This is a complex task that is best accomplished if the marketer has much experience and detailed records of past sales and ticket exchanges. As many subscribers have shown a distinct preference for shorter series in recent years, many performing arts organizations have been modifying their offers to accommodate these patrons.

SETTING GOALS AND STRUCTURING THE CAMPAIGN For each subscription campaign, the marketing director should set specific goals for the numbers of new subscribers, renewing subscribers, and reattracting lapsed subscribers. Objectives should be set realistically so that each campaign's goals are attainable. The target increase may be a small increment, or there may be a major drive to substantially increase the number of subscribers, based on the appeal of an upcoming award-winning play, a new venue, a star performer, or other attraction that may provide extra incentive for new subscribers. When an organization enjoys a large subscriber increase in one year, it rarely can sustain that level of growth in succeeding years. Rather, the organization should focus on renewing as many of the first-year subscribers as possible. If the organization has lost a significant percentage of subscribers recently, it should investigate the reasons and focus on efforts to bring them back.

The campaign should be formulated in detail, considering all opportunities for audience growth and with strategies for targeting each group, from personal selling to mass media. Marketing managers should study the effectiveness of various tactics used in the past when deciding how much effort and budget to commit to each. For example, when an arts organization buys mailing lists from a commercial source or trades lists with other organizations, the manager should code the mailings with the source of each contact so that the effectiveness of each source can be measured.

OFFERING EXTENDED PAYMENT PLANS The actual cost of a subscription series is not only the price of the tickets but the timing of payment. Traditionally, subscribers are expected to make payment in one lump sum when they place their order, typically in the spring before the fall performance season begins. In the San Francisco audience survey, we tested the premise that some single ticket buyers would purchase a subscription series if they had the option to pay for their subscription over a period of several months. The encouraging result was that 23 percent of single ticket buyers for the symphony, ballet, and theater reported that they were very or extremely likely to purchase a subscription if an extended payment plan were offered. These people represented a broad range of demographic characteristics in terms of age, income, length of attendance, and marital status.

To administer this option the organization can charge a modest service fee—$10 should be more than adequate—and a credit card number for each participant should be kept on file with the understanding that this account will be charged monthly over a period of time, which can range from three to six months or even longer, depending on how expensive the organization's ticket prices are.

The arts managers I have spoken with who offer extended payment plans report they have never had anyone fail to pay, even when payments are due well after the season has begun. It is highly worthwhile to offer extended payments even if an occasional patron defaults.

Renewals and Retention

Renewal of past subscribers is the first step in the annual subscription campaign, and the organization should do everything possible to make sure current subscribers renew. The cost of getting a subscriber to renew is a fraction of the cost of recruiting a new one. Past attenders are far more likely to respond to marketing offers than are people who have never attended; furthermore it is much easier to sell a fifth ticket to people who have already purchased four than to sell someone his or her first ticket. When people subscribe to guarantee seeing a star performer or other similar enticement, they are less likely to renew the following year if that season is less exciting. Also, the more gimmicks that are used to lure new subscribers, such as deep discounts, the less likely those subscribers will be to renew, as they may have been coming for the "wrong" reasons. Historically, 50 percent of subscribers renew after the first year, 80 percent after the second year, and 90 percent thereafter. However, in recent years these averages have dropped somewhat as subscriptions are losing popularity. So the organization must work diligently to compensate for attrition before it even begins to increase the subscriber base.

RENEWING FIRST-YEAR SUBSCRIBERS Because it is not uncommon for 50 percent of first-year subscribers to fail to renew their subscriptions, every effort should be made to increase their satisfaction and involvement levels. Increasing first-year renewals by even 10 percent can amount to significant subscriber growth over time. From the time people first subscribe, the organization should welcome them into the subscriber "family" and provide them with in-depth information about the organization, its policies, its artists, and its programs.

Newsletters and other special mailings should be sent on a regular basis. New subscribers should also receive at least one customer-service phone call during the season asking them to evaluate various aspects of their experience and to express any concerns or suggestions they may have. Success with this technique requires that the callers be fully informed about the organization and capable of carrying on a meaningful conversation with the subscriber; they cannot just read a script. The organization should follow up on all customer requests. If seat locations cannot be improved as requested, the organization might offer two complimentary guest tickets to a performance to deflect disappointment. If a patron has missed one or more productions, the organization might offer extra tickets to an upcoming production.

At renewal time all first-year subscribers should receive a personal letter inviting them to renew. Sometimes the renewal effort requires several contacts by mail or phone. Some people will actually express appreciation for being reminded. Others do not want to renew, however, and telemarketers should ask these people their reasons for lapsing, try to find an alternative offer with which to satisfy each person, and then put that household on the "do not call for subscription" list, at least for that season.

RENEWING LONG-TERM SUBSCRIBERS If fewer than 50 or 60 percent of long-term subscribers are renewing, the organization may be in serious trouble. In such cases the organization must carefully determine the reasons for customer dissatisfaction and make dramatic efforts to improve its products or services.

Even though most subscribers renew automatically, their commitment and loyalty should not be taken for granted. The organization can plan anniversary events for subscribers after five years, ten years, and twenty years or more of subscribing. Once a year, subscribers might be invited to enjoy a complimentary dessert with the artists after a performance. On occasion they might be invited for backstage tours or preseason previews, and they can be offered an occasional souvenir. The point is that the organization should show subscribers how special and important they are.

HANDLING LAPSED SUBSCRIBERS Some people who are unfamiliar with an organization and its offerings may try it out for a season and then find it is not for them. Some people are lured to sub-scribe by various benefits and premiums or by a special event or per-former, factors that apply for one season only. These are common explanations for the high attrition rate among first-year subscribers. Among long-standing subscribers who do not renew, most report their reason for lapsing is their dissatisfaction with the programming. Others have schedule conflicts and can no longer conveniently plan in advance.

Some of these factors are in the control of the arts marketer; some are not. The organization should survey all lapsed subscribers by mail or phone to determine their reasons for dropping their subscription. Some people can be encouraged to resubscribe if the organization can remedy their concerns; many others will purchase tickets on a show-by-show basis. It is important for the marketing department to con-tinue to treat lapsed subscribers as valued patrons, even if they purchase only occasional single tickets.

LOYALTY

People are as loyal as *they* think they are. People who have attended one of your performances each year for the past several years may see themselves as loyal attenders. The fact that they do not subscribe should not be seen as a failure; their annual ticket purchase should be viewed as a success. Of course the organization rightfully values dif-ferent levels of loyalty and involvement differently. But subscription is just one type of customer relationship, and it is clear that arts or-ganizations need to build value around other kinds of marketing relationships as well, particularly those that reward loyalty without advance commitment.[10]

Consider that among the respondents to the San Francisco sur-vey, 82 percent of single ticket buyers have been attending for five years or more; among single ticket buyers at the Chicago Symphony Orchestra in the 1996–1997 season, 56 percent had been attending five years or more. Even though these people have not subscribed, they are clearly loyal attenders.

Also consider that loyalty is a two-way street, so patrons deserve loyalty from the organization as well. A couple may be loyal sub-scribers for ten or fifteen years, drop their subscriptions for one or

two years, then resubscribe. When they renew after a hiatus, sometimes the organization will treat them like first-year subscribers, with
the lowest subscriber seating priority. Rather, they should be wel-
comed back with seats as close to their former location as possible.

Some organizations believe that they win customer loyalty by offering a loyalty award program. Says Philip Kotler, "A loyalty program
may be a good feature as part of a customer relationship management
program, but many loyalty schemes do not create loyalty. They appeal
to the customer's rational side of accumulating something free but do
not necessarily create an emotional bond. . . . Some programs are dis-
loyalty programs, as when an airline says the points will be lost unless
the customer flies within two months."[11]

When creating loyalty benefits, consider how to attract those who
may require several seasons to accrue the status of loyal attender, not
just those who accrue the benefits in one season.

LINCOLN CENTER THEATER: BUILDING ATTENDANCE AND LOYALTY WITHOUT SUBSCRIPTIONS

Since it was established in 1985, Lincoln Center Theater (LCT) has
made audience development a cornerstone of its mission. The organization observes founder John D. Rockefeller III's mandate that "the
arts are not for the privileged few, but for the many." LCT began by
offering a traditional subscription, for the same reason that so many
not-for-profit theaters do: subscription was for many decades a tried-
and-true means to build audiences and gain financial security from
up-front ticket income. About 5,000 charter subscribers joined, filling most of the available seats for a modest two-play season.

However, it soon became apparent that it was not enough for
LCT simply to fill seats. From an administrative point of view, the
subscription system was too constricting, as management did not
want to close a popular play simply because the next subscription offering was scheduled to begin. Management also did not want to
limit the theater to the number of plays planned for a subscription
schedule. Management was unhappy with the subscribers too. Even
though the subscribers were avid theatergoers, they were not always
the best audience for some LCT plays because they did not relate
to the subject matter of some plays. The subscription audience was

extremely homogeneous—nearly all white, upper-middle-class, and fifty-five-years old or older. Although this is a common demographic profile for a subscription audience, it was a poor match for LCT's mission and eclectic mix of plays and musicals, which were new and old, traditional and avant-garde. Subscribers' reactions were good for some shows, indifferent for others, and hostile to the rest, which was often disappointing to the artists working on a play.

In 1987, Lincoln Center Theater discontinued its traditional subscription series and pioneered membership offers. There were some angry subscribers from the first two seasons who hated losing "their" seats, but most subscribers converted to member status without incident.

Because members select which shows to see, audience response at individual performances is noticeably more positive than it was when audiences had many subscribers who were attending simply because they had tickets as part of a series, not because they had a particular interest in a production. Because members do not buy tickets to every production, LCT felt it could safely enroll many more members than it could subscribers. Nevertheless, at various times in the program's history, LCT has closed membership so it could be sure to accommodate the members who do want to attend. When a production is highly popular, its run is extended to accommodate more people, something that cannot be done with a subscription series. As of 2005, the membership fee was $40, and members paid $40 per show for tickets. Members of the general public are eligible to purchase tickets after the members' priority ordering period, and they pay $70 to $80 a ticket for plays and $65 to $95 for musicals. Students aged eighteen to thirty-five are given free memberships and pay only $20 per show. With the large number of memberships and the ability to extend the run of popular shows, the membership plan is highly viable financially for the organization.

At first, the people who joined as members were the same people who had subscribed, so LCT solicited theatergoers who were younger, less affluent, or people of color. Based on results of focus groups conducted with people in these target groups, LCT developed appealing brochures and benefits. Because price was a major barrier, the theater devised an *introductory member* promotion in which the first year's fee was waived for qualifying prospects, with the hope that their experience would be so positive that they would become fee-paying regular members in the future. The offer was promoted in newspapers, radio spots, and cable television with high concentrations of readers and listeners in the target groups, and in direct mail to demographically sorted lists. Then word-of-mouth spread these affordable ticket offers to increasingly wide networks of people; more than 73 percent of introductory members reported learning about the program through a friend or relative. The campaign achieved its goals very quickly, enrolling 10,000 introductory members in just six months and was highly successful at attracting the desired audience. Forty-four percent of introductory members were African American, compared to only 3 percent of the regular members. Almost two-thirds of introductory members were aged twenty-five to forty-four, whereas two-thirds of regular members were forty-five years of age or older. And introductory members had much lower household incomes than regular members: only half as many had annual household incomes over $50,000. More than 28 percent of the introductory members renewed as fee-paying members, a percentage the theater was happy to see given the price barrier faced by many in this market. Because the program could not accept an unlimited number of members, new introductory member enrollment was suspended the following year.

Other strategies have been undertaken to attract nontraditional theatergoers to LCT plays, especially production-specific audience outreach. For example, through group sales and ads in community newspapers, the theater drew people from New York's Caribbean American and African American communities to see Mustapha Matura's *Playboy of the West Indies*. The theater sold over 9,000 tickets for that play to people of color—about one-third of the total audiences who saw the play.[13]

Findings from focus groups conducted among all the member categories clearly indicate that members like the flexibility of the membership structure and the control that it gives them in choosing what to see and when, and they prefer it to regular subscription programs. The membership fee is considered reasonable and is not generally kept in mind or mentally added on to the ticket price. Quite a few members think the low ticket price encourages them to take risks and to see many plays that they might not otherwise choose to see. Whether or not they like every play they see, the fact that it was their *choice* and not determined for them as part of a subscription package leaves them with a better feeling about the experience. LCT so strongly positions its membership program against the disadvantages of subscriptions that its membership materials say "Unsubscribe Now!"

ALTERNATIVES TO SUBSCRIPTIONS

A highly significant and growing segment of the arts-going public are unlikely ever to become full-season subscribers. Yet arts organizations can offer many alternatives to full-season subscriptions that build some level of frequency and commitment—offers that are effective when they are designed to meet the specific needs and interests of their target markets. Organizations may choose to offer one or several of these alternatives, according to opportunities identified in the marketplace.

But arts marketers must be careful *not* to build a portfolio of multiple offers to see what might be attractive to their customers. Too many offers can be confusing to people who do not take the time to understand each and compare the differences. Most important, marketing offers should be based in customer research and should be highly targeted to the segments for which they are intended.

Offering more variety in anticipation of potential yet uncertain demand, say Pine and Gilmore in their book *The Experience Economy*, "often represents a last-ditch attempt to preserve the Mass Production mindset in the face of rapidly fragmenting markets." *Variety* means producing and distributing product choices in the hope that customers will come along and buy them. *Customization,* conversely, means producing in response to a particular customer's desires. Pine and Gilmore suggest turning the old supply chain into a *demand chain*.[12] This means listening to customers to learn what might be appealing to them, rather than creating multiple new offers to which marketers think customers will be drawn.

Some of the alternatives to season subscriptions available to marketers are miniseries, flex plans, memberships, and group sales. Although more and more organizations are adopting these alternatives, most often they are offered—and offered for renewal—only after the full subscription campaign has run its full course. This is done in order to give the organization time to try to up-sell small package buyers to larger subscriptions and to avoid tempting full subscribers to switch to a reduced commitment.

The best way to make sure current full-season subscribers renew without being tempted by smaller packages is to send a renewal letter out well before the brochure is mailed—or even printed. Most subscribers will gladly renew in response to a letter that includes information about the upcoming season. Some may require a second or third reminder by letter or phone, but the great majority of subscribers can be renewed by most organizations before the season brochure goes out. Also, for most organizations it benefits both the organization and the patrons to fully value the preferences of all ticket buyers and to invite smaller package buyers to renew at their existing level, not expecting that they will move up to a larger package (although the opportunity and accompanying benefits should certainly be offered).

Miniseries

Miniseries are small packages of performances—often three to five programs—for those who are unable or unwilling to attend a full subscription series. At many organizations they can be designed around specific programming, such as full-length story ballets, modern repertoire, music of the Romantic period, and so on. This serves to attract potential patrons with specific interests and eases the decision process for people who may be attempting to select from a long list of programs. Additionally, miniseries can be packaged around the lifestyle characteristics of certain consumer segments. The Chicago Symphony's Afterwork Masterworks series consists of ninety-minute programs, without an intermission, that start and end early to appeal to people coming directly from work. Some theaters in cold climates offer a snowbird series of fall and spring programs to accommodate people who head to warm climates for the winter. Some arts organizations also allow patrons to create "choose-your-own" series.

Flex Plans

Flex plans are designed to appeal to people who want to select exactly which programs to attend and also plan their attendance at their own convenience. A patron who purchases, say, four flex ticket vouchers may use them for four different shows or all at one time. Flex plan buyers order their tickets whenever convenient, with the understanding that they will get the best available seats at the time of their call. Some organizations allocate some seats for flex plan buyers for each performance, once all subscribers have been seated. With a flex plan, patrons retain certain subscriber benefits, and the organization enjoys a far higher level of frequency and loyalty than with single ticket buyers. The organization also has a viable opportunity with this segment to sell additional tickets and gift certificates.

Some arts marketers report that a number of their flex plan buyers are unhappy with this program because they reach the end of the season with ticket vouchers remaining. The marketing manager should do everything possible to satisfy these customers. Patrons can be sent a midseason e-mail or postcard reminder notice about their remaining flex tickets. The vouchers' expiration date can be extended to the following season and these patrons can be offered alternatives to flex plans for the upcoming season, alternatives that better meet their lifestyles.

Membership Plans

A membership plan is an even more flexible option than the flex plan. Rather than committing to a certain number of seats for the season, members pay an annual fee that makes them eligible for a meaningful discount on tickets to individual performances of their choice and gives them the opportunity to purchase tickets in advance of the general public.

The membership concept gives people a sense of belonging and provides them with a range of benefits, without requiring commitment to specific programming or frequency of attendance.

As we saw earlier in this chapter, the Lincoln Center Theatre abandoned subscriptions altogether in favor of their membership program. Some organizations effectively offer both subscriptions and membership plans. TheatreWorks in Palo Alto, California, offers a membership plan each year, after the subscription campaign has ended, to people who have rejected the subscription offer and to special target groups, namely young couples, people of color, and low-income groups. The membership program has been successful at reaching the desired audience; approximately one-third of members are Asian Americans, and many others are part of other target groups. Regular ticket prices in 2005 ranged from $28 (for weekday preview performances of plays) to $54 (weekend performances of musicals), but members pay $15 for plays and $25 for musicals; prices for youths eighteen and under are $10 and $15. The annual membership fee of $30 is more than paid back to members by the time they attend their second show each season. On average, members attend four performances per season. Each year, about 40 percent of members renew, and some of those who do not renew become subscribers. Most important, the membership offer does not erode the subscriber base at all. Subscribers like to plan in advance, they like to guarantee "their" seats, and they do not value the lower ticket prices enough to give up their subscriber benefits.

Group Sales

Group sales provide arts organizations with the opportunity to target specific audience segments in significant numbers for individual productions. Groups may attend for social, fundraising, or educational purposes; many organizations, corporations, and schools center activities around a performing arts event. Some special interest groups have a natural affinity for the subject of a play, with a key performer, with a composer's nationality, and so on, and are ideal target markets for group promotions. Many people who are unaccustomed to attending the performing arts find the experience comfortable and enjoyable when they are among friends. Therefore group sales offers are a wonderful way to attract people who ordinarily would not attend on their own, and they efficiently sell multiple tickets at one time.

Group sales require a great deal of advance research, planning, and frequent follow-up. Groups typically plan their programs many months or even a year in advance and often require several meetings to make decisions. A person who is knowledgeable about the arts organization and its offerings, is highly organized, and has good follow-through capability should be put in charge of this task.

Vicki Allpress, marketing manager for the NBR New Zealand Opera in Auckland, has reported how she overhauled her company's group booking offer and strategy, resulting in doubling the total number of tickets sold to groups and more than doubling the number of groups who purchased tickets in just one season. Her tips for implementing an effective group booking strategy include (1) get commitment from the whole organization and help third-party ticketing suppliers understand and appreciate the importance of groups, (2) keep good records from the beginning so you have a benchmark against which to compare your results, (3) build a really good database, (4) think laterally—any individuals can get together and come as a group—and (5) invest some decent resources into the program. Ensure you have a staff resource who is responsible for being the groups' liaison person, a phone number specifically for groups to use to call you, the budget to produce a good brochure, and the ability to run some events and add-ons for groups. Give groups generous lead times so they can plan far in advance and not be pressured to pay until they have time to collect money from their members. Invite some organizers whose groups have not yet booked with your company to performances as guests. Group organizers act as ambassadors, assisting with word-of-mouth and awareness—effectively serving as an additional arm of your marketing team. Try to understand what it feels like never to have been to your organization's kind of performance before and what it feels like to be a group organizer, and anticipate the organizers' needs as they plan their group bookings. Then, at the performance, find the organizers in the theater and thank them for arranging the booking and coming along. That makes the group organizer feel good in front of his or her group members. There is also potential for additional contacts, like follow-up letters and calls. Says Allpress, "Arts organizations have to take a more empathetic customer-focused approach because we are going to be here for a long time and we want to build relationships and have long term growth."[14]

THE SEASON BROCHURE

Traditionally, a brochure that offers only the opportunity to subscribe is sent to thousands of people at high cost to the organization. Except for the awareness and interest these brochures build, they are wasted on the people who clearly do not wish to subscribe but who want to attend certain events. So instead of a *subscription* brochure, the marketing manager should offer a *season* brochure, offering miniplans, flex plans, single tickets, or other alternatives to subscriptions in addition to the subscription package. Of course benefits need to be delineated so that people understand, for example, that subscribers get first seating priority. In this way single ticket buyers can order tickets well in advance for the specific events they want to attend, with the knowledge that they will have seating priority over other single ticket buyers but not be assigned seats until subscription orders have been filled. This approach is far more sensitive to the patrons than policies that say, in effect, "If you don't subscribe, we don't want to hear from you until we are so close to the performance dates that we do not expect to sell any more subscriptions and then we will eagerly take your money."

By *allowing* and *encouraging* people to purchase exactly what they want up front, the organization is simultaneously validating their personal preferences (thereby increasing customer satisfaction and involvement), reducing costs later in the season for single ticket marketing, and most likely selling more tickets than it would have otherwise. The exception to this recommendation is that any highly targeted offer, such as memberships offered to appeal to specific segments, should not go out to a general audience.

11

Valuing the Single Ticket Buyer

Trends, like horses, are easier to ride in the direction they are going.

—John Naisbitt

A LARGE PERCENTAGE OF PERFORMING ARTS ATTENDERS *like* being single ticket buyers and their ranks are growing. Yet many arts marketers and managers resist focusing on this segment as a viable, rich source of income and growth. In fact many arts marketers are ingrained with Danny Newman's negative attitude toward single ticket buyers, which he summed up as "The Slothful, Fickle Single Ticket Buyer Versus the Saintly Season Subscriber," the title of Chapter Two in his 1977 book, *Subscribe Now!* Since this book has been published and widely adopted, single ticket buyers have been considered a necessary "evil"; they fill the seats not purchased by loyal subscribers. Until the early 1990s, arts marketers employing Newman's tactics were able to build their subscriber bases, largely by converting single ticket buyers to subscriber status over time. But with the changing consumer attitudes and behavior described throughout this book, it is more and more crucial for arts marketers to treat single ticket buyers as *valued* patrons. This means developing messages and offers that meet the needs, wants, interests, and concerns of occasional ticket buyers.

The Classical Music Consumer Segmentation Study, conducted in 2001, found that overall, half of arts consumers typically plan their live performance attendance within ten days of the event and three-quarters typically plan within several weeks of the event. Arts consumers who are single are 30 percent more likely than their married counterparts to plan within a week of the event.[1]

As pointed out in the earlier discussion of the San Francisco audience survey, *interest in a specific production or repertoire* is by far the most common reason people cite for buying tickets to a performance—64 percent of responses overall. Furthermore, this study found that many single ticket buyers have been subscribers in the past: 38 percent of single ticket buyers at the San Francisco Symphony, 78 percent at the San Francisco Ballet, and 25 percent at the American Conservatory Theater, indicating an extremely high level of defection from subscription status. This huge market definitely does not value seeing all the productions in a season, and the subscriber benefits of guaranteed seats, discounts, and so on are not sufficiently motivating for these people to subscribe. But, most important, they are clearly interested in attending and continue to do so over long periods of time, as we saw in the previous chapter.

W. Chan Kim and Renée Mauborgne say that the business universe consists of two distinct kinds of space, which they describe as red oceans and blue oceans. Red oceans represent the known market space, where boundaries are defined and accepted and the competitive rules of the game are well understood. As the space gets more and more crowded, increasing competition turns the water bloody. Blue oceans denote the unknown market space, untainted by competition. In blue oceans demand is created rather than fought over. In some cases a blue ocean is created when a company gives rise to a completely new industry, as eBay did with the online auction industry. But in most cases a blue ocean is created from within a red ocean when a company alters the boundaries of an existing industry.

As we saw in Chapter Nine, Tiffany & Company created a blue ocean by shifting from demographic to behavioral targeting; repositioning from "baubles for the world's elite" to "timeless gifts for special occasions and special people." By changing its marketing and branding strategies, Tiffany discovered a blue ocean of new market segments for its products.

Say Kim and Mauborgne, "There is no consistently excellent company; the same company can be brilliant at one time and wrongheaded at another. Likewise, there is no perpetually excellent industry; relative attractiveness is driven largely by the creation of blue oceans from within them."[2] The authors' research shows that blue ocean creators offer a leap in value for both buyers and the company itself.

An obvious blue ocean opportunity for arts marketers is to focus on building audiences among single ticket buyers, a major source of audience growth in recent years and in the foreseeable future. The Theatre Communications Group reports that from 2000 to 2004, the average number of season ticket holders per theater in its *trend theatre* group dwindled by 3 percent, and the average subscription renewal rate dropped consistently over the five-year period, from 75 percent in 2000 to 65 percent in 2004. But during this same period, single ticket sales at these theaters rose 3 percent. In the 2003–2004 season, single ticket sales funded 24 percent of 192 *profiled theatres'* expenses, whereas subscription income funded 20 percent of expenses.[3] Imagine how many more tickets would be sold if marketers would implement more strategies geared to single ticket buyers.

Furthermore, as was illustrated in Table 10.1, many fewer single ticket buyers than subscribers make donations to the arts organizations they attend, yet their numbers are significant and encouraging. Fundraising efforts that include valued benefits and are targeted to single ticket buyers, especially those who have attended over a period of time, will certainly be effective in increasing contributions from current donors and attracting new monetary gifts from those who have not given in the past.

Thankfully, the Internet and e-mail make single ticket marketing incredibly inexpensive. Most arts organizations have not yet realized significant cost savings from high-technology marketing on their bottom line, as the electronic media have been added to other marketing media, not replaced them. Before long, it is likely that the marketplace will be ready for arts marketers to reduce expensive direct-mail and newspaper advertising, as more and more customer segments adopt the Internet and e-mail as their primary and preferred sources of information and promotions. In the meantime, frequent contacts with customers via the Internet and e-mail can be effectively added to other ongoing communications without additional cost. And as discussed in

Chapter Ten, if single ticket buyers have the opportunity to purchase tickets for *what* they want to see and *when* they are motivated to make the purchase—even during the subscription drive—an organization's marketing messages serve a much broader audience.

During the run of its first production of the season, one organization's advertisements promoted a much-anticipated third production, saying that tickets for this show were available only to subscribers. The ads were placed in a publication well targeted to people who would be likely to be interested in trying out the organization by seeing this show. I expressed my concern to the executive director about how such an ad was likely to turn away people who would have eagerly purchased tickets for that show. He replied that subscriptions were up somewhat this season, which made him happy given the current downtrend. In response, I asked how many single ticket buyers were lost due to that ad.

There is no way to know the answer to my question, of course. The best and only way to come close to an answer is to offer single ticket sales early for the next show that is similar in style and appeal to the one for which the ad appeared (with the understanding that subscribers will be seated first), and then compare the ticket sales for the two shows. I firmly believe that a focus on the subscriber segment to the *exclusion* of infrequent buyers is damaging to any arts organization.

STRATEGIES FOR ATTRACTING SINGLE TICKET BUYERS

Arts organizations can employ many different strategies for attracting single ticket buyers and building their frequency of attendance. In addition to using Internet and e-mail marketing (discussed at length in Chapter Eight) and appealing to initiators and responders (discussed in Chapter Three), marketers can use options like the following, designed to meet single ticket buyers' needs and lifestyles.

Offering a Ticket Exchange Option for Single Ticket Purchases

Arts organizations have been so effective at communicating the scarcity of their tickets (even when this is not the case!) that many potential patrons do not even consider trying to buy tickets close to the performance date. A common marketing refrain is "Subscribe now!

Guarantee your seats! Guarantee good seats!" As a result, many performing arts organizations face empty seats that would have sold with a different marketing approach.

Communicating scarcity is a mixed blessing; the organization hopes this approach will create a sense of urgency so people will purchase tickets well in advance, but it can also deter people from even trying to see if seats are available. I have a friend who, as an officer of the Joseph Jefferson Committee (which gives the Jeff awards, Chicago's version of the Tonys), is a highly sophisticated theatergoer. I received an e-mail from her one day asking if I knew how she could get tickets to an opera she and her husband wanted to see the following month at Chicago's Lyric Opera. The Lyric has a long-standing history of communicating messages that encourage people to act now, before all tickets are sold. These messages were so effective in communicating scarcity that when I asked my friend if she had tried the box office, she responded, "I never thought of that!"

When respondents to the San Francisco study were asked their reasons for attending fewer performances than in the past, about 40 percent overall reported that they have difficulty scheduling in advance. Many people are eager to attend a performance and would like to purchase tickets early enough to get good seats but face the risks of missing the show and of losing the monetary value of their tickets if other circumstances take priority.

The option to exchange tickets will stimulate advance ticket purchase among those who are interested in attending but uncertain whether they will be able to attend and do not want to take the risk that tickets (or good seats) will be available at the last minute. Ticket exchange privileges mean that no sale is final and therefore no patron needs to be stuck with an unusable ticket.

In the San Francisco survey we asked single ticket buyers if they would be more likely to purchase tickets if they could exchange their tickets up until noon on the day of their performance for tickets to a different performance, for a handling fee. On average, 25 percent of respondents indicated that they would be very likely to take advantage of this ticket exchange option. Marketers consider any strategy that is anticipated to increase sales 5 to 10 percent as highly attractive; a 25 percent response is phenomenal. Respondents indicated a preferred fee for this option averaging four dollars; the variations in the amounts between the three organizations corresponded to their ticket price differences. A significant percentage of respondents reported that they would be happy to pay a fee of as much as ten dollars, and we found that this response was more common among people with lower income levels. Obviously, the ticket value is worth much to them.

The appropriate ticket exchange fee is dependent on each organization's average ticket price and the exchange fee charged to subscribers, if any. A lower fee will be likely to attract more single ticket buyers and increase their satisfaction. A higher fee makes the free ticket exchange privilege for subscribers seem more valuable. Organizations may offer a per order fee, rather than a per ticket fee, to minimize the cost to people who have purchased multiple tickets.

Marketing managers have resisted offering ticket exchange privileges to single ticket buyers for two reasons: first, ticket exchange is a subscriber benefit, and second, it incurs box office expense in terms of personnel time. However, with a fee attached to a ticket exchange offer, there are no negative implications for the free subscriber benefit, and the fee will defray any costs incurred.

Most performing arts organizations should offer a ticket exchange option to single ticket buyers. However, those organizations that enjoy near-capacity or full-capacity sales and have difficulty reselling the seats that result from last-minute exchanges may not find such a policy in their best interest. Requiring a longer lead time on exchanges may make this offer attractive to those organizations.

Some managers say that they are willing to make a ticket exchange when a patron phones with a problem, but they are not willing to advertise the offer. Getting the word out loud and clear is key to the success of this venture, meaning that the ticket exchange offer should appear in all ads and brochures and on the Web site. People *expect* ticket sales to be final; they will not even consider ordering a ticket in some cases unless they know of the new policy. Typically, the last words a caller hears when purchasing tickets by phone are, "All sales are final. There are no refunds or exchanges." Imagine the customer satisfaction and potential for increased future sales if instead people hear: "No sale is final. If you are unable to attend, please phone us at least twenty-four hours before the performance, and for a small fee, we will be happy to exchange your tickets for another performance this season. We hope you enjoy the show."

Positioning on Occasions

Arts marketers traditionally capitalize on occasions that are centered on the artistic offering, featuring a composer's birthday, a music director's anniversary with the organization, or the opening of a new performance hall. These and similar events are meaningful and worth featuring, but they focus on occasions relevant to the organization, not to most ticket buyers.

Arts marketers should consider ways to attract patrons for their *own* special occasions. For many people, attending a performing arts event is special. Price may be an obstacle when it comes to a usual evening out; but to celebrate certain occasions this expenditure is highly worthwhile. Even regular attenders may select a performing arts event as something special to do on an occasion.

Marketers should encourage people to celebrate special occasions by attending a performance and should offer benefits that acknowledge these occasions in meaningful ways: a note of congratulations in the program book or on a program insert, a rose or candies on the patron's seat. Tickets specially wrapped before being mailed make tangible the nature of the intangible experience to come. Packages can be offered with local restaurants; the organization can offer refreshments before or after the show or during intermission in a special room at the venue. Gift certificates for tickets and subscriptions can be vigorously promoted to current attenders for holidays, birthdays, anniversaries, wedding gifts, graduation gifts, Mother's Day or Father's Day—any time someone wants to make someone else feel special. An obvious corollary is that the art itself will take on a more special significance.

As we saw in Chapter Nine, Tiffany's branding takes the acts of shopping, gift giving, and gift receiving to a high level of personal value and emotional appeal for a broad range of customer segments. The arts, like Tiffany, have historically been viewed as elitist in content and as intended for the elite. By focusing on the *special* rather than the elite aspects of attending the arts, we can help more people feel comfortable that the arts are for them. Furthermore, communicating that art inspires us, enriches us, broadens us, and becomes a part of us, is reminiscent of the timeless quality that adds to Tiffany's attractiveness.

STRATEGIES FOR INCREASING
FREQUENCY OF ATTENDANCE

In a 2003 U.K. study of arts attendance, arts participation, and attitudes to the arts commissioned by Arts Council England, 68 percent of the respondents who had attended an arts or cultural event in the preceding year said they would be interested in attending more often. Cost was a significant factor for this group, mentioned by 41 percent of those who expressed a desire to increase their attendance.[4]

Yet people who have attended an arts organization's performances and enjoyed them are among the most likely people to purchase in the future and to increase their frequency of attendance, given the right conditions. People who have become highly interested in the organization and its offerings may be encouraged to purchase a miniseries, flex plan, or rush tickets (described in Chapter Ten). People who do not want to risk attending something unfamiliar may be enticed with a version of the airlines' frequent flyer programs.

Offering Frequent Ticket Buyer Benefits

The policy of rewarding frequent users with free tickets, commonly used by the airlines, has been adopted successfully by many arts organizations. In the arts, these programs encourage people to experiment and to attend programs with which they are unfamiliar. The experienced marketing director will usually know before the season starts which programs are likely to have excess capacity and are good candidates for free ticket offers. Patrons taking advantage of this offer may discover that they enjoy something they have not as yet experienced, such as Handel's operas or modern dance.

Typically, once an individual has purchased tickets for four to eight performances (the number depends on the organization and its offerings), he or she is offered one complimentary ticket, to be chosen from a list of specific performances. The organization should address the issue of expiration when designing the program. If single ticket buyers attend only one performance a year, it is unlikely that the frequent ticket buyer program will motivate them to go four times in one season just to get a free ticket. However, these patrons may choose to go to two performances per year for two years to take advantage of the program and should be offered extended time to earn this reward.

Targeting Attenders More Strategically and Directly

Thanks to a marketing communication strategy called Audience Builder, the U.K.'s Royal Liverpool Philharmonic Orchestra (RLPO) enjoyed a 44 percent increase in attendance from 2001 to 2004. Audience Builder, developed by the Philharmonic in conjunction with consultancy firm Morris Hargreaves McIntyre, first analyzes the types of people who attend concerts in order to target the different segments in specific ways. The audience is segmented according to attendance frequency and the type of event attended. A customized database also reveals how much money people spend. Then each segment is targeted with special messages and in a particular style. The aim is both to encourage people to return to see more of the same and to try new types of programs.

RLPO marketing director Helen Dunnett describes the approach as *holistic,* as it covers all aspects of marketing and communications. Among the initiatives is one called Test Drive, which allows people to try new things for free initially and then gradually build up to paying full price. Test Drive uses spare capacity—a valuable resource that is cost free to the organization. This is not a new strategy for the Philharmonic, but focusing on follow-through is key to the success of the program. Typically, 30 percent of these first-timers are retained as regular attenders. Says Andrew McIntyre of Morris Hargreaves McIntyre, "There is a consensus that traditional box office marketing has failed audiences. People are recognizing that we need to be more sophisticated with marketing."[5]

McIntyre has several recommendations for making Test Drive a success. The free ticket offer should not be broadcast, so as not to alienate regular ticket buyers. Instead, screen potential attenders by phone to establish genuine interest and qualification. Make them feel welcome and make them feel important. Choose accessible entry-level productions, even if few seats remain, yet give free ticket recipients the best available seats in the house. Follow up with a letter and new offer—an offer that demands a commitment, such as "two shows in two months for $25." These offers will sort out the interested people from the maybes. Make a second offer to those who did not respond the first time, but then cut your losses and focus on other people with more potential. Obtain and use feedback and box office data to track, measure, and evaluate the impact, then refine your program accordingly. Start small and set aside only the number of seats you know will be available to be given away and for the number of people you have staff time to contact.

Activating Infrequent Attenders

TelePrompt, also developed by McIntyre, is an initiative to activate infrequent attenders. Typically, half the single ticket buyers on a database attend only once a year. Research shows that they generally get the brochure and mailings but tend to purchase tickets only for major shows or for ones they already know they'll like. With TelePrompt, patrons are telephoned periodically and given a menu of shows about which they can order more information—information that goes into more depth and is more persuasive than the general direct-mail pieces. TelePrompt uses a deliberately soft-sell approach that is designed to build a trusting relationship. Typically, 70 percent of patrons called join the plan. For every dollar invested by the organization, patrons have spent three dollars at the box office. The program could be further developed to promote value-added offers such as backstage tours, preperformance talks, incentives for patrons to introduce new people to the organization, or to convert seasoned TelePrompt patrons to more cost-effective e-mail prompts.

Targeting Single Ticket Buyers for Subscriptions

Jim Royce, director of marketing and communications at the Center Theater Group in Los Angeles, claims that the best subscriber prospects are recent single ticket buyers. Royce suggests phoning first-time attenders within a few days after they attend their first performance. During these calls it is important for the callers to *listen* to what patrons have to say, rather than just give a scripted spiel. The patrons' feedback should then be used in designing a customized series that meets their interests and needs. This strategy will require an advanced selection process for identifying people to call and extra training for qualified phone personnel but will be well worth the effort. To this purpose, some organizations enlist their own performers and volunteers to contact audience members.

In most cases, says Royce, the patron will not subscribe, but do not stop your efforts to keep your company top-of-mind. Send postcards, e-mails, and other promotions as appropriate and consider following up with another phone call in a few months. At the least, people are likely to purchase tickets to one or two shows.[6]

In addition to up-selling, which is the act of encouraging patrons to purchase tickets to more programs throughout the season, marketers should also take advantage of the opportunity to cross-sell when reaching out to patrons. Examples of cross-selling are encouraging symphony attenders to also attend chamber music concerts or regular theatergoers to attend performances on the second stage. The effectiveness of cross-selling depends on the affinity these programs have for one another in the customer's mind. Some arts patrons love all dance; some love modern repertory and not full-length story ballets. Special price offers may encourage patrons to try something they would not try otherwise.

Capitalizing on Cultural Tourism

Whether traveling for business or for pleasure, a huge percentage of tourists attend arts and cultural events. In Peoria, Illinois, it is estimated that 80 percent of arts attenders are locals; the other 20 percent are visitors. In major cities like New York City, the percentage of tourists attending many of the arts attractions is much higher. Large institutions get the word out to travelers through the publicity they receive in guide books and hotel room magazines and through advertisements in local papers. Of course the Web has opened up a world of possibilities for all organizations, no matter what their size.

A highly effective approach for exposing people to all that is available in a region is to encourage people to use the Web sites of local arts councils and tourist bureaus. The Artsopolis Web site (www.artsopolis.com) is a comprehensive source for all cultural events, classes, workshops, auditions, organizations, venues, and individual artists in Silicon Valley. It is a project of the Arts Council Silicon Valley in partnership with the San José Convention and Visitors Bureau and the Norman Y. Mineta San José International Airport. The site makes it easy to search the calendar or to search by type of event in thirteen different categories.

Each organization should keep tourists in mind when designing its own Web site and should anticipate the questions that newcomers to both the organization and the city may have. Arts marketers should also consider attracting tourists, business travelers, and conference-goers through strategies that involve working with local hotels, conference planners, corporate officers, and so on, implementing these strategies as part of their marketing efforts.

Participating in Festivals

Arts festivals around the world are making headlines for their ability to break box office records and for their contribution to branding certain cities for the vitality and variety of their arts offerings. Although the New York Philharmonic has to struggle to sell tickets for its Summertime Classics at Avery Fisher Hall in New York City, tickets for its residency at the Bravo! Vail Valley Music Festival in Colorado sell out in advance. Successful festivals tend to generate their own momentum, and in a medium-sized city where they can really gain some profile, there are significant economic benefits.

Festivals have four special attributes, says Tim Joss, director of the Bath Festivals Trust and chairman of the British Arts Festivals Association. First, unlike performing arts companies, they are not constrained by having to work with a particular group of artists. Second, unlike arts venues, they enjoy the freedom to present a wide variety of arts and nonarts at indoor and open-air spaces. Third, at their best they are rooted in their locality, building partnerships founded on a rich understanding of the region's cultural qualities, problems, and aspirations. Finally, their freedom from year-round contracts with artists and from the burdensome overheads of running buildings means they are typically quite efficient. Some festivals are moving toward being year-round arts development agencies, with occasional programs throughout the year and the festival itself as the high point.[7] This strategy helps marketers keep the festival top-of-mind with customers and builds interest and excitement.

Festivals are typically curated and fully presented but are more and more being accompanied by *fringe* festivals, which are typically open access and provide umbrella marketing and a framework in which artists and audiences can engage. Since their inception in the late 1940s, the Edinburgh International Festival and Edinburgh Fringe Festival have been joined by the Book Festival, the Film Festival, and the Military Tattoo, which together are estimated to generate almost £140 million ($264 million) annually for the Scottish economy. The marriage of festival and fringe proves to be good for the box office. In 2003, the Edinburgh Fringe Festival alone sold more than a million tickets, worth £9.3 million. In 2004, the Adelaide Festival of Arts garnered AUS$3.45 million ($2.62 million) while Adelaide's fringe festival brought in receipts of AUS$3 million ($2.29 million). Festivals with fringes seem to attract the most tourism because of the breadth of access across the cultural spectrum that they provide.

Festivals and fringes cooperate best when they recognize their differences and pool their energies on noncompetitive activities. Directors of the Hong Kong Arts Festival and the Hong Kong Fringe Club have collaborated by offering venues to one another for preshow talks and for meet-the-artist sessions after shows, by recommending programs to one another, and by collaborating on sponsorship benefits. Says Fergus Linehan, director of the Sydney Festival, "The public perceives that it is festival time. People don't necessarily make the distinction between the component parts, so whether they are attending the children's season, the fringe, the festival, conferences, etc., it all serves to feed into the idea that there is something exciting happening."[8]

Festivals expose people to art forms and organizations they may not have attended otherwise and often create a carryover effect to stimulate attendance among both residents and tourists during the regular season of performances.

Leveraging the Database

Modern databases offer marketers the power to record and build on patrons' interests and preferences. Marketers should capture all the information they can about people's purchasing behavior and leverage this information by reaching out to people with programs and offers that are likely to be highly appealing. Box office personnel, when not busy receiving calls, can contact customers via phone or e-mail. This is similar to the method so effectively used by Amazon.com and Netflix.com when they tell a customer, "Since you liked this book [or film], we think you will like this one as well." One morning while reading the *New York Times* I came across a review of a book that sounded fascinating. Before ordering the book from Amazon.com, I checked my e-mail, and lo and behold, there was a message from Amazon.com saying, "Joanne, we think you will like this book!" Creative and industrious arts marketers can be right on target in the same way.

Focusing on the Customer Experience and Delivering Great Customer Service

The marketing imperative is unambiguous: get control by giving up control to consumers. This is the path to success.

—J. Walker Smith, Ann Clurman, and Craig Wood

Your most unhappy customers are your greatest source of learning.

—Bill Gates

ALL THE ARTS MARKETING STRATEGIES, TACTICS, AND principles I have covered in this book—and those I have not— can be boiled down to one phrase: *focus on the customer experience.* Too many marketing departments focus primarily on the products and services their organizations offer, without realizing that the total customer experience is what matters most in attracting, retaining, and delighting customers. Focusing on the customer experience requires marketers to think holistically about every single customer touch point and every stage in the customer life cycle. It also demands a total quality approach to designing and improving the customer experience. It is the marketing director's responsibility to ensure that every employee in the organization understands how he or she affects the customer experience. And it is the responsibility of marketing to orchestrate the customer experience across every aspect of the organization's functions and through all the stages in the customer's buying cycle.[1]

It also means that relationship marketing is key. The marketer must take advantage of every opportunity to get close to customers; to seek regular, direct contact with them; to anticipate their needs; and to develop a reputation for responsiveness—in other words, to build strong relationships. It means that the organization should deliver the highest-quality service possible and serve customers more fully.

Consumer Power

People are happier when they believe they have some control over a process. Being a marketer in the new information age means rethinking the role of the customer in the exchange process; customers are shifting from passive receivers of the marketer's offers to initiators of the contact and even active cocreators of the offer.

Say marketing experts C. K. Prahalad and Venkatram Ramaswamy, "Business competition used to be a lot like traditional theater: On stage, the actors had clearly defined roles, and the customers paid for their tickets, sat back, and watched passively. . . . Now the scene has changed, and business competition seems more like the experimental theater of the 1960s and 1970s; everyone and anyone can be part of the action." Continuing the theatrical metaphor, Prahalad and Ramaswamy explain: "Thanks largely to the Internet, consumers have been increasingly engaging themselves in an active and explicit dialogue with manufacturers of products and services. What's more, that dialogue is no longer being controlled by corporations. . . . Consumers can now initiate the dialogue; they have moved out of the audience and onto the stage."[2] It is ironic that the performing arts, the very industry from which this metaphor was drawn, may be among the slowest to understand and respond to this dramatic change in how customers expect to do business.

An example from my own experience is the conversation I had with a telemarketer representing a large, well-respected theater to which I had subscribed for many years. She phoned to encourage me to renew my subscription, as I had not responded to several direct-mail pleas. I explained that I was not interested in seeing three of the five plays being offered the following season, two of which I had recently seen in other cities, but I offered to purchase tickets to the two plays I was eager to see. My offer to buy those tickets was refused. I could only buy all or none. I explained that I understood that subscribers were eligible to be seated before single ticket buyers, but that I would like my order to be taken at that time for convenience and so that I could have seating preference over other single ticket buyers. I also understood that telemarketers are trained only to handle specific situations, so I suggested she ask someone in the marketing department to contact me about this matter. I received no follow-up contact. This situation is not uncommon in the performing arts, but to me it is as ludicrous as if a department store salesperson were to tell me that if I wanted black socks only, I could purchase them in three months if any remained; if I wanted them today, I must also purchase blue and brown ones. Of course, arts organizations that sell most of their capacity to subscribers may not want to commit to single tickets during the subscription campaign. However, they should follow up with any customer interested in purchasing tickets or they may find themselves without resources to draw upon when it is time to fill unsold seats.

Customers increasingly want to shape their experiences by themselves or with their companions. Performing arts managers and marketers must understand that by involving their customers as cocreators of the marketing product experience, they have the best chance of broadening their audience, building loyalty and satisfaction, and increasing frequency of attendance.

CUSTOMER RELATIONSHIP MANAGEMENT

Customer relationship management (CRM) has been considered a marketing panacea since the sophistication of databases has allowed marketers to capture detailed information about individual customers. CRM involves examining a customer's past purchases and certain demographic information so that the organization can improve customer acquisition, cross-selling and up-selling with highly targeted, specific offers. Yet Smith, Clurman, and Wood say that "with the emergence of self-invention, marketers must do more than simply customize;

marketers must facilitate self-customization. . . . Finding profitable ways of giving power to consumers is now the only way to succeed at giving consumers what they want."[3]

In a similar vein Frederick Newell, in his book *Why CRM Doesn't Work,* accuses CRM of falling far short of serving customers well. Newell claims that CRM projects are more concerned with which customer segments are going to deliver the most value to the organization and with internal efficiency in handling customers rather than with the real needs of the customer. As a result some customers may be treated even worse than before.[4]

Similarly, the authors of an article titled "Preventing the Premature Death of Relationship Marketing" say that "ironically, the very things that marketers are doing to build relationships with customers are often the things that are destroying those relationships." Companies ask their customers for friendship, loyalty, and respect, but too often they don't give those customers friendship, loyalty, and respect in return. As a result many marketing initiatives seem trivial and useless instead of unique and valuable.[5]

Newell calls for a change, suggesting that companies *empower* customers, not *target* them. He advocates replacing *customer relationship marketing* (CRM) with *customer management of relationships* (CMR), which has a goal of humanizing relationships and delivering better solutions to customers.

Newell summarizes the journey from CRM to CMR in these terms: from the company being in control to putting the customer in control; from making business better for the company to making business better for the customer; from tracking customers by transaction to understanding customers' unique needs; from treating customers as segments to treating customers as individuals; from forcing customers to do what you believe they want to letting customers tell you what they care about; from making customers feel stalked to empowering customers; from organizing around products and services to organizing around customers.[6]

The next generation of CRM won't be found in bringing significant new products to market. Rather, it will be found in better applying technology to myriad existing problems. This is the *holistic marketing concept,* through which marketers develop contextual offerings of products, services, and experiences to match individual customers' requirements.

A key factor in facilitating this process is to focus on consumer lifestyles, attitudes, and insights, rather than just on transactions, as is common in CRM. The fact that nowadays lifestyle is central to people's choices of products, services, and experiences is good news for arts marketers. Arts events provide innumerable opportunities and associations for meaningful lifestyle satisfactions.

GREAT CUSTOMER SERVICE

A patron's experience with a theater, symphony, dance, or opera performance does not begin when the curtain rises, nor does it end with the last applause. Rather, the total experience begins when a potential patron first becomes aware of an organization's offering; it is ideal for the marketer to consider this the beginning of a long-standing relationship between the customer and the organization. Meeting the demands of sophisticated, educated audience members who want specialized and individualized services means more creative, out-of-the-box thinking and more staff to implement these services. The process of learning what is important to your customers and developing customized communications and services will involve some new costs. But, says Newell, "most companies waste money in their communication with customers. . . . When priorities change in order to shift investments to what is critical for the customer, the value of each marketing dollar spent must be measured in terms of its value to the customer. This means dollars saved as well as dollars spent."[7]

Every contact the patron has with the organization's personnel, including box office personnel and ushers, and with the organization's communications, whether mass advertising, the Web site, e-mail, or direct mail, affects the person's satisfaction level. Also, every organization must have policies in place for handling any problems that may arise with customers.

On the following page is the story of one theater director's experience in customer service that turned an unfortunate incident into an opportunity to build a loyal customer.

A commonly accepted principle of marketing holds that people who have had a bad experience remedied are more satisfied than those who never had a bad experience. (This does not mean that we should orchestrate bad experiences!) Marketing researchers claim that people

From Dismay to Delight in North Carolina

A long-standing subscriber to the North Carolina Blumenthal Performing Arts Center purchased eight tickets to a performance so she could take her family as part of her special birthday celebration. When the family arrived at the theater, other people were sitting in several of the subscriber's seats. Unfortunately, the seats had been double sold—one set through the box office, the other set through Ticketmaster. Because it was impossible, just before the curtain was to rise, to determine which set of tickets had been sold first, management decided to allow the people who had arrived first to retain their seats, and they placed the subscriber's family in equally good seats but scattered throughout the hall in pairs.

Two days later, Judith Allen, then president of the center, received a letter from the subscriber saying that her birthday celebration had been ruined when her family had to be split up and seated around the hall. As a result of her great disappointment, she was canceling her subscription and writing a letter of complaint to the editor of the local newspaper.

Allen sent the subscriber a bouquet of flowers with a note of apology. After receiving no response, Allen sent the subscriber another note. In this second note she acknowledged that she couldn't recreate the subscriber's birthday celebration but said she would like to offer her eight seats together for another production. This time the subscriber replied, saying that it was clear to her that Allen truly cared about her feelings and about reaching out to her personally. Along with her appreciative acceptance of the ticket offer, she enclosed her subscription renewal for the following season. When the family arrived for the performance, a staff member greeted them at the door and escorted them to their seats. Shortly thereafter the subscriber sent the center a contribution of $500, and the next season she increased her contribution to $1,000.[8]

who are happy with an experience tell three others; unhappy people tell eleven others. Clearly, turning around a customer's negative experience should be a high priority for marketers. Furthermore, acquiring new customers can cost five to ten times more than satisfying and retaining current customers. In this era when it is increasingly difficult to attract new audiences and develop among them some level of loyalty, the most crucial task of managers and marketers is to nurture and build relationships with current attenders one by one. Deepening the bond with current patrons by going well beyond expectations in serving them is the best way for the organization to guarantee that it will increase frequency of attendance and maintain a healthy base of patrons and contributors.

Jim Royce, director of marketing and communications at the Center Theatre Group in Los Angeles, says he would like the words "No" and "Sorry, we can't do that" eliminated from his employees' sales vocabulary. In every instance, says Royce, an alternative must be offered, even if they physically cannot do a requested action. For example, his box office personnel may say, "We're sold out; however, I have seats for this other event or performance." Royce says that if anyone sends him a complaint letter—about anything—he replies personally with an apology and "thanks for letting us know" letter, along with a complimentary certificate for two tickets, usually for a preview performance of an upcoming show, with the idea of getting these people back in the theater again.[9]

Royce's policy is in keeping with the *finish strong* principle. Behavioral science research shows that the ending of an encounter is more important than the beginning because it is what remains in the customer's memory. This means that customer service personnel should get unpleasant news out of the way early in the conversation and enhance the customers' experiences during the process, ending with a highly satisfactory result, so that people will have positive recollections of the process after it is completed.[10]

Measure Customer Satisfaction

A customer-centered organization always asks: How satisfied are our customers with our offering? In what ways can we make them more satisfied? In what ways can we create and market satisfaction for other potential audiences as well?

A common result of a customer-centered orientation is that the people who come in contact with such organizations report high personal satisfaction. Jan Carlzon, former chief executive officer of Scandinavian Airlines, once said, "Our aim goes beyond satisfying the customer. Our aim is to *delight* the customer." This higher standard may well be the secret of the great marketers. They go beyond meeting the mere expectations of the customer; they inspire the customer to rave.

Many organizations institute customer satisfaction surveys to gather an understanding of the general needs of their customer base. However, say Gilmore and Pine in their book *The Experience Economy,* such techniques do not go far enough, as they measure the *market,* not *individual* customer satisfaction. The surveys are typically designed to make tabulation easy, not to gain true insight into customer-specific wants and needs. As a result, people who fill out these surveys gain little or no direct benefit. Furthermore, customer satisfaction surveys rarely ask for information about the particular needs and wants of the respondents. Rather, they ask customers to rate how well the organization and its personnel are performing on a series of predefined categories. As a result managers gain too little insight into what people truly want and need.[11]

Dave Power III, of J. D. Power & Associates, says, "when we measure satisfaction, what we're really measuring is the difference between what a customer *expects* and what the customer *perceives* he gets."[12] What organizations must seek to analyze is *customer sacrifice,* the gap between what a customer settles for and what he or she wants exactly. At a certain point the customer believes that the sacrifice is too great—whether it involves the ticket price, the time commitment, a lack of interest in the offerings, disappointing customer service, or any combination of myriad factors—and decides not to purchase tickets or renew a subscription. Some of these factors, of course, are out of the marketing manager's control, but it is the responsibility of the organization to ascertain that each customer receives as close to what he or she expects, needs, and wants as possible.

Pine and Gilmore also suggest going beyond what people expect by *staging the unexpected.* This doesn't mean offering an improvement that customers may then expect to see institutionalized. It means arousing customer surprise by staging memorable experiences. Some examples of the unexpected are moving patrons to a better seat location when there are empty seats available just before the curtain rises; offering patrons two-for-the-price-of-one tickets to a preview performance of the upcoming show, available during the intermission; and offering complimentary beverages (compliments of a sponsor of course). At Chicago Shakespeare Theater, actors in costume mingled with patrons before the performances of one production. This created a level of excitement and got people into the mood of the show even before the real action began. Similarly, members of a dance company warmed up for the performance on stage with the curtain open so patrons would feel like insiders, observing what is typically out of view. Thus audience anticipation and excitement is enhanced.

Referring to the world of business, Pine and Gilmore say that "companies must realize that they make *memories,* not goods.[13] Performing arts organizations, by their nature, make memories with their core products: the works of art on their stages. Arts organizations need to realize the importance of engaging their audiences and creating satisfying, memorable experiences with the business, off-stage aspects of their work as well.

Capture and Use Service Quality Information

Where do you begin once a commitment has been made to offer great customer service? The answer, of course, is to listen to the customers, to truly understand their experiences with your organization and your competitors. Researchers—either staff members or outside consultants, or both—should also play the role of the customer to have first-hand experience with each encounter with the organization.

CREATE A SERVICE STRATEGY Service listening reveals what is important to customers, what is occurring in service performance and why, and what should be done to improve service; it also provides the basis for establishing an overall strategic direction.

To determine a service strategy ask: What attributes of service are—and will continue to be—most important to our customers? On what important service attributes is the competition strongest?

On which ones is it weakest? What are the existing and potential service capabilities of our organization?[14]

CONCIERGE SERVICE IN LOS ANGELES

The Mark Taper Forum offers a concierge service for upper-level patrons and donors. The concierge has a private number and the ability to book hotel rooms, restaurant reservations, theater tickets in London and New York, and provide other services. Over time the concierge service will be available to a wider and wider group of patrons.

Offering a concierge service is feasible only for the large arts organizations that have the infrastructure and sizable audience base to make this offer worthwhile. Every organization, large and small, should start planning its service strategy by investigating how it can improve procedures that already exist, such as for contacts with ushers and box office staff.

MEASURE SERVICE QUALITY It is crucial to measure customers' service expectations, as expectations are the basis for their satisfaction level. Service quality may stay the same or even improve; expectations may continue to rise even more.

Also measure the relative importance of service quality attributes to customers. When is good good enough? The organization should prioritize its customer service efforts according to what matters most to the people it serves.

Finally, the organization should measure the market impact of its service offerings.

STEPS IN SERVICE RECOVERY Systems should be put in place for handling customer complaints and should be clearly explained to all employees. Details should be developed for responding to a variety of situations, but in general be sure always to offer a sincere apology, offer a fair fix for the problem, treat the customer in a way that shows the organization cares about the problem and about helping the customer to solve it, and if possible, offer recompense equivalent to or higher than the burden the customer has endured. The manager should ascertain that the organization actually gives the promised level of service recovery rather than one that falls short. The story earlier in this chapter that described how Judith Allen recovered the loyalty of a very unhappy patron is exemplary in all these regards.

Managers should try their best to anticipate and plan for problems. With a controversial work on stage or a new marketing offer, try to identify the negative reactions that may result and develop a plan to deal with them. Whenever possible, of course, deflect the potential problem before it occurs.

Conduct Internal Marketing

Implementing a customer service strategy requires internal marketing—the marketing conducted with staff at every level in the organization. Leonard Berry, in his book *On Great Service,* recommends that leaders employ the following methods to establish an overall service strategy.[15]

CREATE A VISION   A broad vision is worth believing in, is challenging, provides emotional energy, generates commitment, and helps create a sense of teamwork and belonging that is sustaining on difficult days. Short-term pressures encourage service mediocrity; keeping a vision in mind helps employees focus on the big picture.

STRESS PERSONAL INVOLVEMENT   Management guru Peter Drucker defined a leader as someone who has followers. A leader who has a strong, clear vision and who listens to his or her employees is the one who gains trust and succeeds. To be effective, people need to have to think on the job, be creative, and venture outside their routine; they need to be encouraged to take the initiative. This is true even for the lowest-paid employees, such as the box office personnel and the ushers, those who have the most direct contact with the patrons. These people play a crucial role in providing excellent customer service, in developing goodwill, and in bringing issues of concern back to their managers. Granting employees some autonomy and allowing them to show what they can do requires trust. They may make some mistakes, but overall this strategy will pay off well.

EMPLOYEE FIELD REPORTING Employee field reporting involves asking employees to report what customers are saying and doing. Are people who have phoned the box office hanging up without buying tickets? Are they unhappy with available seat locations? Are they asking questions that employees cannot answer?

CONDUCT EMPLOYEE RESEARCH Ask employees to rate service quality as they see it. The employees who are in direct communication with customers can help reveal why problems occur and what to do to solve them. Ask such questions as these: What is the biggest problem you face day in and day out trying to deliver a high quality of service to your customers? If you were the organization's executive director and could make only one change to improve service quality, what change would you make? What other problems do you encounter, and how would you suggest managing them? Provide a suggestion box so employees can comment anonymously.

SHARE VALUES Schedule sessions on a monthly or bimonthly basis to share ideas and experiences and to evaluate them together. Bring in all levels of employees, including upper-level management. Reaffirm every employee's role in quality improvement. Make presentations, which may include skits with role playing.

HOLD BOOK DISCUSSION GROUPS Management can select a variety of service quality books and ask employees to discuss one chapter per week in group meetings. It is important that discussion facilitators understand the technical and theoretical issues and be able to conceptualize ways to make the principles a book presents apply to their organization.

SET UP QUALITY IMPROVEMENT TASK FORCES The best way to help people learn quality is to engage them in solutions to real organizational problems. Employees and managers can be invited to conduct mystery shopping or real shopping at their own organization or competitors' organizations. It is often a revelation for people to see how they respond to a customer service experience themselves.

ELICIT EMPLOYEE SUGGESTIONS Encourage employees to make suggestions to improve customer service within their departments or anywhere else in the organization. Also ask them: If you could make one change to improve employee motivation, what change would you make? Give prizes such as recordings, books, or gift certificates for the best suggestions of the month. Employee performance reviews should take into consideration the degree of involvement in such activities.

In this era when it is increasingly difficult to attract new audiences and develop some level of loyalty among current attenders, the most crucial task of managers and marketers is to build and nurture one-on-one relationships with customers. Deepening the bond with current patrons and going well beyond expectations in serving them is the best way for an arts organization to guarantee that it will maintain and grow a healthy base of patrons and contributors.

Epilogue

We must cultivate our garden.

—Voltaire

Before he was appointed president of the Kennedy Center in Washington, D.C., Michael Kaiser had been the executive director of the Royal Opera House in London, American Ballet Theatre (ABT) in New York City, and the Alvin Ailey Dance Theater Foundation. During his tenure at ABT the company eliminated its accumulated deficit of more than $5 million, increased income from both box office sales and sponsorships, increased its touring activities, inaugurated a junior company and three summer schools, and expanded its education, access, and outreach programs considerably. The Alvin Ailey American Dance Theater was also in dire financial straits when Kaiser took the helm. Under Kaiser's leadership the Ailey company's $1.5 million deficit was wiped out and it accumulated $5 million. Kaiser has developed programs in arts management at the Kennedy Center and attracts arts managers from all over the globe who are eager to glean his wisdom.

Says Kaiser, "Troubled arts organizations invariably get themselves into a vicious spiral. They reduce spending on art and marketing, lessening the interest of audiences and patrons, thereby reducing box office revenue and private contributions. In response, they cut back further, receive less, and so on and so on. Most problems facing arts organizations have to do with inadequate flow of income, not spendthrift artistic directors."

Kaiser firmly believes the solution to these problems is to search relentlessly for new sources of revenue, not to cut costs. Kaiser has never seen "a sick arts organization economize its way to health." This does not mean that reducing expenditures is not important; money must be saved when the organization faces financial shortfalls. But savings should be made on staff costs and administrative costs, *not* on artistic initiatives or marketing. The money Kaiser saves through cost-cutting efforts is devoted to creating vibrant artistic projects and to marketing these projects and the institution in exciting and contemporary ways. Concludes Kaiser, "Box office revenue and contributed funds result from good art, well marketed. Quite simply, effective marketing is an absolute prerequisite for consistent success in the arts."[1]

SOME FINAL INSIGHTS

Remember that markets are changing faster than marketing. Embrace change. When it comes to the future, resistance is ultimately futile.

Have vision; pay attention and respond to the trends in the world around you. Gordon Sullivan and Michael Harper, authors of *Hope Is Not a Method*, say that "doing the same thing you have always done—no matter how much you improve it—will get you only what you had before."[2]

Stretch yourself and those around you—stretch your imagination, ingenuity, and curiosity.

Take risks—risks grounded in your mission and values and driven by well thought out strategy.

Believe passionately in what you do—it is only through the expression of your passion that you will incite passion in others.

Insist on rigorous adherence to standards of excellence.

Put your customers first. *Listen;* pay attention to their words and to their actions. Be rigorous about visitor satisfaction.

Focus on insights, not on processes. That being said, make sure the processes you use are current and that they leverage the continually advancing technology of our times.

Most important, offer compelling art of great quality that resonates in people's lives.

All the rest is marketing.

"WE MUST CULTIVATE OUR GARDEN"

In the Prologue, I wrote about Candide's misfortunes as a metaphor for the struggles faced by arts marketers in building and retaining their audiences. To continue the metaphor, Voltaire's *Candide* concludes with Candide's philosophy teacher, Pangloss, saying to him: "All events are interconnected in this best of all possible worlds, for if you hadn't been driven from a beautiful castle with hard kicks in the behind, . . . if you hadn't been seized by the Inquisition, if you hadn't wandered over America on foot, if you hadn't lost all your sheep from the land of Eldorado, you wouldn't be here eating candied citrons and pistachio nuts."

In the final song of Leonard Bernstein's musical version of *Candide,* the cast sums up the story's philosophy by singing:

Let dreamers dream what worlds they please;
Those Edens can't be found.
The sweetest flowers, the fairest trees
Are grown in solid ground.
We're neither pure nor wise nor good;
We'll do the best we know;
We'll build our house, and chop our wood
And make our garden grow.

Now, reader, may your garden grow.

Notes

Book epigraph: From a talk given Nov. 19, 2005, at Next Theater, Evanston, Ill. Used with permission.

CHAPTER ONE

Chapter epigraph: Gary Hamel and C. K. Prahalad, *Competing for the Future* (Boston: Harvard Business School Press, 1994), p. 25.

1. Samuel Lipman, *Music and More: Essays, 1975–1999* (Evanston: Northwestern University Press, 1992), p. 25.

2. Norman LeBrecht, *Who Killed Classical Music? Maestros, Managers, and Classical Music* (Secaucus, N.J.: Birch Lane Press, 1997), pp. 5, 12.

3. William Bolcom, "Trouble in the Music World," *Musical America,* 1990, *110*(3), 20.

4. K. Robert Schwartz, "The Crises of Tomorrow Are Here Today," *New York Times,* Oct. 31, 1993, pp. AR31–AR32.

5. Heloisa Fischer, personal e-mail to the author, Mar. 17, 2005.

6. Douglas Dempster, "Wither the Audience for Classical Music?" *Harmony,* Oct. 2000, *11,* p. 45.

7. Barbara Jepson, "Classical, Now Without the 300-Year Delay," *New York Times,* Mar. 26, 2006, p. AR23.

8. Douglas Blackmon, "From Small Towns to Big Cities, America Is Becoming Cultured," *Wall Street Journal,* Sept. 17, 1998, p. A1.

9. Performing Arts Research Coalition, *The Value of the Performing Arts in Ten Communities,* June 2004, retrieved from http://www.operaamerica.org/about/parc/parc.html.

10. National Endowment for the Arts, *2002 Survey of Public Participation in the Arts,* 2002, p. 60, retrieved from http://www.arts.gov/pub/NEASurvey2004.pdf.

11. Zannie Giraud Voss and Glenn B. Voss, *Theatre Facts 2004* (New York: Theatre Communications Group, 2005), retrieved from http://www.tcg.org/pdfs/tools/theatrefacts_2004.pdf. The 2004 TCG survey report divides nonprofit, professional theaters into groups (universe, profiled theatres, and trend theatres), defined by the amount of information available.

12. Edward Jay Epstein, "The Vanishing Box Office," *Slate,* July 5, 2005, retrieved from http://www.slate.com/id/2122000.

13. Quoted in Ben Pesner, *Eyeing the Horizon: "A Digest of Theatre Facts 2002": As They Cope with a Troubled Economy, Theatres Position Themselves for the Future,* retrieved from http://www.tcg.org.

14. Quoted in Pesner, *Eyeing the Horizon.*

15. Zannie Giraud Voss and Glenn B. Voss, *Theatre Facts 2005* (New York: Theatre Communications Group, 2006), retrieved from http://www.tcg.org. The 2005 TCG survey report divides nonprofit, professional theaters into three groups (universe, profiled theatres, and trend theatres), defined by the amount of information available.

16. Voss and Voss, *Theatre Facts 2005.*

17. Joli Jensen, *Is Art Good for Us?* (Lanham, Md.: Rowman & Littlefield, 2002), pp. 2–4.

18. Kathleen Watt, "Charles Wuorinen: New Wine, Old Skins," *USOPERAWEB,* retrieved from http://www.usoperaweb.com/2004/autumn/wuorinen.htm.

19. Performing Arts Research Coalition, *The Value of the Performing Arts in Ten Communities.*

20. Arts Council England, *Arts in England: Attendance, Participation and Attitudes in 2001,* Research Report No. 27, Oct. 2002, retrieved from http://www.artscouncil.org.uk.

21. "New Harris Poll Reveals That 93 Percent of Americans Believe That the Arts Are Vital to Providing a Well-Rounded Education," Americans for the Arts Press Release, June 13, 2005, retrieved from http://ww3.artsusa.org/information_resources/press/2005/2005_06_13b.asp.

22. Cheryl Newman, "Travelers Seek Byway Experiences," *Public Roads,* May/June 2001, retrieved from http://www.tfhrc.gov/pubrds/mayjun01/byway experiences.htm.

23. Alan Brown, "The Shifting Sands of Demand: Trends in Arts Participation," *Arts Reach,* 2004, *13*(1), 10; excerpted from *Magic of Music,* Issues Brief No. 5, *Smart Concerts: Orchestras in the Age of Edutainment* (Miami, Fla.: John S. and James L. Knight Foundation, Dec. 2004), retrieved from http://www.knightfdn.org.

24. Steve McMillan, presentation at the Kellogg School of Management Marketing Conference, Evanston, Ill., Jan. 29, 2003.

25. B. Joseph Pine II and James H. Gilmore, *The Experience Economy: Work Is Theatre & Every Business a Stage* (Boston: Harvard Business School Press, 1999).

26. Philip Kotler, Dipak C. Jain, and Suvit Maesincee, *Marketing Moves* (Boston: Harvard Business School Press, 2002), pp. x, 21.

27. Kotler, Jain, and Maesincee, *Marketing Moves,* p. 45.

28. Kotler, Jain, and Maesincee, *Marketing Moves,* p. 36.

29. J. Walker Smith, Ann Clurman, and Craig Wood, *Coming to Concurrence: Addressable Attitudes and the New Model for Marketing Productivity* (Evanston, Ill.: Racom Communications, 2005), pp. 25–29.

30. Smith, Clurman, and Wood, *Coming to Concurrence,* pp. 32–33.

31. Adapted from Mohanbir Sawhney, *Insights into Customer Insights,* 2004, retrieved from http://www.mohansawhney.com.

32. Douglas W. Kinsey, "The Death of Performing Arts Subscriptions—Or Not?" *Arts Reach,* 2006, *14*(3), p. 18.

33. Quoted in Thomas L. Friedman, *The World Is Flat: A Brief History of the Twenty-First Century* (New York: Farrar, Straus & Giroux, 2006), p. 451.

CHAPTER TWO

Chapter epigraph: Robert Brustein, personal e-mail to the author, July 17, 2006.

1. *Some Like It Hot, Some Like It Cold, Most Like It Here: Forecasting Retirement in Chicago,* Report of the Metro Chicago Information Center, Nov. 2000, retrieved from http://info.mcfol.org/WWW/Datainfo/hottopics/HHS/somehot_summary.asp.

2. Ken Dychtwald, "Inspired, Not Retired," *New York Times Magazine,* May 22, 2005.

3. Pauline Taylor, *Getting There: Equal Arts Taxi for the Over Sixties,* Evaluation Report, Mar. 2003, retrieved from http://www.newaudiences.org.uk.

4. Katherine Khalife, "Ten Reasons Why You Should Be Marketing to Grandparents," Museum Marketing Tips, 2002, retrieved from http://www.museummarketingtips.com.

5. Karen Akers, "Gen X & Y: Life After the Big Boom," 2001, retrieved from http://www.logomall.com/imprintPM/issues/fall-2001/features3.htm.

6. Onpoint Marketing & Communications, "Generation X Definition," n.d., retrieved from http://www.onpoint-marketing.com/generation-x.htm.

7. Wynne Delacoma, "Classical Artists See Titanic Potential in Bypass of Traditional," *Chicago Sun Times,* Feb. 11, 2001.

8. Adam Bregman, "Classical and Casual Fridays," *Los Angeles Times,* May 2, 2002, p. F12.

9. Baltimore Symphony Orchestra, "Symphony with a Twist," 2006, retrieved from http://www.baltimoresymphony.org.

10. Canberra Arts Marketing, "U27," n.d., retrieved from http://www.canberraarts.com.au/text/u27.cfm and http://www.canberratheatre.org.au/pages/page41.asp.

11. Claudia Keenan, personal e-mail to the author, Feb. 8, 2005. For a thorough discussion of this program, see Marianne Stone, "What's Got Gen-Xers Heading to the New York City Opera," *Arts Reach*, 2002, *10*(10).

12. Dan Pankraz, "Going Online to Get Through to Teenagers," *B&T,* May 14, 2002, retrieved from http://www.bandt.com.au/articles/68/0C00D768.asp.

13. Karen Hill, "Back to School Guide: Kids' Education Set to Music," *Atlanta Journal Constitution,* July 28, 2005, p. SN4.

14. Chris Jones, "Child's Play," *Chicago Tribune,* May 18, 2003, Arts and Entertainment p. 1.

15. Jack McAuliffe, "Voyage of Discovery," *Symphony,* Nov./Dec. 2004, pp. 18–19.

16. Brian Sternthal and Alice Tybout, "Segmentation and Targeting," in Dawn Iacobucci (ed.), *Kellogg on Marketing* (Hoboken, N.J.: Wiley, 2001), pp. 7–18.

17. Martha Barletta, *Marketing to Women* (Chicago: Dearborn Trade, 2002), pp. 4–8.

18. Barletta, *Marketing to Women,* p. 175.

19. Faith Popcorn and Lys Marigold, *EVEolution* (New York: Hyperion, 2000), pp. 4, 18–19.

20. Joel Henning, "Joffrey Ballet: Back on Its Feet," *Arts Reach,* 2006, *14*(3), p. 5. This article originally appeared in the *Wall Street Journal,* Jan. 11, 2006.

21. Forrester Research, *Gays Are the Technology Early Adopters You Want,* 2003, retrieved from http://www.forrester.com/ER/Research/Brief/Excerpt/0,1317,17004,00.html.

22. Robin Wallace, "Does Spending Power Buy Cultural Acceptance?" Sept. 16, 2003, retrieved from http://www.foxnews.com/story/0,2933,97293,00.html.

23. Wilde Marketing, *Pink Dollars,* 2002, retrieved from http://www.wildemarketing.com/pink_dollars.html.

24. gaymarketexpress.com, *Marketing to Reach the Gay and Lesbian Community,* n.d., retrieved from www.gaymarketexpress.com.

25. David Brooks, "Questions of Culture," *New York Times,* Feb. 19, 2006, p. WE12.

26. Paul Stuart Graham, "Marketing to Asians," *Arts Reach,* 2004, *13*(1), p. 3.

27. *American Demographics,* Apr. 2003, as cited in Packaged Facts, *Report on the U.S. Hispanic Market,* 4th ed., Oct. 2003, retrieved from http://www.marketresearch.com.

28. Packaged Facts, *Report on the U.S. Hispanic Market.*

29. Packaged Facts, *Report on the U.S. Hispanic Market.*

30. Packaged Facts, *The U.S. African American Market,* 5th ed., Jan. 2004.

31. Securities Industry Association, *The African-American Market,* n.d., retrieved from http://www.sia.com/hrdiversity/html/african-american.html.

32. Securities Industry Association, *The African-American Market.*

33. Packaged Facts, *The U.S. Asian-American Market,* Mar. 2002, retrieved from http://www.marketresearch.com.

34. Packaged Facts, *The U.S. Asian-American Market.*

35. Xing Jin, comments made in the online Audience Development Forum sponsored by Fuel4arts.com, June 25, 2003.

36. Emanuel Rosen, *The Anatomy of Buzz: How to Create Word of Mouth Marketing* (New York: Currency, 2002), p. 62.

37. Jesse McKinley, "Lincoln Center Goes A-Courting," *New York Times,* July 12, 2005, p. B1.

38. McKinley, "Lincoln Center Goes A-Courting," p. B1.

CHAPTER THREE

Chapter epigraphs: Ben Cameron, former executive director, Theatre Communications Group, keynote address to the Dance/USA Winter Council meeting, New Orleans, La., Jan. 2003; David Ogilvy's statement cited from brainyquote. com, retrieved from http://www.brainyquote.com/quotes/quotes/d/davidogilv103081.html.

1. Malcolm Gladwell, *The Tipping Point: How Little Things Can Make a Big Difference* (Boston: Little, Brown, 2000), pp. 96–98.

2. Mohanbir Sawhney, "Don't Homogenize, Synchronize," in *Harvard Business Review on Customer Relationship Management* (Boston: Harvard Business School Press, 2001), pp. 86, 101.

3. Felicia R. Lee, "Breaking the Motherhood Drama with a Drama on Motherhood," *New York Times,* Nov. 24, 2004, retrieved from http://www.nytimes.com.

4. Morton Smyth, *Not for the Likes of You: How to Reach a Broader Audience,* May 2004, retrieved from http://www.newaudiences.org.uk.

5. Alex Ross, "Listen to This," *New Yorker,* Feb. 16 and 23, 2004, retrieved from http://www.therestisnoise.com/2004/05/more_to_come_6.html.

6. Daniel Kahneman, Nancy Hanks Memorial Lecture, presented at the Kellogg Graduate School of Management, Evanston, Ill., May 19, 2004.

7. Daniel Kahneman, "Maps of Bounded Rationality," prize lecture presented at Stockholm University, Dec. 8, 2002, retrieved from http://nobelprize.org/economics/laureates/2002/kahneman-lecture.html.

8. Anne Midgette, "Decline in Listeners Worries Orchestras," *New York Times,* June 25, 2005, p. A15.

9. Janelle Gelfand, "Orchestra League Leader Takes Industry to Task," *The Enquirer,* June 6, 2005, retrieved from http://www.Cincinnati.Com.

10. Tim Baker and Heather Maitland, *Profile of Dance Attenders in Scotland: Section 3. Qualitative Research Report* (Edinburgh: Scottish Arts Council, Oct. 9, 2002), p. 6.

11. Gordon E. Butte, "Increasing Opera Attendance: The 2002 American Express Audience Research Project," *Opera America Newsline,* June 2002.

12. Gerald Zaltman, *How Customers Think: Essential Insights into the Mind of the Market* (Boston: Harvard Business School Press, 2003), pp. 8–9.

13. Gary Klein, *Sources of Power: How People Make Decisions* (Cambridge, Mass.: MIT Press, 1999).

14. John S. and James L. Knight Foundation, *Classical Music Consumer Segmentation Study: How Americans Relate to Classical Music and Their Local Orchestras,* Final Report, Oct. 2002, retrieved from http://www.knightfdn.org/music/consumersegmentation/pdf/KF_Classical_Consumer_Report.pdf.

15. J. Walker Smith, Ann Clurman, and Craig Wood, *Coming to Concurrence: Addressable Attitudes and the New Model for Marketing Productivity* (Evanston, Ill.: Racom Communications, 2005), p. 95.

16. Smith, Clurman, and Wood, *Coming to Concurrence,* p. 95.

17. Kazuaki Ushikubo, "A Method of Structure Analysis for Developing Product Concepts and Its Applications," *European Research,* 1986, *14*(4), 174–175.

18. Alan Brown, "Classical Music Consumer Segmentation Study: How Americans Relate to Classical Music and Their Local Orchestras," *Arts Reach,* 2003, *11*(3), p. 18.

19. Butte, "Increasing Opera Attendance."

20. Smith, Clurman, and Wood, *Coming to Concurrence,* p. 211.

21. Alan Brown, *Magic of Music,* Issues Brief No. 4, *Initiators and Responders: A New Way to View Orchestra Audiences* (Miami, Fla.: John S. and James L. Knight Foundation, July 2004), p. 7, retrieved from http://www.knightfdn.org/default.asp?story=research/cultural/index.asp.

22. Brown, *Magic of Music,* Issues Brief No. 4, p. 4.

23. Brown, *Magic of Music,* Issues Brief No. 4.

24. Brown, *Magic of Music,* Issues Brief No. 4.

25. Rebecca Krause-Hardie, a principal with SymphonyWorks, telephone conversation with the author, Oct. 22, 2004.

26. Cleveland Foundation, *Marketing the Arts in Cleveland: An in-Depth Survey* (Cleveland, Ohio: Cleveland Foundation, 1985).

27. Baker and Maitland, *Profile of Dance Attenders in Scotland,* p. 6.

Chapter Four

Chapter epigraphs: Jay Conrad Levinson, "The Process of Marketing," *Marketing Magic,* 2005, retrieved from http://www.marketing-magic.biz/archives/archive-marketing/process-of-marketing.htm; Henry Ford's statement cited from brainyquote.com, retrieved from http://www.brainyquote.com/quotes/quotes/h/henryford145978.html.

1. Adrian J. Slywotzky, *Value Migration* (Boston: Harvard Business School Press, 1996), p. 1.

2. Slywotzky, *Value Migration,* pp. 39–40.

3. Helgi Tomasson, "Introduction," in *Building on Success: San Francisco Ballet's Long Range Plan 1998–2003* (San Francisco: San Francisco Ballet, 1997).

4. Glenn McCoy, executive director, and other San Francisco Ballet managers, personal conversation with the author at the San Francisco Ballet offices, Aug. 9, 2004.

5. Al Ries and Jack Trout, *Positioning: The Battle for Your Mind* (New York: McGraw-Hill, 1986), p. 34.

6. Patricia Seybold, "Get Inside the Lives of Your Customers," in *Harvard Business Review on Customer Relationship Management* (Boston: Harvard Business School Press, 2001), p. 30.

7. Seybold, "Get Inside the Lives of Your Customers," p. 46.

8. Leonard Berry, "The Old Pillars of New Retailing," in *Harvard Business Review on Customer Relationship Management* (Boston: Harvard Business School Press, 2001), p. 51.

9. Philip Kotler and Fernando Trias de Bes, *Lateral Marketing* (Hoboken, N.J.: Wiley, 2003), p. 98.

10. Kotler and Trias de Bes, *Lateral Marketing,* p. 88.

Chapter Five

Chapter epigraphs: Flint McGlaughlin's statement cited from Museum Marketing Tips, *Motivational Quotes: Marketing and Advertising,* retrieved from http://www.museummarketingtips.com/quotes/quotes_ac.html; Daniel Boorstin, *The Image: A Guide to Pseudo-Events in America* (New York: Vintage, 1992), p. 232.

1. Robert Lauterborn, "New Marketing Litany: 4P's Passé; C-Words Take Over," *Advertising Age,* Oct. 1, 1991, p. 26.

2. Mohanbir Sawhney, "Winning Strategies for E-Commerce," Lecture at the Kellogg Graduate School of Management, Evanston, Ill., Apr. 1999.

3. Philip Kotler, *Marketing Insights from A to Z* (Hoboken, N.J.: Wiley, 2003), p. 109.

4. Quoted in Theodore Levitt, *The Marketing Imagination* (New York: Free Press, 1986), p. 85.

5. Levitt, *The Marketing Imagination,* p. 128.

6. Greg Sandow, personal e-mail to the author, Apr. 9, 2006.

7. Andrew Druckenbrod, "Music Preview: National Critic and PSO Aim to Involve Audience with the Music," *Pittsburgh Post-Gazette,* Oct. 20, 2004, retrieved from http://www.post-gazette.com/pg/04294/398513.stm.

8. Greg Sandow, *The Future of Classical Music?* Book 2.0, Episode 3, retrieved from http://www.gregsandow.com.

9. Peter Dobrin, "Delaware Symphony Sets Its Sales Pitch to Music," *Philadelphia Inquirer,* Oct. 10, 2004, p. H16.

10. Steve McMillan, presentation at the Kellogg School of Management Marketing Conference, Evanston, Ill., Jan. 29, 2003.

11. Nina Large, "Orchestras Set for Annual Effort to Spread Classical Music in Britain," Adante.com, Mar. 8, 2002, retrieved from http://www.adante.com.

12. BBC Philharmonic, "Pop-Up Projects," retrieved from http://www.bbc.co.uk/orchestras/philharmonic/learning/working_with_us.shtml; BBC, "Superstore Co-Commissions UK's First Supermarket Symphony," Press Release, retrieved from http://www.bbc.co.uk/pressoffice/pressreleases/stories/2003/03_march/10/asda_philharmonic.shtml.

13. Eugene Carr, *Sign-Up for Culture* (New York: Patron, 2004), pp. 16–17.

14. Andrew Druckenbrod, "Music Preview," *Pittsburgh Post-Gazette,* retrieved from http://www.post-gazette.com/pg/04294/398513.stm

15. Tim Baker and Heather Maitland, *Profile of Dance Attenders in Scotland: Section 3. Qualitative Research Report* (Edinburgh: Scottish Arts Council, Oct. 9, 2002), p. 24.

16. Alex Ross, "Listen to This," *New Yorker,* Feb. 16 and 23, 2004.

17. E. B. White, *Charlotte's Web* (New York: HarperCollins, 2004), pp. 77–81.

18. Marjorie Garber, *Symptoms of Culture* (New York: Routledge, 1998), p. 36.

19. White, *Charlotte's Web,* pp. 81–83.

20. Richard A. Posner, "Bad News," *New York Times Book Review,* July 31, 2005, pp. 1, 8.

21. Marc A. Scorca, "Preface," in Performing Arts Research Coalition, *The Value of the Performing Arts in Ten Communities,* June 2004, retrieved from http://www.operaamerica.org/parc.

22. Tom Harris, *The Marketer's Guide to Public Relations* (Hoboken, N.J.: Wiley, 1991), p. 12.

23. J. Walker Smith, Ann Clurman, and Craig Wood, *Coming to Concurrence: Addressable Attitudes and the New Model for Marketing Productivity* (Evanston, Ill.: Racom Communications, 2005), p. 95.

24. Arts Victoria, *Arts Audiences in Victoria* (Melbourne: Arts Victoria, 1996), retrieved from http://www.arts.vic.gov.au/arts/general/archive/factsheets/amtf1.htm.

25. Marylynne Pitz, "Analyst Helps Arts Groups Target Likely Ticket Buyers," *Pittsburgh Post-Gazette,* Dec. 30, 2004, retrieved from http://www.post-gazette.com.

26. Emanuel Rosen, *The Anatomy of Buzz: How to Create Word of Mouth Marketing* (New York: Currency, 2002), p. 6.

27. Rosen, *The Anatomy of Buzz,* p. 249.

28. Malcolm Gladwell, *The Tipping Point: How Little Things Can Make a Big Difference* (Boston: Little, Brown, 2000), pp. 35, 54.

29. Seth Godin, *Unleashing the Ideavirus* (New York: Hyperion, 2001).

30. Rosen, *The Anatomy of Buzz,* p. 261.

Chapter Six

Chapter epigraph: Warren Buffett's statement quoted in Roger Lowenstein, *Buffett: The Making of an American Capitalist* (Pella, Iowa: Main Street Books, 1996), p. 114.

1. William J. Baumol and William J. Bowen, *Performing Arts: The Economic Dilemma* (Cambridge, Mass.: MIT Press, 1968), pp. 162–165.

2. Robert Hewison and Henley Centre for Forecasting, *Towards 2010: New Times, New Challenges for the Arts* (London: Arts Council England, 2000).

3. Institute for Public Policy Research, "Thinktank Says Cheap Opera Tickets Will Not Bring in the Poor," Press Release, Apr. 11, 2004, retrieved from http://www.ippr.org.uk/pressreleases/?id=786.

4. New York City Center, "New York City Center *Fall for Dance Festival* Past Press," 2005, retrieved from http://www.nycitycenter.org/ffd/ffdpress.cfm.

5. Chris Blamires, "What Price Entertainment?" *Journal of the Market Research Society,* Oct. 1992, *34*(4), 378–379.

6. Arts Council of Great Britain, *Omnibus Arts Survey,* conducted by Research Surveys of Great Britain (London: Arts Council of Great Britain, 1991).

7. Data from an unpublished study conducted by the Writers' Theatre Marketing Department with the assistance of Sean Ryan, a Northwestern University student, who reported the results in coursework, May 2005.

8. Saint Paul Chamber Orchestra, "SPCO Lowers Prices in Neighborhoods," News Release, Feb. 2, 2005, retrieved from http://www.thespco.org.

9. David Anderson, "Sell All of Your Holiday Performances," *Arts Reach,* 2004, *12*(3), pp. 6, 15.

10. Penn Trevella, comments made in the Fuel4Arts Pricing Forum, Nov. 2002, retrieved from http://www.fuel4arts.com.

11. Merryn Carter, comments made in the Fuel4Arts Pricing Forum, Nov. 2002, retrieved from http://www.fuel4arts.com.

Chapter Seven

1. Anthony Tommasini, "Choice Words in Protest of Spelling It All Out," *New York Times,* July 3, 2005, sec. 2, p. 26.

2. Tommasini, "Choice Words," sec. 2, p. 26.

3. See Philip Kotler and Joanne Scheff, *Standing Room Only: Strategies for Marketing the Performing Arts* (Boston: Harvard Business School Press, 1997), chap. 6, for a comprehensive overview of marketing research and references to some major texts in this field.

4. Leonard Berry, *On Great Service: A Framework for Action* (New York: Free Press, 1995), pp. 39–40.

5. Gerald Zaltman, *How Customers Think: Essential Insights into the Mind of the Market* (Boston: Harvard Business School Press, 2003), p. 11.

6. Philip Kotler, *According to Kotler* (New York: AMACOM, 2005), p. 97.

7. For further details on the findings of this study see Joanne Scheff, "Factors Influencing Subscription and Single-Ticket Purchases at Performing Arts Organizations," *International Journal of Arts Management,* 1999, *1*(2), 16–26.

CHAPTER EIGHT

1. Frank Barnako, "Study: Life Without Net Is Unbearable," Sept. 22, 2004, retrieved from http://www.CBS.MarketWatch.com.

2. Katie Hafner, "For Some Internet Users, It's Better Late Than Never," *New York Times,* Mar. 25, 2004, p. E1.

3. Jeffrey Boase, "The Strength of Internet Ties," Pew Internet and American Life Project, Jan. 25, 2006, retrieved from http://www.pewinternet.org.

4. Eugene Carr, *Wired for Culture: How E-Mail Is Revolutionizing Arts Marketing* (New York: Patron, 2003), p. 16.

5. "FC-Roper Starch Survey: The Web," *Fast Company,* Sept. 1999, p. 302.

6. Mark Smith, "Europe Pushes Online Buttons to Streak Ahead of US Sales," *The Herald,* Dec. 2, 2002, p. 18.

7. Jupiter Research, "Jupiter Research Reports U.S. Online Retail Will Reach $65 Billion in 2004 . . . ," Press Release, Jan. 20, 2004, retrieved from http://www.jupitermedia.com/corporate/releases/04.01.20-newjupresearch.html.

8. Jim Royce, "Building an Online Presence for Live Theatre: Experience from the Field," Theatre Communications Group, *Centerpiece,* July 2001.

9. "Where Are You on the Web?" *Fast Company,* Sept. 1999, pp. 300–312.

10. Royal Scottish National Orchestra, Web site home page, retrieved from http://www.rsno.org.uk/news/archive/archive035.html.

11. John F. Welch Jr., quoted in General Electric Corporation, *1999 Annual Report,* Feb. 11, 2000.

12. Sarah Jones, "Ringtones? MP3s? Beethoven Would Have Been Proud," Mar. 26, 2006, retrieved from http://www.Living.Scotsman.com.

13. Julie Aldridge and Roger Tomlinson, *Pump Up Your Website: Improving the Effectiveness of Your E-Marketing,* Arts Marketing Association of Great Britain, seminar presented across the U.K., Oct. and Nov. 2004, retrieved from http://www.a-m-a.co.uk/pumpupyourwebsite. Aldridge and Tomlinson draw some of their information from Roger Tomlinson and Vicki Allpress, *Practical Guide to Developing and Managing Websites,* Arts Council England, available for free download at www.artscouncil.org.uk/publications/publication_detail.php?sid=4&id=407.

14. Aldridge and Tomlinson, *Pump Up Your Website.*

15. John C. Sawhill and Liz Kind, *San Francisco Opera,* Harvard Business School Case Study 9-300-095, Apr. 14, 2000.

16. Data provided by Kevin Giglinto, director of marketing, and Stephen Scully, director of revenue management, Chicago Symphony Orchestra, personal e-mails to the author, Aug. 28, 2003.

17. Data provided by Kevin Giglinto, vice president of marketing and sales, Chicago Symphony Orchestra, personal e-mail to the author, Aug. 1, 2005.

18. Data provided by Angus Watson, ticketing manager, Ravinia Festival, personal e-mail to the author, Aug. 2003.

19. Andrew Goldberg, marketing director, Florida Grand Opera, personal e-mail to the author, Aug. 3, 2005.

20. Laurie Windham, *The Soul of the New Consumer* (New York: Allworth Press, 2000), p. 45.

21. Aldridge and Tomlinson, *Pump Up Your Website.*

22. Carr, *Wired for Culture,* pp. 32–33.

23. Aspirational Arts Partnerships, *Communication and Audience Development: A Report Highlighting Communication and Promotional Tools Taken from Arts Council England's New Audiences Programme* (Aspirational Arts Partnerships, Nov. 2003).

24. "Your Music Lesson Is in the Mail," *Los Angeles Times,* Aug. 21, 2005.

25. Carr, *Wired for Culture,* p. 34.

26. Seth Godin, *Permission Marketing: Turning Strangers into Friends, and Friends into Customers* (New York: Simon & Schuster, 1999), p. 130.

27. Nick Usborne, "It's Not About Permission, It's About Trust," *ClickZ,* Aug. 14, 2000, p. 2.

28. Julie Aldridge, *Word of Mouse: Practical Online Marketing* (London: Arts Marketing Association, 2002).

29. Carr, *Wired for Culture,* p. 38.

30. Carr, *Wired for Culture,* p. 36.

31. Carr, *Wired for Culture,* p. 68.

32. Godin, *Permission Marketing,* p. 98.

33. Carr, *Wired for Culture,* p. 65.

34. Carr, *Wired for Culture,* p. 66.

35. Carr, *Wired for Culture,* p. 68.

36. Judith James, *Sauce: Hot Tips for Effective Arts Promotion, E-mail Promotions,* 2001, retrieved from http://www.fuel4arts.com.

Chapter Nine

Chapter epigraph: Roy Williams, "Top 12 Advertising Mistakes to Avoid," *Entrepreneur.com,* May 5, 2003, retrieved from http://www.entrepreneur.com/article/0,4621,308364,00.html.

1. Philip Kotler, *Marketing Insights from A to Z* (Hoboken, N.J.: Wiley, 2003), p. 9.

2. Scott Bedbury, *A New Brand World: 8 Principles for Achieving Brand Leadership in the 21st Century* (New York: Viking, 2002), p. xiii.

3. Bedbury, *A New Brand World,* p. 21.

4. Ars Viva, "Mission," 2006, retrieved from http://www.arsviva.org.

5. Philip Kotler, *Kotler on Marketing: How to Create, Win, and Dominate Markets* (New York: Free Press, 1999), p. 55.

6. Gerri Morris, *It's a Vision Thing* (Manchester, U.K.: Morris Hargreaves McIntyre Consultancy and Research, 2004), retrieved from http://www.lateralthinkers.com.

7. Bedbury, *A New Brand World,* p. 105.

8. Wanda Goldwag, "Loyalty Schemes," keynote presentation at *Stairway to Heaven,* conference of the Arts Marketing Association of Great Britain, Nov. 19, 2002, retrieved from http://www.a-m-a.co.uk/event_detail_archive.asp?cat=2&id=25.

Chapter Ten

Chapter epigraph: Philip Kotler, *Marketing Insights from A to Z* (Hoboken, N.J.: Wiley, 2003) p. xiii.

1. Danny Newman, *Subscribe Now!* (New York: Theatre Communications Group, 1983), pp. 17–24.

2. Zannie Giraud Voss and Glenn B. Voss, *Theatre Facts 2004* (New York: Theatre Communications Group, 2005), retrieved from http://www.tcg.org/pdfs/tools/theatrefacts_2004.pdf.

3. Alan Brown, "Classical Music Consumer Segmentation Study: How Americans Relate to Classical Music and Their Local Orchestras," *Arts Reach,* 2003, *11*(3), p. 16.

4. Femke Colborne, "Subscriptions Under Scrutiny as Opera Europa Meets in Latvia," *International Arts Manager,* Dec. 2004/Jan. 2005, p. 13.

5. Voss and Voss, *Theatre Facts 2004.*

6. Patricia Horn, "On the Edge of Their Seats," *Philadelphia Inquirer,* Dec. 30, 2004, retrieved from http://www.philly.com.

7. Statistics provided by Stephen Belth, former vice president of marketing for the Chicago Symphony Orchestra, personal conversation with the author, Jan. 28, 1998.

8. Brown, "Classical Music Consumer Segmentation Study," p. 16.

9. Jim Royce, personal e-mail to the author, June 24, 2004.

10. Alan Brown, *Magic of Music,* Issues Brief No. 4, *Initiators and Responders: A New Way to View Orchestra Audiences* (Miami, Fla.: John S. and James L. Knight Foundation, July 2004), retrieved from http://www.knightfdn.org.

11. Philip Kotler, *Marketing Insights from A to Z* (Hoboken, N.J.: Wiley, 2003), p. 98.

12. B. Joseph Pine II and James H. Gilmore, *The Experience Economy: Work Is Theatre & Every Business a Stage* (Boston: Harvard Business School Press, 1999), p. 76.

13. Thomas Cott, *New Audiences Now! A Report on Lincoln Center Theater's Introductory Membership Program* (New York: Lincoln Center Theater, 1994).

14. Vicki Allpress and Andrew Ross, *Opera for Groups,* Apr. 5, 2006, retrieved from http://www.fuel4arts.com.

CHAPTER ELEVEN

Chapter epigraph: John Naisbitt's statement cited from Museum Marketing Tips, *Motivational Quotes: Marketing and Advertising,* retrieved from http://www.museummarketingtips.com/quotes/quotes_ac.html

1. John S. and James L. Knight Foundation, *Classical Music Consumer Segmentation Study: How Americans Relate to Classical Music and Their Local Orchestras,* Final Report (Miami, Fla.: John S. and James L. Knight Foundation, Oct. 2002), p. 117.

2. W. Chan Kim and Renée Mauborgne, "Blue Ocean Strategy," *Harvard Business Review,* Oct. 2004, p. 81.

3. Zannie Giraud Voss and Glenn B. Voss, *Theatre Facts 2004* (New York: Theatre Communications Group, 2004), retrieved from http://www.tcg.org. As mentioned in Chapter One, Note 11, the 2004 TCG survey report divides nonprofit, professional theaters into groups (universe, profiled theatres, and trend theatres), defined by the amount of information available. Also see Robin Pogrebin, "Uncertain Times: Impulse Buyers Replace Ticket Subscribers," *New York Times,* Oct. 16, 2002.

4. Andrew McIntyre and Helen Dunnett, *Practical Guide: Move on Up: How Test Drive and TelePrompt Develop Audiences,* 2003, retrieved from http://www.newaudiences2.org.uk/downloads/move_on_up.pdf.

5. Caroline Bishop, "Marketing Strategy Success for RLPO," *International Arts Manager,* May 2005, p. 8.

6. Jim Royce, "Marketing Strategies for Uncertain Times," *Arts Reach, 11*(6) pp. 1, 13–14.

7. Tim Joss, "International Rescue," *International Arts Manager,* June 2001, p. 26.

8. Sophie Travers, "Stronger Together," *International Arts Manager,* May 2004, pp. 13–14.

CHAPTER TWELVE

Chapter epigraphs: J. Walker Smith, Ann Clurman, and Craig Wood, *Coming to Concurrence: Addressable Attitudes and the New Model for Marketing Productivity* (Evanston, Ill.: Racom Communications, 2005), p. 98; Bill Gates, *Business @ the Speed of Thought: Succeeding in the Digital Economy* (New York: Warner Business Books, 2000), p. 200.

1. Mohanbir Sawhney, *A Manifesto for Marketing: What Ails the Profession and How to Fix It,* Summer 2004, retrieved from http://www.mohansawhney.com.

2. C. K. Prahalad and Venkatram Ramaswamy, "Co-Opting Customer Competence," in *Harvard Business Review on Customer Relationship Management* (Boston: Harvard Business School Press, 2001), pp. 2–5.

3. Smith, Clurman, and Wood, *Coming to Concurrence,* p. 98.

4. Frederick Newell, *Why CRM Doesn't Work: How to Win by Letting Customers Manage the Relationship* (Princeton, N.J.: Bloomberg Press, 2003).

5. Susan Fournier, Susan Dobscha, and David Glen Mick, "Preventing the Premature Death of Relationship Marketing," in *Harvard Business Review on Customer Relationship Management* (Boston: Harvard Business School Press, 2001), pp. 134–137.

6. Newell, *Why CRM Doesn't Work,* pp. 7–8.

7. Newell, *Why CRM Doesn't Work,* p. 183.

8. Judith Allen, personal conversation with the author, July 8, 1999.

9. Jim Royce, personal e-mail to the author, June 24, 2004.

10. Richard B. Chase and Sriram Dasu, "Want to Perfect Your Company's Service? Use Behavioral Science," in *Harvard Business Review on Customer Relationship Management* (Boston: Harvard Business School Press, 2001), pp. 67–68.

11. B. Joseph Pine II and James H. Gilmore, *The Experience Economy: Work Is Theatre & Every Business a Stage* (Boston: Harvard Business School Press, 1999), pp. 77–78.

12. Quoted in Clayton Collins, "Five Minutes with J. D. Power III," *Profiles,* Oct. 1996, p. 23.

13. Pine and Gilmore, *The Experience Economy,* p. 100.

14. Leonard Berry, *On Great Service: A Framework for Action* (New York: Free Press, 1995), pp. 20–22.

15. Berry, *On Great Service,* pp. 33–48.

Epilogue

1. Michael Kaiser, speech to the Arts Marketing Association of Great Britain, Cardiff, Wales, July 1999.

2. Gordon R. Sullivan and Michael V. Harper, *Hope Is Not a Method* (New York: Random House, 1996), p. 152.

Index